Reviews of Note
from colleagues and professionals

"SERVES AS A STATUS REPORT ON THE ECO-
NOMIC, SOCIAL, AND POLITICAL CONDITION OF
FEMALE EMPLOYEES. . . . The authors present
practical information on myriad issues confronting women of all ages at work. Will serve as a
valuable resource and training guide to EAP
practitioners and managers alike. Most importantly, it increases the sensitivity of women's
issues as they relate to the workplace."
— R. Paul Maiden, PhD, Chair, Occupational Social Work, Jane
Addams College of Social Work, University of Illinois at Chicago

"This book is timely and valuable for understanding a range of stressful challenges confronting
female employees. The authors offer clear, practical guidelines for relevant and responsive
employee assistance services. I HIGHLY RECOM-
MEND IT FOR ALL WHO CARE ABOUT THE WELL-
BEING OF WOMEN IN THE WORKPLACE."
— Froma Walsh, PhD, Professor and Co-Director, Center for
Family Health, The University of Chicago

Empowering Women in the Workplace: Perspectives, Innovations, and Techniques for Helping Professionals

Empowering Women in the Workplace: Perspectives, Innovations, and Techniques for Helping Professionals

Marta Lundy, PhD
Beverly Younger, MSW
Editors

Empowering Women in the Workplace: Perspectives, Innovations, and Techniques for Helping Professionals, edited by Marta Lundy and Beverly Younger, was simultaneously issued by The Haworth Press, Inc., under the title *Women in the Workplace and Employee Assistance Programs: Perspectives, Innovations, and Techniques for Helping Professionals*, as a special issue of the *Employee Assistance Quarterly*, Volume 9, Numbers 3/4 1994, Keith McClellan, Journal Editor.

Harrington Park Press
An Imprint of
The Haworth Press, Inc.
New York · London · Norwood (Australia)

ISBN 1-56023-062-2

Published by

Harrington Park Press, 10 Alice Street, Binghamton, NY 13904-1580

Harrington Park Press is an imprint of The Haworth Press, Inc., 10 Alice Street, Binghamton, NY 13904-1580, USA.

Empowering Women in the Workplace: Perspectives, Innovations, and Techniques for Helping Professionals has also been published as *Employee Assistance Quarterly*, Volume 9, Numbers 3/4 1994.

The development, preparation, and publication of this work has been undertaken with great care. However, the publisher, employees, editors, and agents of The Haworth Press and all imprints of The Haworth Press, Inc., including The Haworth Medical Press and Pharmaceutical Products Press, are not responsible for any errors contained herein or for consequences that may ensue from use of materials or information contained in this work. Opinions expressed by the author(s) are not necessarily those of The Haworth Press, Inc.

Library of Congress Cataloging-in-Publication Data

Empowering women in the workplace: perspectives, innovations, and techniques for helping professionals / Marta Lundy, Beverly Younger, editors.
     p. cm.
   "Has also been published as Employee assistance quarterly, volume 9, numbers 3/4 1994"–T.p. verso.
     Includes bibliographical references.
     ISBN 1-56023-062-2 (acid-free paper)
     1. Employee assistance programs–United States. 2. Women–Employment–United States. 3. Women–Services for–United States. I. Lundy, Marta. II. Younger, Beverly.
HF5549.5.E42E497 1995
658.3'82–dc20
                                         94-43715
                                            CIP

INDEXING & ABSTRACTING

Contributions to this publication are selectively indexed or abstracted in print, electronic, online, or CD-ROM version(s) of the reference tools and information services listed below. This list is current as of the copyright date of this publication. See the end of this section for additional notes.

- *EAP Abstracts Plus*, EAP Information Systems, P. O. Box 1650, Yreka, CA 96097

- *Excerpta Medica/Electronic Publishing Division*, Elsevier Science Publishers, 655 Avenue of the Americas, New York, NY 10010

- *Human Resources Abstracts (HRA)*, Sage Publications, Inc., 2455 Teller Road, Newbury Park, CA 91320

- *Inventory of Marriage and Family Literature (online and hard copy)*, National Council on Family Relations, 3989 Central Avenue NE, Suite 550, Minneapolis, MN 55421

- *Medical Benefits*, P. O. Box 1007, Charlottesville, VA 22902

- *NIAAA Alcohol and Alcohol Problems Science Database (ETOH)*, National Institute on Alcohol Abuse and Alcoholism, 1400 Eye Street NW, Suite 600, Washington, DC 20005

- *Personnel Management Abstracts*, 704 Island Lake Road, Chelsea, MI 48118

- *Psychological Abstracts (PsycINFO)*, American Psychological Association, P. O. Box 91600, Washington, DC 20090-1600

(continued)

- *Public Affairs Information Bulletin (PAIS)*, Public Affairs Information Service, Inc., 521 West 43rd Street, New York, NY 10036-4396

- *Social Planning/Policy & Development Abstracts (SOPODA)*, Sociological Abstracts, Inc., P. O. Box 22206, San Diego, CA 92192-0206

- *Social Work Abstracts*, National Association of Social Workers, 750 First Street NW, 8th Floor, Washington, DC 20002

- *Sociological Abstracts (SA)*, Sociological Abstracts, Inc., P. O. Box 22206, San Diego, CA 92192-0206

- *SOMED (social medicine) Database*, Institute fur Dokumentation, Postfach 20 10 12, D-33548 Bielefeld, Germany

- *The Brown University Digest of Addiction Theory and Application (DATA Newsletter)*, Project Cork Institute, Dartmouth Medical School, 14 South Main Street, Suite 2F, Hanover, NH 03755-2015

- *Urban Affairs Abstracts,* National League of Cities, 1301 Pennsylvania Avenue NW, Washington, DC 20004

- *Work Related Abstracts*, Harmonie Park Press, 23630 Pinewood, Warren, MI 48091

(continued)

SPECIAL BIBLIOGRAPHIC NOTES

related to special journal issues (separates)
and indexing/abstracting

- ☐ indexing/abstracting services in this list will also cover material in any "separate" that is co-published simultaneously with Haworth's special thematic journal issue or DocuSerial. Indexing/abstracting usually covers material at the article/chapter level.

- ☐ monographic co-editions are intended for either non-subscribers or libraries which intend to purchase a second copy for their circulating collections.

- ☐ monographic co-editions are reported to all jobbers/wholesalers/approval plans. The source journal is listed as the "series" to assist the prevention of duplicate purchasing in the same manner utilized for books-in-series.

- ☐ to facilitate user/access services all indexing/abstracting services are encouraged to utilize the co-indexing entry note indicated at the bottom of the first page of each article/chapter/contribution.

- ☐ this is intended to assist a library user of any reference tool (whether print, electronic, online, or CD-ROM) to locate the monographic version if the library has purchased this version but not a subscription to the source journal.

- ☐ individual articles/chapters in any Haworth publication are also available through the Haworth Document Delivery Services (HDDS).

ABOUT THE EDITORS

Marta Lundy, PhD, a licensed Clinical Social Worker and faculty member at Loyola University of Chicago School of Social Work, specializes in women's issues and women and families. She teaches graduate clinical courses in family therapy, practice with women, and human sexuality. Dr. Lundy has initiated research projects on women's health care, the therapeutic relationship, and on social workers' ideas about feminist theory. She is currently collaborating on a research project about non-offending mothers of children who have been sexually abused. She has presented and published articles about clinical practice with adult survivors of incest, the dilemma of women's health care, the process of therapy, and gender issues that pervade family relocation. Dr. Lundy also maintains a private practice in Chicago.

Beverly Younger, MSW, worked as an Independent Employee Assistance Consultant for nearly five years. A licensed Clinical Social Worker, she has moved into an internal position in Employee Assistance and Health Services at Continental Bank, Chicago, Illinois. Ms. Younger has provided community clinical services and acted as a Director of Administration at a community mental health agency. She has a strong interest in research and has completed two studies in collaboration with faculty at Jane Addams College of Social Work at the University of Illinois, on the response of business to federal legislation affecting employee practices.

CONTENTS

Preface

This volume addresses three important blind spots in services to women workers. First, many people in the work world do not see the gender issue and the special needs of women workers. Their lenses are focused on a workforce undifferentiated by gender. Second, many professionals in EAPs do not see the woman worker as one who has multiple roles and multiple stresses beyond the work world. Their sights often do not include the woman in her family and wider roles. Third, many human service professionals outside the work world do not see women as workforce participants. Their tunnel vision is restricted to the woman in her family and interpersonal relationships only. The result has been that all three views obscure the real circumstances of women who work both inside and outside their homes.

The impact on services to women of these restricted views is crucial. Women are joining the workforce in increasing numbers, without relinquishing their family responsibilities. Women continue to be the majority of clients whom most human services personnel serve, and more and more of those women clients are in the work place. Services to all those women must be informed by a perspective which sees women whole. This volume provides such a perspective on a wide-ranging set of issues.

Each of the chapters compels the EAP reader to see the many facets of women's lives beyond the work place. As these contributors tie these issues to work place situations, readers who are social workers or psychotherapists practicing outside the work situation

[Haworth co-indexing entry note]: "Preface." Gottlieb, Naomi. Co-published simultaneously in *Employee Assistance Quarterly* (The Haworth Press, Inc.) Vol. 9, No. 3/4, 1994, pp. xiii-xiv; and: *Empowering Women in the Workplace: Perspectives, Innovations, and Techniques for Helping Professionals* (ed: Marta Lundy, and Beverly Younger) Harrington Park Press, an imprint of The Haworth Press, Inc., 1994, pp. xiii-xiv. Multiple copies of this article/chapter may be purchased from The Haworth Document Delivery Center [1-800-3-HAWORTH; 9:00 a.m. - 5:00 p.m. (EST)].

xiii

can also see the interplay between family and work. The message to both groups is clear–these women are not just family members, nor are they just work force employees. Women have the demanding job of combining the two roles.

Although focused on EAPs, this volume is relevant to several branches of the human services field. It speaks to all those who counsel women, who, far more than men, feel the tension between their personal, family and work responsibilities. At the very least, all professionals who serve women should acknowledge the stress inherent in women's multiple roles. This volume provides valuable insights into the many facets of a woman's world.

Naomi Gottlieb
School of Social Work
University of Washington

Foreword–
Women:
The Invisible Majority

AND THEN ALL THAT HAS DIVIDED US

And then all that has divided us will merge
And then compassion will be wedded to power
And then softness will come to a world that is harsh and unkind
And then both men and women will be gentle
And then both women and men will be strong
And then no person will be subject to another's will
And then all will be rich and free and varied
And then the greed of some will give way to the needs of many
And then all will share equally in the Earth's abundance
And then all will care for the sick and the weak and the old
And then all will nourish the young
And then all will cherish life's creatures
And then all will live in harmony with each other and the Earth
And then everywhere will be called Eden once again

–Judy Chicago[1]

One of the greatest difficulties women have faced is in gaining acknowledgement from the socio-political, legal and economic system that women are a disadvantaged group. Of course, gains have been made and as women now have a substantial presence in the

[Haworth co-indexing entry note]: "Foreword–Women: The Invisible Majority." Lundy, Marta, and Beverly Younger. Co-published simultaneously in *Employee Assistance Quarterly* (The Haworth Press, Inc.) Vol. 9, No. 3/4, 1994, pp. xv-xxvi; and: *Empowering Women in the Workplace: Perspectives, Innovations, and Techniques for Helping Professionals* (ed: Marta Lundy, and Beverly Younger) Harrington Park Press an imprint of The Haworth Press, Inc., 1994, pp. xv-xxvi. Multiple copies of this article/chapter may be purchased from The Haworth Document Delivery Center [1-800-3-HAWORTH; 9:00 a.m. - 5:00 p.m. (EST)].

xv

workforce many people may feel that focusing on the specific needs of women is no longer necessary. But within the workforce in 1990, even as we make up 47% of the total labor force, we still struggle to obtain an equal footing with men (Landes, Foster, & Jones, 1992, p. 16). In 1988, women's hourly wages were 74% of men's, and the annual wage was 66% of men's (ibid., p. 76). In 1990, women make $.71 for every $1.00 that a man makes (ibid., p. 73). The median income in 1990, for a woman with four years of college, working full-time, year-round, was $28,017, while a man with the same background made $39,238 (ibid., p. 73). Female elementary teachers earn 90.3% of a man's salary; a female engineer earns 85.7% of the male engineer's salary (ibid., p. 76). No matter how men's and women's earnings are compared, women earn less than men.

Within the ranks of women, racial minorities face even greater obstacles. Known as double and triple jeopardy, these terms refer to the intersection of race, gender and class, all of which combine to oppress women of color. Even so, the labor participation rate compiled in 1991, indicates that nearly equal levels of women are working, with 57 percent of black women (6.7 million), 57.6 percent of white women (48 million), and 52 percent of Hispanic women (3.8 million) in the labor force (ibid., 1992, p. 24). Historically, African-American women have always been in the labor force, dating back to the time of slavery. In 1990, African-American women working full time earned an average of $18,518. Hispanic women who work year-round, full-time earn 21 percent below the median income for all women, an average of $16,186 in 1990, and 16 percent below the median income of Hispanic men (ibid., p. 25).

In 1960, not even 20% of married women with children under six years of age were in the workplace. In 1991, almost 60% of married women with small children were working outside the home. The largest occupational category of employed women is administrative support or clerical; 31% of all women are in these positions, with a median weekly salary of $348. These figures remind us that despite the influx of women in the labor force over the last 50 years and despite the significant increase of women into managerial and professional positions, women still encounter the "glass ceiling."

According to the Department of Labor, in *A Report on the Glass Ceiling Initiative*, the glass ceiling is defined as "artificial barriers based on attitudinal or organizational bias that prevent qualified individuals from advancing upward in their organization into management level positions" (Landes, Foster, & Jones, 1992, p. 29). Women are segregated vertically within occupations preventing promotion to higher ranks, rarely achieving the inner circle of power.

For a female-headed family, the income differential of $497 per week for men and $368 per week for women is particularly devastating. Besides making less money, women are often the sole supporters of their children and are less likely to be financially able to sustain a job loss. Furthermore, women maintain multiple roles as caregivers and wage earners. In the last thirty years there has been a 40% increase of women in the work force, a trend which indicates that women maintain their caregiving roles while adding on a full time job, all of which contributes to an increase in stressors brought on by the demands of multiple roles. Moreover, 7.4 percent of widowed, divorced, or separated women have multiple jobs, with the number of women who work at more than one job totaling 3.1 million in 1991 (ibid., p. 26).

It is an old but no less startling realization that women carry a disproportionate amount of the responsibility for families, and therefore, women receive concomitant blame for family problems. The pervasiveness of judgments against women for environmental or societally imposed circumstances is rampant. For example, victims of incest are blamed for not stopping the abuse, and mothers of victims of incest are denigrated as "silent colluders." Single mothers who miss work due to unreliable child care, or who do not apply for promotion due to family responsibilities, are evaluated poorly on job performance when fathers are given no judgement for failure to support or provide care. Mothers have been blamed for childhood schizophrenia, labeled as "schizophrenogenic mothers." The list goes on and on with over 72 different psychological problems of children attributed to mothers (Caplan & Hall-McCorquodale, 1985).

As we grapple with the system in order to achieve some equity in the workplace, we also struggle with ourselves to blend traditional caregiver roles with the responsibility of making money. The joys of motherhood are dimmed by the lack of safe and adequate child care; by the need for better women-focused and women-researched medical care. The feelings of competence derived from work well done are negated by the lack of solutions available for the pain of sexual harassment and verbal abuse. The values of hearth and home are threatened by endless physical abuse, financial insecurity, and minimization of the role of motherhood, except under certain circumstances. Yes, women have made gains, but much remains to be done.

The old adage, strength in numbers, should be reassuring. Not only are women anticipated to be 47% of the work force by 2000 (Landes, Foster & Jones, 1992, p. 32), but the Bureau of Census estimates that in the total population there will be 12.5 million more women than men in 2050 (ibid., p. 32). In addition, minorities, women, and immigrants will comprise 90 percent of the increase in the labor force in the year 2000 (ibid., p. 32). However, in spite of our growing numbers, we seem to lack socialized ways of supporting each other at work. Unity and cohesiveness appear to be difficult to achieve. The Old Boy Network has served its function well for men climbing the ladder to success. Maybe we need an Old Girl Network, without all the implications of nepotism, but with successful ways to use the strength of our numbers. Mentoring is one excellent opportunity to assist young women maturing in professional paths. Advocacy and social activism on workplace issues is another way to change the status quo. Preventative education may help women already hurt by the injustices of the system. And we definitely need more female researchers, in health, mental health, family violence, and alcohol and drug abuse; we need more women politicians, judges, and legislators; and there is a need for more mothers to speak out about the circumstances of the modern day family.

Employee Assistance professionals have a special position in the workplace from which to assist female employees with their unique struggles. EAPs are a substantial number of trained and sensitive professionals who are available to create a change in the workplace. With the large number of women in the field, EAP professional associations have always included women, not only as part of the membership, but also in leadership roles. Similarly, EAPs have kept their focus on the needs of minorities, culturally diverse groups and special populations. But perhaps we too easily assume that the needs of women have already been met, that equity has been gained in the workplace and on the home front. The following articles will present some of the circumstances of women in the workplace. Some of the articles in this volume will represent the unique perspective and experience of particular women; some will describe experiences across women.

THE CHOICE OF TOPICS

Women do have special needs, but women's experiences are diverse. Our choice of topics reflects and celebrates women's diversity. Adrienne Rich helps us to understand the world of women in her eloquent description:

> Women both have and have not had a common world. The mere sharing of oppression does not constitute a common world. Our thought and action, insofar as they have taken the form of difference, assertion, or rebellion, have repeatedly been obliterated, or subsumed under "human" history, which means the "publicity of the public realm" created and controlled by men. Our history is the history of a majority of the species, yet the struggles of women for a "human" status have been relegated to footnotes, to the sidelines. Above all, women's relationships with women have been denied or neglected as a force in history.[2] (Rich, 1979, p. 203-204)

The rates of sexual abuse, rape, battering and homicide against women, as well as the fear that women express regarding everyday living, indicate the reality that women are at risk (Gordon & Reiger, 1989). The lists of injustices continue within the work place where women experience daily discrimination institutionalized in the form of insufficient access to opportunity. However, women are not a special population; we *are* the invisible majority. We compose 51.3% of the total population, making us potentially a powerful force in shaping the future (Rix, 1990, p. 349). In order for women to feel and focus their potential, there must be direct education, intervention and prevention against the onslaught of violence and discrimination against women.

We are concerned about the long history of inequity women have struggled with in society in general, and at work, specifically. Power and income differentials create unique hazards for women at work. Women are potential victims for a variety of abuse at work; sexual harassment, verbal abuse and even physical violence, fostered by an imbalanced distribution of power among men and women at work. Beverly Younger was inspired by actual cases of workplace violence against women to research this problem and to begin the documentation needed to understand why women are at risk for abuse. Additionally, inequities in income lead to particular problems for women trying to maintain financial security, the nature of which was discussed by almost every contributing author.

That women have faced abuse at home is fairly well known but is not researched well. We asked our authors to consider topics which draw attention to the types of family abuse which may affect the lives of female employees. In response, Mary Jo Barrett, Wayne Scott, Joanna Gillespie and Becky Palmer provide an article on female incest victims, aimed at providing an effective model of intervention which can also be applicable to EAP assessments of potential incest victims.

Female employees bring to work with them a variety of other family issues as well. The perception that women are responsible for it all–parenting, home care, elder care, in addition to earning an income–perpetuates a significant amount of strain on female employees. Judith Casey and Marcie Pitt-Catsouphes discuss the concerns of single parent mothers and the implications for employers to assist with their distinctive needs at work. Linda Duxbury and Chris Higgins present the results of a large survey of Canadian parents, examining the relationship of gender and career status as it relates to family to work and work to family interference, role overload, and stress. Marie Raber outlines potential solutions for much needed child care that concerned employers may want to consider implementing. Focusing on the harmful effects of relocation on women as they struggle to maintain family stability without losing personal ground, Marta Lundy unveils a largely ignored concern for women. We found that the efforts women make to maintain a balance between work and family are both necessary and stressful, and little considered by society, researchers and employers.

As half of the population, women deserve to have attention paid to their experiences. Women's health needs lag behind in empirical research initiatives; women are stereotypically diagnosed with mental health problems that may be more indicative of their socioeconomic and gender status than their mental health. Beth Reed addresses the intersection of women's health and mental health problems with a comprehensive discussion of women's use of alcohol, tobacco and other drugs. Diagnostic labels may be intended to be helpful, but instead may trap and ensnare women in a web that veils the real problems. Sally Mason introduces us to the unspoken, but ever present reality of AIDS. Until recently, women with AIDS were only minimally recorded by the Center for Disease Control. Sally alerts us to the dangers of this disease and how it is manifested in women. Women are expected to anticipate and to focus on the needs of the family, but women are not educated about their own needs. Kathleen Perkins reveals the shocking economic status of older women, and the lack of preparation and education for retirement provided for women in the work force, another issue affecting great numbers of women which receives little attention.

Women are over half the population, but women do not share identical experiences, nor do women all think the same thoughts. Betty Reddy begins this special volume by providing an overview of the history of EAP through the evolution of her own thoughts and experiences within the occupation. Barbara Jackson introduces us to the circumstances of African-American women within the work place, both from the perspective of the EAP professional and the employee. Nan Van Den Bergh discusses the circumstances of lesbians in the work place, women who often must remain invisible within the work environment.

As two women editors working together to create a special volume focused on women at work, we learned a tremendous amount from the process of compiling this work. We requested articles from women authors primarily because they had already established an area of expertise in their topic area specific to women. We also wanted to provide an opportunity for women to write about their experiences in the workplace. With great disappointment, we discovered that we could not include in this volume everything that we felt was important for women. For example, there are no articles on the following topics: sexual harassment, which women are learning to fight against in the workplace, and for which we need models of success; trauma of acquaintance, date and marital rape; Hispanic and other culturally and ethnically diverse women's experiences; and, lastly, the empowerment of women and our need to empower one another. We are saddened by the absence of these topics, but heartened that the *Employee Assistance Quarterly* is open to women's concerns and committed to their publication.

As we talked and worked with the authors, we learned about some of the difficulties that female professionals face. During the course of this journal composition, three potential authors were laid off from their positions, one due to the downsizing of a women's treatment program. Others faced relocation, illness, family crises and responsibilities, and most commonly, tremendously overloaded schedules. We experienced both personally, and from observation, the stress of trying to make it as a professional woman. We discussed among ourselves whether the need to compulsively overdo was related to the need to prove ourselves worthy of our occupations, or was required in order to receive minimal acknowledgment in our respective areas of expertise.

The primacy of this project took over certain aspects of our lives. We became even more aware of the lack of attention paid to women's issues. It was extremely difficult to find enough resources, enough data, enough theory relevant to some of the issues that were specific to women as a population. At times it was even difficult for potential authors to define issues relevant to women from within their area of expertise. We realized how hard it is for women and men to make strong statements about the special plight of women at work, and how easy it is to buy into society's denial of women's unique needs. But mostly we learned how much we can gain from valuing and supporting each other. Within the ranks of all working women, we have great resources just waiting to be tapped. As editors, we acquired a deep respect for each other's abilities, struggles, and uniqueness.

We are pleased to be able to bring these topics together in one special volume on women and the work place. Their relevance springs to life on the pages of the authors' works, castigating us for our previous complacency; alerting us to the potential dangers;

warning us to take care, in a world that moves very rapidly, with little concern for the human beings, the women, who nurture the rest of our world. Women's realities are different. We are not an amorphous mass that acts as a body. Each of us struggles to find value and meaning in our particular world. If the reader takes away nothing else, it is our hope that this will be remembered.

ACKNOWLEDGEMENTS

We want to acknowledge the pleasure we both had in working with the contributors to this special volume. All were respectful and invested in the topic of women in the work place, and in the publication needs of the volume; of our time line for the work; and of the process of working together toward an important goal. While we acknowledge the bright and earnest people we worked with, we also want to acknowledge two very important men in our lives.

Beverly would like to gratefully acknowledge the support and assistance of Blake Osborne, who stood by her side with both emotional and grammatical contributions.

Marta expresses gratitude and appreciation for the nurturance and support given by Jim Weiss, who offered helpful suggestions and was always available to listen.

Beverly and Marta also extend their appreciation to Keith McClellan for responding to the need for this topic, and for supporting our efforts.

Marta Lundy
Beverly Younger

NOTES

1. Reprinted by permission of the author, Judy Chicago. This poem is available as an illuminated poster by Judy Chicago. To purchase contact: Through the Flower, P.O. Box 8138, Santa Fe, New Mexico 87504.

2. Rich, A. (1979) "Conditions for work: The common world of women (1976)." ON LIES, SECRETS, AND SILENCE: SELECTED PROSE 1966-1978. New York: W.W. Norton, p. 203-214.

REFERENCES

Caplan, P. J. & Hall-McCorquodale, I. (1985). Mother-blaming in major clinical journals, *American Journal of Orthopsychiatry, 55*, 345-353.

Gordon, M.T. & Riger, S. (1989). *The Female Fear.* New York: Free Press.

Landes, A., Foster, C. D., & Jones, N. H. (1992). Women's Changing Role. Wylie, Texas: Information Plus.

Rix, S. E., ed. (1990). *The American woman, 1990-1991: A status report.* New York: Norton.

RECOMMENDATIONS FOR FURTHER READING

Violence Against Women

Bass, E. & Davis, L. (1989). *The Courage to Heal: A Guide for Women Survivors of Child Sexual Abuse.* New York: Harper & Row.

Bograd, M. (1984). Family systems approaches to wife battering: A feminist critique, *American Journal of Orthopsychiatry, 54*(4), 558-568.

Briere, J. (1989). *Therapy for adults molested as children; beyond survival.*

Carter, B. (1993). Child sexual abuse: Impact on mothers. *Affilia, 8,* 72-90.

Courtois, C. (1988). *Healing the incest wound.* New York: Norton.

Elbow, M. & Mayfield, J. (1991). Mothers of incest victims: Villains, victims, or protectors: *Families in Society: The Journal of Contemporary Human Services,* 78-86.

Gordon, M. T. & Riger, S. (1989). *The Female Fear.* New York: Free Press.

Herman, J. (1992). *Trauma and Recovery.* New York: Basic Books.

James, K. & MacKinnon, L. (1990). The "incestuous family" revisited: A critical analysis of family therapy myths. *Journal of Marital and Family Therapy, 16,* 71-88.

Koss, M.P. (1990). Violence against women. *American Psychologist,* 374-380.

Lundy, M. (1993). Explicitness: The unspoken mandate of feminist social work. *Affilia,* 8(2), 184-200.

Walker, L. (1989). Psychology and violence against women. *American Psychologist, 49* (4), 695-702.

Women and Health/Mental Health

Belle, D. (1990). Poverty and women's mental health. *American Psychologist, 45* (3), 385-389.

Brody, C. M. (1984). *Women Therapists Working with Women.* New York: Springer.

Caplan, P. J. & Hall-McCorquodale, I. (1985). Mother-blaming in major clinical journals, *American Journal of Orthopsychiatry, 55*, 345-353.

Collins, B. G. (1993). Reconstruing codependency using self-in-relation theory: A feminist perspective. *Social Work,* 38 (4), 470-476.

Kaplan, M. (1983). A woman's view of DSM-III. *American Psychologist*, 786-792.

Kaspar, B. (1989). Women and AIDS: A psychosocial perspective. *Affilia: The Journal of Women and Social Work*, 7-22.

Kutchins, H. & Kirk, S.A. (1989). DSM-III-R: The conflict over new psychiatric diagnoses. *Health and social work, 14,* 91-101.

Lewittes, H.J. (1989). Just being friendly means a lot: Women, friendship, and aging. *Women & Health,* 14, 134-140.

Lundy, M. & Mason, S. (1994). Women's Health Care Centers: Multiple Definitions, *Health and Social Work,* 19 (3/4) (in press).

McBride, A.B. (1990). Mental health effects on women's multiple roles, *American Psychologist, 45*(3), 381-383.

Rubenstein, H. & Lawler, S.K. (1990). Toward the psychosocial empowerment of women. *Affilia: The Journal of Women and Social Work, 5* (3), 27-38.

Yama, M., Fogas, B., Teegarden, L., & Hastings, B. (1993). Childhood sexual abuse and parental alcoholism: Interactive effects in adult women. *American Journal of Orthopsychiatry, 57,* 93-101.

Women's Personal/Professional Experiences

Berzoft, J. (1989). Therapeutic value of women's adult friendships. *Smith College Studies in Social Work: Women and Clinical Practice,* 59 (3), 267-279.

Bricker-Jenkins, M., & Hooyman, N. eds. (1986). *Not For Women Only.* Silver Spring, MD: National Association for Social Workers.

Bricker-Jenkins, M., Hooyman, N.R., & Gottlieb, N. (1991). *Feminist Social work practice in clinical settings.* Newbury Park, CA: Sage.

Faludi, S. (1991). *Backlash: The undeclared war against American women.* New York City: Crown Books.

Freeman, J. (Ed.). (1989). *Women.* 4th ed. Mountain View, CA: Mayfield Publishing Co.

Hagen, J.L., & Davis, L.V. (1992). Working with women: Building a policy and practice agenda, *Social Work, 37* (6), 495-502.

Hull, G.T., Scott, P., & Smith, B. (1982). *All the Women are White, All the Blacks Are Men, But Some of Us Are Brave.* Old Westbury, New York: The Feminist Press.

Moraga, C., & Anzaldua, G. (1983). *This Bridge Called My Back: Writings by Radical Women of Color.* New York: Kitchen Table: Women of Color Press.

Van Den Bergh, N., & Cooper, L.B., eds. (1986). *Feminist visions for social work.* Silver Spring, MD: National Association of Social Workers.

Women and the Family

Hochschild, A, (with Anne Machung) (1989). *The Second Shift.* New York: Viking Press.

Lerner, H.G. (1985). *The Dance of Anger: A Woman's Guide to Changing the Patterns of Intimate Relationships.* New York: Harper & Row.

McGoldrick, M., Anderson, C., & Walsh, F. (1990). *Women in Families.* New York: Norton Press.

Siegel, R.J. (1988). Women's 'dependency' in a male-centered value system: Gender-based values regarding dependency and independence. *Women & Therapy,* 113-123.

Slater, S., & Mencher, J. (1991). The lesbian family life cycle: A contextual approach. *American Journal of Orthopsychiatry, 61*(3), 372-382.

Women's Development

Barbach, L. (1975). *For yourself: The fulfillment of female sexuality.* New York: Signet.

Berzoff, J. (1989). From separation to connection: Shifts in understanding women's development. *Affilia, 4* (1), 45-58.

Duerk, J. (1989). *Circle of Stones.* San Diego, CA: Lura Media.

Rossi, A.S. (Ed.) (1985). *Gender and the Life Course.* New York: Aldine Press.

Shibley-Hyde, J. (1991). *Half the Human Experience.* 4th ed. Lexington, MA: D.C. Heath & Co.

Porcino, J. (1983). *Growing older, getting better.* Reading, MA: Addison-Wesley.

Women and Work

Burgos, N. (1986). Women, work and family in Puerto Rico. *Affilia, 1* (3), 17-28.

Delgado, A.K., Griffith, E.E.H., & Ruiz, P. (1985). The black woman mental health executive, *Administration in Mental Health, 12*(4), 246-251.

Kaufman, D.R. (1989). Professional women: How real are the recent gains? In Freeman, J., (Ed.) *Women,* 4th edition. California: Mayfield Publishing Company, pp. 329-346.

Landes, A., Foster, C.D., & Jones, N.H. (1992). *Women's Changing Role.* Wylie, Texas: Information Plus.

Maypole, D. (1987). Sexual harassment at work: A review of research and theory. *Affilia: Journal of Women and Social Work,* 2 (1), 24-38.

Rich, A. (1979). *On lies, secrets, and silence (Selected prose, 1966-1978),* pp. 203-204. New York: Norton.

Rix, S.E., ed. (1990). *The American woman, 1990-1991: A status report.* New York: Norton.

The Emergence of Women
as a Force for Change in EAP's

Betty Reddy

SUMMARY. For about 15 years women professionals in both the Employee Assistance and alcohol/drug addiction treatment fields have attempted to raise awareness in the workplace about the specific problems faced by women. In this article, the author has traced a brief history of both a personal and a professional emergence of the awareness of women's issues. She has also outlined the organizational efforts that have been planned and actualized by the EAP field to bring about positive changes for women.

For about fifteen years women professionals in both the Employee Assistance and the alcohol and drug addiction treatment fields have diligently pursued efforts to raise awareness in the workplace about the specific problems faced by women. They have worked to identify both problems and reasonable changes which when implemented can benefit both women and the workplace. Some of the issues which surfaced in the early 80's—equality in pay, opportunities and training for advancement, and recognition and respect for gender differences—still have not been resolved. Sexual

Betty Reddy, CSADC, CEAP, is affiliated with Rush Behavioral Health Center, The Institute for Mental Well-Being, Rush-Presbyterian St. Luke's Medical Center, Chicago, IL.

Address all correspondence to: Betty Reddy, 9351 Bay Colony Road, #2E, Des Plaines, IL 60016.

[Haworth co-indexing entry note]: "The Emergence of Women as a Force for Change in EAP's." Reddy, Betty. Co-published simultaneously in the *Employee Assistance Quarterly* (The Haworth Press, Inc.) Vol. 9, No. 3/4, 1994, pp. 1-9; and: *Empowering Women in the Workplace: Perspectives, Innovations, and Techniques for Helping Professionals* (ed: Marta Lundy, and Beverly Younger) Harrington Park Press an imprint of The Haworth Press, Inc., 1994, pp. 1-9. Multiple copies of this article/chapter may be purchased from The Haworth Document Delivery Center [1-800-3-HAWORTH; 9:00 a.m. - 5:00 p.m. (EST)].

1

harassment has become much more visible since the Hill-Thomas hearings. As society continues to be educated about women's issues, a broader spectrum of human issues has emerged. The lack of availability of child care to working parents, either single parents or couples, is a problem that communities and corporations are beginning to grapple with. The work force is continuing to become more diverse in the sexual, cultural and racial composition of workers. We must become understanding and accepting of cultural differences and develop skills in working well together. It is satisfying to note that the topics in this volume will shed light on some of the very difficult subjects having to do not only with women's issues, but also with racial and cultural differences.

As I thought about my own involvement in the EAP field, I realized that I have been interested and involved in women's issues since 1978. In my own experience as a working woman, I did not face serious discrimination. Yet my life experiences have taught me about the nature of prejudice. My deep conviction was, and still is, that no one should face discrimination because of gender, race, culture or religion. My involvement in women's committees grew as I listened to other women in the EAP field calling attention to women's rights, supporting the ERA amendment and focusing on a variety of workplace injustices, such as pay scale differences. The education and mentoring I received from other women leaders taught me that we need a continued focus on women's issues.

Taking a trip down memory lane, I can trace my own evolving awareness of women's needs. So many things have drastically changed since I was born that I am often amazed at what I've seen and experienced. When I was young we lived in the town of Casper, Wyoming, in a four-room house with an outhouse. Weekly baths were in a big tub set on the kitchen table. When I was about seven years old, we moved to Aurora, Illinois. There we had a bathroom and a telephone. I finally learned to overcome my fear of talking on the phone. Imagine, now I'm often on it most of the day.

Throughout my growing-up years, our family entertainment often consisted of listening together to radio programs or going for a car ride with the whole family in the country. There was open country in the Chicago area in those days. Other times we would play baseball in the street in front of our house, roller skate, or hike in the woods.

I was the oldest in our family, with two younger brothers and a little sister. Our parents were loving, but strict. Dad taught us to be responsible, to face consequences and learn from mistakes. I was a good student and very inquisitive. My father always took time to talk over my questions, encouraging me to learn. He was an active booster of my self-esteem, something I needed in my teens.

In many ways Dad was a self-made man, having moved up from a timekeeper on the Chicago, Burlington and Quincy Railroad to a staff officer in Labor Relations and, eventually, to the Western Division of the National Railway Relations board. He told us often of the prejudice he faced at work–the glass ceiling–because he was Irish Catholic. Prejudice against Catholics, especially Irish Catholics, was a fact then.

Mom was fun-loving and the heart of our family. She softened my Dad's strictness and kept our family close and happy. We grew up with the usual family roles for men and women that were expected at that time. I was astonished when, about a year ago, I went through a photo album my mother kept when she was about seventeen to twenty years old. I had never thought about what her life was like as a young woman. The whole album was filled with pictures of her and several girlfriends sightseeing across the United States and Canada. She had worked at the Chicago, Burlington and Quincy Railroad offices in LaCrosse, Wisconsin from age fifteen until she and my dad were married during World War I. She and her friends could travel on railroad passes. In the pictures, they were dressed in very smart outfits and always seemed full of high spirits, obvious from both the pictures and the witty captions. I had never realized my mother had that kind of freedom and independence as a young woman.

Before World War II most women naturally did not plan to go into business. We expected to get married, quit any job we had taken, and raise a family. Because of our tight finances, Dad did not think it was as important for me to graduate from college as it was for my brothers. I didn't consider that a problem. I graduated from Junior College and worked at the Burlington Transportation Company for three years before getting married. This was during World War II and I had a job previously held by a married man who had children. The war opened the road for women into many positions that had been closed to them before.

The lifestyle of wife and mother was normal then. I think that we did not feel limited by the roles we took because we *wanted* to get married and raise children. I felt raising children and all the activities that go hand in hand with that were very important. My husband and I had five children and I was busy with them and their school activities and community programs until the late sixties. I went back to work outside the home only because at one point we had three in college and two in high school.

During the twenty-five years I was at home, our family lived through my dear husband's struggle with alcoholism, and my struggle to cope with its effects on him and the rest of our family. During those years, my husband's alcoholism defined my horizon and it was difficult to focus on anything else. Fortunately, Al-Anon was available in Houston, Texas where we lived and I found the life-line I needed. Three years later Bill gave up his battle with alcoholism and joined A.A. He had twenty-six years of contented sobriety when he died in 1989.

In 1969, Lutheran General Hospital opened a new building dedicated to treatment, research and training for alcoholism. I began working there two weeks after it opened. I was a secretary, but one of my duties was to manage volunteer programs comprised of Al-Anon members. In the early 70's, we provided training for social workers, the Illinois Occupational Program Consultants, and Occupational Nurses, among others. I was often called upon to describe Al-Anon and to play the part of a wife of an alcoholic, in role-plays demonstrating assessment interview techniques that could capture the alcoholic's motivation for treatment.

When I started at Lutheran General, my hope was to receive training to become a counselor. I soon became intrigued by the ability of employers to motivate an alcoholic to enter treatment and follow a recovery plan. And, I had begun to recognize my own abilities in communication and outreach that developed through my Al-Anon work, and my organizational skills that came from running a household.

In the early 70's, the senior staff members of the Center worked with the Illinois State Occupational Program Consultants to introduce executives to the value of Occupational Alcoholism Programs and to provide training programs for supervisors and employees. In 1974, I was promoted and trained to represent the Center in these consulting activities to companies. I was happy to reach professional goals that had sprung out of my own personal growth.

I have revealed this personal history about how I entered the EAP field as it may be similar to the career paths that many other women have taken. My history also shows how my own awareness and recognition of specific gender issues, the ones affecting a great number of women moving into the workforce, have been just as slow in developing as that of many others. In spite of the gradual pace of growth of my own awareness of women's issues, I have been involved since 1978 in ALMACA's (now EAPA) Committees on Women's Issues. In the same time frame that my understanding of women's issues was growing, the impact of women's issues in the workplace was emerging as a legitimate concern for EAPs.

In 1975, I joined the Counselor's Round Table in Chicago, a group of about twenty people in the new field of Occupational Alcoholism Programs. Later, in 1976, this group became charter members of the Illinois Chapter of ALMACA. Nationally, the field was just beginning to shift from Occupational Alcoholism Programs to Employee Assistance Programs.

Among this group in Chicago was one of the first women in this field, Dr. Fern Asma, who was the Associate Medical Director at Illinois Bell Telephone. Begun in 1950, the program she directed was one of the first programs to provide solid statistics on the efficacy of EAP's and later became a broadbrush EAP during the seventies. In 1972, Dr. Asma was one of the trainers for the Occupational Program Consultants, otherwise known as the Thundering One-Hundred, who were trained to promote EAP's in business, industry and government. As companies became interested in EAP's, many people were referred to her to discuss EAP issues and learn how Illinois Bell's program was organized. Through the years, Fern Asma has been one of the leaders in the EAP field and in Illinois, a role model and mentor to many of us, both women and men.

Even though there were few women in the field in the early years there were some women, like Dr. Asma, in leadership positions.

From 1974 to 1976, three women served on the board and executive committee of ALMACA. Women have continued in these positions since then, making significant contributions to employee assistance practices and the development of standards and technologies that identify this profession.

The Employee Assistance Society of North America (EASNA), organized in 1983, indicated their awareness of women's issues by making the inclusion of both women and minorities on the board and executive committee one of its permanent policies. EASNA's first Executive Director was a woman. Further, women comprised about 30% of its first board and now represent about 50% of its current board. Later this year, a woman, currently the Executive Vice-President, should become first president of EASNA. Curiously, EAPA elected its first woman president last fall; in fact, three of the top officers are women. Women have already achieved a prominent place in the field both in numbers and in leadership.

A formal recognition of the need to investigate and learn about the differences between a woman's reality at work and a man's began in the EAP field when ALMACA appointed a steering committee on women in the workplace in 1978. Later, an ad hoc committee was formed which hosted discussions at several national conferences to identify the concerns of women. At the 1983 annual conference, over 100 women and men attendees overwhelmingly supported a motion to strongly request the board to change the ad hoc women's committee to a standing committee, giving the chairperson voting rights and, thereby, placing concerns about women's issues within the formal structure of the organization. The board agreed and the Committee on Women's Issues was established.

The Committee immediately began efforts to achieve the following goals, some of which continue to this day:

1. identify the key issues that impact women at work;
2. provide education, raise awareness and suggest solutions through the use of conference and seminar presentations and articles in magazines and journals;
3. promote outstanding women as keynote speakers at major conferences;

4. place women in leadership roles in the professional organization;
5. promote research on women; and
6. develop recommendations for EAP's, clinicians and corporate America on how to address workplace issues with a gender sensitive approach.

Early Committee activities involved identifying the problems which concerned women most, using surveys that eventually indicated that ACOA problems, co-dependency, women and alcoholism, child care, career paths, and equal pay were some of the primary concerns.

In 1985, the Committee began to solicit articles on these topics and received a commitment from the *ALMACAN* (now the *EAPA Exchange*) to print the articles. From 1985 to 1990, at least three articles appeared each year. In 1987, this committee proposed the development of a bibliography about research on women's issues to the board, and received a commitment from the Illinois Chapter to finance it. "Women, Alcohol, Drugs and Workplace Issues, An Annotated Bibliography of Research" was published in 1988 and had two foci: Women and Alcoholism, and Women in the Workplace. One remarkable result was that it clearly showed how little research in these two areas, using adequate numbers of female subjects, had been done until 1987. The need for more research still exists.

Constant efforts were made to educate EAPs about women's issues and about the knowledge and skills needed to accomplish solutions. The committee also networked with chapter and regional committees, to ensure that papers, seminars and workshops on women's issues continued regularly in each region. Each year the committee has searched for and proposed women keynote speakers for the annual national conference. For instance, last fall a special session was held with Coretta Scott King as the speaker. Over 400 participants attended and were inspired by her talk about civil rights. The Women's Issues Committee of EAPA is another encouraging example of women as a force for change.

As a liaison from ALMACA to the Alcohol and Drug Programs Association (ADPA), I was a member of the planning committee when ADPA held its first annual National Conference on Women's Issues in 1987. In September of 1986, the first planning meeting for the 1987 conference was held. Two women conference co-chairs, Jan Johnson and Rebecca Brownlee, had also scheduled a workshop for women, called "Women on the Way Up," that same weekend. I decided to attend the workshop, which was one of the nicest presents I have ever given myself. The program was designed to help us look at the myths we grew up with about a "woman's place." We explored how we saw ourselves as still controlled or not controlled by these images, what internal barriers to achievement blocked our way, the nature and feel of power and what were our personal feelings about success. We closed by setting realistic goals for ourselves, evaluating their importance and deciding how to achieve them.

During the mid 80's, ALMACA's Committee on Women's Issues assisted the Association of Junior Leagues with a three year alcohol awareness and education campaign called "Woman to Woman." They undertook this project to bring to light some facts about the sex-related differences in the use and effects of alcohol. The Junior Leagues developed a broad-based informational network to get data into the media, corporations and community organizations. It was a well thought-out and expertly implemented campaign.

On the subject of women and alcohol, I just recently came across the *Alcohol Alert* newsletter published by the National Institute on Alcohol Abuse and Alcoholism in April of 1992. It stated that body structure differences in women and men cause women to become more intoxicated than men who have used an equal dose of alcohol, due to stomach enzyme and body fat differences. Based on these findings the article defined moderate drinking for women as no more than one drink a day. It makes me shudder to think that neither I, nor people in my generation or others, knew these facts until the 90s! I wonder, too, how many women know them today.

Recent media articles convince me that we still have a long way to go with research and education on women's issues. The front page of the May 31, 1993 Business Section of the *Chicago Tribune* had an article on the glass ceiling, stating that a 1990 survey indicated that women in Fortune 500 and Service 500 companies make up less than 5% of all managers at or above the level of vice president. We need to continue moving forward to empower women as a force for change; and continue to decrease discrimination and prejudice against not only women, but also toward people of any variety of diverse backgrounds and cultures.

African-American Women in the Workplace: A Personal Perspective from African-American Female EAPs

Barbara McKinney Jackson

SUMMARY. This article looks at the perceptions and professional perspectives of African-American female EAPs who work with African-American women in various industries. It provides an exploration into the attitudes of African-American women about several workplace and personal issues including:

- sexual harassment and discrimination
- racial discrimination
- career opportunities
- work assignment disparity
- organization culture and sensitivity
- organizational supports

These concerns have been examined against a backdrop of actual demographic changes that have occurred for minority and all women over the last decade.

The author has used her own experiences as an EAP professional for the last ten years, in addition to those of other African-American

Address correspondence to: Barbara McKinney Jackson, Jackson & Associates, 8941 South Western Avenue, Chicago, IL 60620.

[Haworth co-indexing entry note]: "African-American Women in the Workplace: A Personal Perspective from African-American Female EAPs." Co-published simultaneously in *Employee Assistance Quarterly* (The Haworth Press, Inc.) Vol. 9, No. 3/4, 1994, pp. 11-19; and: *Empowering Women in the Workplace: Perspectives, Innovations, and Techniques for Helping Professionals* (ed: Marta Lundy, and Beverly Younger) Harrington Park Press an imprint of The Haworth Press, Inc., 1994, pp. 11-19. Multiple copies of this article/chapter may be purchased from The Haworth Document Delivery Center [1-800-3-HAWORTH; 9:00 a.m. - 5:00 p.m. (EST)].

11

women EAPs, in order to highlight and identify the central issues of concern for African-American female clients. The data were gathered through in-depth, face-to-face interviews with six African-American female Employee Assistance professionals. Their experiences illustrated the difficulty that EAPs are still having in effecting the problems of sexual discrimination and harassment, racial discrimination, and general career barriers that African-American women face in the workplace. As our current cadre of intervention strategies are not yet successful, new approaches are called for as we move toward the next century, especially if EAPs are to enhance our effectiveness in helping clients confront some of the most significant problems they face.

As we all approached the 1992 elections there was constant assertion in the media that we were definitely in the "year of the woman." It is true that women made substantial gains in the political arena. Last year the first African-American woman, Carol Mosely Braun, was elected to the U.S. Senate. There are six female senators in all now, the highest number ever elected in the history of this country. In addition, 48 women now serve in the Congress, 24 more than last term. The political advancement of women has come on other fronts as well. There have been substantial gains in the last decade. We now have thousands of female elected officials at the local, state, and national levels.

Outside of politics, women have also seen gains. In corporate America, in government and public institutions, law firms and other professions, women have taken on higher level jobs with apparently better pay than they had ten years ago. Overall, women are making gains, but the question that still begs to be answered is how African-American women have fared in the workplace and elsewhere.

According to data found in the *Statistical Record of Black Americans* (1989), 52% of all African-American women were employed. Indeed, 54% of all women were employed, including 55% of all white women. African-American women were most highly represented in clerical (29%), service (25%) and professional (14%) positions. This compares to 36% (clerical), 16% (service) and 17% (professional), respectively, for white women. The median income in 1983 of $16,000 for full-time employed African-American females was lower than the median incomes of $19,010 for African-American males, $26,680 for white males and $17,030 for white females. So African-American women are still at the lowest end of the economic and occupational hierarchy (Horton & Smith, 1990).

Diversity is the order of the day and it seems clear that the EAP professional is in a position to be on the cutting edge of facilitating diversity awareness, intervention, and cultural change within the workplace. Raising our own consciousness and sensitivity is the first order of business. We have to be aware that within our ranks is a valuable resource waiting to be tapped. Employee Assistance counselors have a unique vantage point from which to view the situation of the clients they service. Employees confide a broad spectrum of personal and professional information that allows counselors to constantly monitor the pulse of change within organizations, at least as it is perceived by the clients. For this reason, an exploration of how African-American female EAPs understand and identify the concerns of their African-American female clients was undertaken. This valuable body of data could help us all increase our sensitivity to the issues that confront African-American women in their personal and professional lives.

METHOD

To initiate this exploration, interviews were conducted with six experienced African-American female EAP professionals. Their total years of EAP practice ranged from 2.5 to 10 years, and averaged 6.8 years. However, the total years of their entire clinical experience ranged for 2.5 to 25 years, and averaged 12.4 years. A questionnaire was constructed to gather data highlighting critical areas of personal and professional concerns presented by African-American female clients in the workplace. The participants were asked the following questions in face-to-face sessions.

- What percentage of your clients are African-American women?
- What issues or concerns are presented to the EAP by African-American women?
- What EEO concerns were brought up by African-American women, including sexual harassment and racial discrimination?

- What workplace advancement concerns do African-American female clients have?
- What are the workplace culture concerns of your African-American women clients?
- What factors or characteristics of the organization are identified as helpful to or supportive of African-American females?
- What strategies have you used as an EAP to help these clients resolve any of the above issues?
- How successful have these strategies been to assist African-American female clients?
- What prior or current other thoughts have you had about these issues?
- What, if any, nagging concerns do you still have about these issues?
- What EAP strategies or interventions would you propose to have EAPs be even more effective on behalf of African-American female clients?

The six interviews were conducted over six weeks with African-American female EAPs from a variety of settings. The sample included counselors from a large corporate in-house program; two from governmental agencies; two from external EAP providers (one from a large national firm and the other from a small independent local firm) and the last from a large union-sponsored program. All participants are based in a midwest metropolitan area and serve employees located in urban, suburban and rural settings.

RESULTS AND DISCUSSION

The percentage of African-American female clients served by the six EAP counselors ranged from 3% to 75% of the total client population. The character of the organization and the demographic mix of the employee base seemed to be the most critical variable in explaining the vast range of percentages.

When asked to identify the issues most often presented by their clients, the six EAPs concluded that 50% to 100% of all presenting problems were personal concerns. These would include (1) finances;

(2) substance abuse (their own or family members); (3) marital and family conflict; (4) mental health/mental illness; and (5) the general stress of managing work and home pressures. When work related issues were identified by clients, they most often included (1) job opportunities; (2) issues of fairness; (3) advancement; (4) burnout; (5) interpersonal conflict (co-workers and supervisors); and, less frequently, (6) harassment or discrimination.

When solicited specifically about the EEO concerns of their clients, the EAP counselors noted racial discrimination, as the primary presenting problem, was raised by 0% to 10% of their African-American female clients. Similar percentages existed with respect to sexual harassment. Fifty percent of the women sampled indicated that sexual harassment and racial or sexual discrimination tended to be raised by clients after first identifying other concerns (i.e., a desire for a promotion because of financial need). The EAPs interviewed felt that these vital concerns were probably minimized by their clients out of a need to focus on other immediate threats to personal or family stability and out of a sense of powerlessness to change their work environments.

Similarly, workplace advancement was raised as a primary presenting problem in less than 5% of all the EAP's cases. When this issue was raised, it seemed to be connected to (1) difficulties experienced with other employees prior to or after promotion; (2) highly political environments where the general perception is that women and/or African-Americans are automatically locked out of higher positions; or (3) in a few cases, situations where advancement is actually used by management to "get rid of" problem employees. Just as harassment and discrimination problems were minimized, the inequities that African-American women face in the workplace were not easily or directly addressed by the EAP clients.

Workplace culture issues were seldom raised by this client population. Many seemed to perceive the culture of the organization as something impervious to their intervention or input. Each participant identified only a few clients who actually focused on cultural disparities or value differences. When workplace culture issues were noted, however, the organizational culture was most often described as negative or oppressive. Employees who had identified a cultural conflict were perceived as more likely to leave the organization as a way of resolving the disparity.

The identification of what employees saw as supportive or helpful about the environment was complex. In work organizations where a diversity of personnel exist–for example, professional, service or manufacturing personnel–the perceptions seem to follow job lines. In these instances, professionals identified child care assistance and personnel policies which allow for compensatory time as helpful, whereas service personnel did not. The most frequently cited positive factors were employee benefits, including health, pension, insurance and credit unions. Occasionally, supportive relationships with co-workers were mentioned as being helpful. The most striking observation made by the EAPs was that employees seldom felt compelled to mention any positive attribute of the work organization or environment.

To begin to distill out effective techniques for finding resolutions to the problems faced by African-American female clients, the question regarding intervention strategies was raised. When the primary presenting problems were of a personal nature, most of the EAPs applied traditional strategies–assessment and referral for counseling or treatment, assisting clients with problem solving, journaling, and the use of support networks.

However, when the primary concerns were identified as work-related or organizational, a variety of strategies were used. The EAPs seemed to intervene at three levels; the first is consultation with, or referral to, other departments within the organization (Human Resources, Employee Relations, Equal Employment Officers, Ethics departments, etc.). In extreme cases, employees were advised or, at least, informed of the right to go to the agencies outside of the company which are mandated to deal with these discrimination issues, including the Department of Labor, the EEOC, and the Human Rights Commissions.

Secondly, EAPs would attempt further internal intervention by collaborating directly with supervisors or managers and, conjointly, by offering training in EEO laws and regulations, such as those related to sexual harassment or the ADA. More training has been offered on the broader topics–managing organizational change, stress management, communication, anger management and team building–that impinge upon these issues.

The last intervention strategy mentioned by the EAPs required them to remain sensitive to the personal impact of the work environment on the client. Focusing on individual needs, the EAPs would implement strategies to help the African-American women cope, using problem solving, stress management, role playing, journaling, and general supportive counseling.

When the EAPs evaluated the benefits of their cadre of interventions, there was decidedly more confidence in the success of their strategies to help curb personal problems; most EAPs noted that this type of intervention was helpful to clients the majority of the time. In contrast, the strategies implemented to help with work-related issues were seen as helpful in only fifty percent of the cases overall. This appeared to be the result of a few factors: (1) the clients' resistance to taking the necessary steps; (2) the organizational rigidity; and (3) the characteristics of the population (blue collar vs. professionals).

It was evident that the majority of the African-American female Employee Assistance professionals in this sample had given a great deal of thought to these issues. Their concerns were summarized in the following terms: (1) how to impact the culture of the organization; (2) how and where to intervene with diversity issues; (3) how to empower employees appropriately; and (4) generally how to help reduce the stress of the work environment. In spite of the concerns expressed by the sample of EAPs, many problems continue to exist in most of the employment settings of our sample. Some of the EAPs raised the added concern that we as a professional group do not let our effectiveness be undermined by issues like downsizing, organizational resistance and the dilemma of being caught in the middle between management and employees.

Their proposals for what EAPs should do to become more effective almost always included an increase of training within the organization, an added focus on diversity, options for career development, and personal life skills education. But in addition, it is suggested that EAPs rethink and, at times, renegotiate their roles within the organization. A change in role perception would then effect how we market ourselves to the organization.

CONCLUSION

The most striking result of this survey was that 100% of the sample agreed that sexual harassment, racial and sexual discrimination. and career barriers still exist for African-American females in the workplace. EAPs may be having limited success in helping clients with these issues. Our failure is occurring on two levels: (1) developing and implementing strategies to intervene with these problems; and (2) effecting problem resolution.

The ineffectiveness of our profession in mediating the problems affecting African-American females should be extremely troubling to all EAPs. This exploratory study was a "wake up call" to this author, and will hopefully awaken other EAPs. A moral imperative exists that compels us to open up dialogue, pursue training, and restructure our agenda to more appropriately reflect the urgency of this need.

The need to heighten awareness extends to the clients themselves. As our data showed, African-American females seldom raised issues of sexual discrimination or harassment, and when they did, they presented these issues only after raising other issues or concerns. At least two reasons exist for this tendency. First, the issues most often raised by the clients–finances, family relationships, or chemical dependency in the family–are issues that most immediately threaten the integrity of the family. In other words, if these concerns are not addressed, the family's functioning becomes impaired. Secondly, African-American women may have become accommodated to racism and sexism in the workplace, since such problems are so institutionalized in society. In other words, the clients may not expect the workplace to be any other way. These women would never expect that they could change the organization, because they have not been able to do so in the past.

It seems likely that both EAPs and their clients are immobilized by the dilemma of how to strategically exercise power without running the risk of being perceived as "biting the hand that feeds them," thereby threatening their own position and security. However, it is encouraging to know that at least among our sample of African-American female EAPs, these issues have been a focus of their attention, and this significant area of their clients' lives is not being ignored or overlooked.

Admittedly, the sample for this first exploration of these issues was narrowly defined. It seems apparent that the next explorative steps should include evaluating the experience of this same population of African-American women with other groups of EAPs, and looking at other employee populations (i.e., African-American males, and males and females of other backgrounds). It may be instructive to formalize sample selection in future studies, in addition to broadening the geographical area. Hopefully, these results will serve as a base for further dialogues on the issues and concerns of African-American women at work.

REFERENCE

Horton, C. P. & Smith, J.C. (Eds.). (1990). *Statistical Record of Black America.* Detroit: Gale Research, Inc.

Women in the Workplace:
Implications for Child Care

Marie J. Raber

SUMMARY. This study examined the influence of employee sponsored child care service on employee stress level and job satisfaction. The findings revealed that women who used company sponsored child care services manifested significantly lower levels of
stress and higher levels of job satisfaction than women who were not
utilizing this service. In addition, a higher level of satisfaction with
child care arrangements was associated with women involved in
company sponsored child care service compared to women who had
to make their own child care arrangements.

Women employees with young children often need assistance in
balancing the conflicting demands of work and family. In response
to this well-documented problem (Fernandez, 1986; Friedman,
1985; Kamerman, 1987), nearly 5000 employers have offered some
type of child care service as part of their employee benefits package
or referral services available through their employee assistance program. While some offer on-site child care, the majority have opted
for resource and referral programs through which employees obtain
information about licensed child care services that are available and

Marie J. Raber, DSW, CSW, is Assistant Dean, Chair Baccalaureate Social
Work Program, The Catholic University of America.
Address all correspondence to: Dr. Raber at The Catholic University of Ameri-
ca, Shahan Hall, Room 117, Washington, DC 20064.

[Haworth co-indexing entry note]: "Women in the Workplace: Implications for Child Care." Raber,
Marie J. Co-published simultaneously in *Employee Assistance Quarterly* (The Haworth Press, Inc.) Vol. 9,
No. 3/4, 1994, pp. 21-36; and: *Empowering Women in the Workplace: Perspectives, Innovations, and
Techniques for Helping Professionals* (ed: Marta Lundy, and Beverly Younger) Harrington Park Press an
imprint of The Haworth Press, Inc., 1994, pp. 21-36. Multiple copies of this article/chapter may be pur-
chased from The Haworth Document Delivery Center [1-800-3-HAWORTH; 9:00 a.m. - 5:00 p.m. (EST)].

21

geographically accessible. The degree to which these programs reduce women's conflicts in combining work and child-rearing has yet to be systematically measured. This study was designed to examine the relative effectiveness of these two approaches in assisting women in balancing the demands of work and family.

More than one-third of the employed women respondents in a large Boston, Massachusetts, study, reported significant difficulties in managing work and family responsibilities including: (a) not being home when children return from school; (b) need to be absent from work when a child is sick; (c) need to attend school events during the work day; (d) need to take children to health care appointments; and (e) problems of transportation to and from child care (Googins & Burden, 1987). A comparable percentage (33%) of the employed women respondents with children in the greater Kansas City, Missouri, area reported similar difficulties in combining work with family responsibilities (Emlen & Koren, 1984). In this study, 56 percent of the women employees reported serious problems locating child care.

Employer responses to the dilemma of finding quality child care vary widely. Employers prefer to assist employees by providing information on child care facilities through seminars and workshops or by participating in a referral and placement system, but not by providing on-site child care, or cafeteria type benefit options. A community-based resource and referral network provides employees with data on the entire supply of centers, nursery schools, family day care, summer day camps, and many other programs in the community. When combined with the services of a local child care expert, a computerized data base provides more options than the parent could otherwise identify. Indeed, a parent cannot find some of these forms of care in any other way.

Given the variety and the cost of benefit options available, it is not surprising that information services are considerably more popular among employers than subsidies and on- or near-site day care. Resource and referral services avoid the substantial start-up cost, involvement, and liability issues inherent in on- or near-site day care. The caveat is that the new or inexperienced parent may falsely assume that the child care programs recommended by the resource and referral service are of high quality status, whereas the reality is that the employer only assures that the programs are duly licensed. The quality must be assessed by the parent in relation to the needs of his or her child. The positive side of this assumption is that the ultimate choice of the child care arrangements is left with the parent.

BALANCING JOB AND FAMILY

Stress

A Kansas City Child Care Study found that women with young children had the highest incidence of absenteeism of all employees (Emlen & Koren, 1984). The study noted that there was an observable relationship between the company's response to employees' needs and the employees' compliance with work expectations (for example, attendance, lateness, early departures and interruptions). This study also found that women with children reported experiencing more overall stress in life than did men with children. Findings from surveyed employees in thirty-three companies indicate that women employees assumed most of the responsibility for providing or arranging for child care. Emlen and Koren (1984) stated that "absenteeism for men was low *because* women's was high. . . . In families where both spouses earned income, women still appeared to carry a disproportionate share of the child care responsibilities (p. 65)," including work interruptions twice as often as men with children.

A major survey of 5,000 management and non-management employees found that 43 percent of the women employees who were attempting to balance work and family responsibilities experienced more stress at home than at work (Fernandez, 1986). Fernandez also reported that children's ages affected the degree of stress experienced by working mothers attempting to balance both worlds. In addition, 58 percent of the women employees with young children attributed unproductive time at work to child care concerns. The Quality of Employment Survey (Quinn & Shepard, 1974) reported that more than one-third of all workers living in families experienced moderate or severe conflict between work and family life. These conflicts most often concerned excessive hours, inflexible schedules, fatigue and irritability caused by work. These workers also were significantly less satisfied with both their jobs and their family life. Six hundred-fifty employees in a large, Boston-based corporation attributed occasional depression to the stress of balancing work and family responsibilities (Friedman, 1985).

Job Satisfaction

Job satisfaction reflects a complex interaction of demographic, organizational and situational variables (Berg, 1980; Fernandez, 1975; Steers & Porter, 1979). It is important that research on women and their employment treat women's work with sufficient complexity. A review of recent quantitative research on the relationship of women's employment to family adjustment reveals that job-specific variables rarely are examined. Research on job satisfaction for women has primarily considered the impact of women's family situation in explaining their job satisfaction. Prestige, recognition, participation in decision-making, job demands and complexity and other organizational variables have been studied almost exclusively for men. This job model approach has either excluded women as subjects or did not analyze sex differences (Lennon & Rosenfield, 1992).

A few studies have examined the interaction of job conditions related to control and family situation. Lowe and Northcott (1988) find that women postal workers experience more symptoms of distress when they are married and when they have job variety and challenge. Other research finds that jobs that have little control, variety and challenge are related to poorer mental health (Hibbard & Pope, 1986). Barnett and Marshall (1989) find that having a rewarding job can protect women against the psychological distress associated with troubled family relationships. Finally, Repetti (1988) finds that the relationship between depressive symptoms and work quality in terms of social climate, supervisor support, and job satisfaction is strengthened when the division of labor at home is inequitable.

This research clearly indicates that family demands have a significant impact on women's job satisfaction but provides little reliable information on the organizational indicators of women's job satisfaction. For this reason the author utilized research addressing job satisfaction with men in order to operationalize the job satisfaction variable for analysis within this study.

Researchers have examined a variety of organizational variables such as working conditions and the type of supervision in relation to job satisfaction experienced by men. Results from previous research indicate that the following organizational variables are conducive to high levels of job satisfaction: (1) opportunities for interaction with other workers on the job; (2) democratic style of leadership in which workers are allowed to participate in decision making about matters which affect them; and (3) fringe benefits.

Generally, in studies of men and their employment, opportunity for advancement has been recognized as one of the most influential determinants of job satisfaction. Herzberg (1959) found that achievement, recognition, and perceived opportunities for advancement were the main factors affecting job satisfaction among men. Other researchers (Quinn & Shepard, 1974), have confirmed the finding that job satisfaction and self-perceptions of the likelihood of promotion are strongly correlated.

Quinn and Shepard (1974) claimed that occupational status is the single most powerful predictor of job satisfaction. It is not clear, however, if it is the variable of occupational status *per se*, or other variables associated with it that produces the relationship. For example, high-status job positions are generally associated with a variety of rewards: high incomes, good opportunities for advancement, challenging work, and possibilities for achievement and recognition. Any of these variables could interact with the occupational status variable to modify the relationship between position and job satisfaction.

One wonders if women would identify the same variables. Women continue to fill traditional jobs, like secretary, social worker, teacher, which allow them to be available for family and work, but offer little upward mobility. Upward mobility is most available through management training seminars and career-oriented job responsibilities, investments that companies may not offer to women due to their assumed family obligations. Women continue to have the societal mandate for primary care of the family, burdening them with multiple roles. Neither role provides much status for women.

In addition to organizational variables, studies of job satisfaction have also factored in such demographic variables as age, income and education. Studies describing the relationship between age and job satisfaction have appeared frequently in the literature. This research has consistently shown that older workers are more satisfied with their jobs than younger workers (Quinn & Shepard, 1974). This same study found the general positive correlation between age and job satisfaction to hold regardless of job classification. However, this work does not consider the social role or the family responsibility of women. As women grow older, they continue with their responsibilities for children and often add to that, the responsibility of aging parents. It is not clear that there would be the same findings for women.

Income level is another variable that has been researched in relationship to job satisfaction. Studies have shown that workers with high incomes are generally more satisfied with their jobs than are workers with low incomes (Quinn & Shepard, 1974). Generally, women make $.64 for every $1 that a man makes. The pay inequities are well-known and notorious, so women may well desire greater opportunity and higher rewards, but they also may be discouraged by the continual low status. Caring for one's family presumably brings its own rewards, therefore, there is no monetary compensation.

Researchers have found that among workers with less than a college degree, there is not a linear relationship between education and job satisfaction. By contrast, the research has shown that a significant relationship between job satisfaction and education occurs among workers with at least a college degree. Generally, more highly educated workers have been able to obtain jobs in which economic and psychological rewards are available.

In spite of potential conflict between work and family life, the advantages of mothers' employment are substantial and consequently beneficial for many families. Hoffman (1979) reports that studies have indicated that the working mother is more satisfied with her life than the non-working mother (McBride, 1990). Both older and more recent studies show that the mother's satisfaction with her job increases her effectiveness as a parent (McBride, 1990). Hoffman and McBride concluded that the family with a working mother may be better suited than the traditional family for preparing children to fill changing adult roles–roles in which parents share work and family functions.

METHODS

This effectiveness study uses an *ex post facto* design to test a hypothesis regarding child care and women employees' levels of stress and job satisfaction. Specifically, we wanted to know if women's levels of stress would be lower and job satisfaction higher if their children participated in child care programs located through the company's resource and referral program or through independent child care arrangements. This survey was limited to employees of one major insurance corporation and targeted women with at least one child less than sixteen years of age. Surveys were mailed to 450 employees: 150 who had used the company's child care resource and referral program and 300 who had not. One hundred thirty-nine survey instruments were returned for an overall response rate of 31 percent.

Survey Instrument

The data collection instrument consisted of a four-part structured questionnaire of 82 items:

Demographic Information. The 14 selected characteristics focused on the women and their children.

Child Care Arrangements. Five items were on child care arrangements and reasons for selection. A set of 27 items explored characteristics (such as suitability, affordability, staffing, programming) related to the quality of the child care arrangement.

Employee Stress Level. These questions were designed to identify stress, for example, self doubt, worry, guilt, and pressure. Other respondents expressed feelings of contentment, fulfillment, self-respect and balance in regard to job and family obligations (Bohen & Viveros-Long, 1983; Bronfenbrenner & Cochran, 1976; Colletta, 1978; Pearlin, 1975). The Employee Stress Level Scale used within this study was comprised of two sub-scales (Komarosky, 1977): (1) The Job-Family Role Strain Scale consisted of eight items reflecting four specific aspects of role related stress–(a) ambiguity about norms; (b) inadequate resources provided by community social structure; (c) low rewards for role conformity; and (d) conflict between normative phenomena (Komarosky, 1977); (2) The Family Management Scale consisted of six items in four categories–health, education, retail services, and family interaction. All items in both sub-scales were rated on a four point Likert-type scale with choice alternative labels of *very easy, somewhat easy, somewhat difficult* and *very difficult.*

Level of Job Satisfaction

These questions covered the relationship between family and work responsibilities. Items were selected from a job satisfaction measure developed by the University of Michigan Institute for Social Research (ISR) (Quinn & Shepard, 1974). The ISR measure was developed by integrating data from previous factor analytic studies of job satisfaction and responses to interview questions about the specific qualities that describe the ideal job. Two factors of job satisfaction emerged from these efforts: (1) facet-free job satisfaction, which probed the worker's general affective reaction to the job, and (2) facet-specific job satisfaction, which tapped the worker's satisfaction with distinct aspects of the job such as pay, benefits, opportunity for promotion, and supervision.

FINDINGS

The ages of the 139 female respondents ranged from 22 to 44 years with a mean age of 34.2 years. Of the all white, middle-class respondents, 33.1% had completed a graduate degree; 40.3% completed their college education; and 23% finished high school.

Thirty-nine (39.6%) percent of the respondents were in management positions, 42.4 percent in professional/supervisory jobs and 18 percent in clerical/secretarial positions. With regard to the family structure of participants, 44.6 percent had one child, 43.9 percent had 2 children, 9.4 percent had 3 children and 2.2 percent of the respondents had 4 children (see Table 1).

Two groups (users versus non-users of resource and referral programs) were identified based on responses to the item "Is your

TABLE 1
Demographic Characteristics of Subjects

Demographic Characteristics		Frequency (n = 139)	Percentage of Valid Cases
<u>Age (in years)</u>	22-30	30	21.7
	31-40	94	68.1
	41-46	14	10.1
	Missing	1	
<u>Education</u>	H.S. graduate	32	23.9
	Undergraduate Degree	56	41.8
	Graduate Degree	46	34.3
	Missing	5	
<u>Marital Status</u>	Single	4	2.9
	Married	119	85.6
	Separated	1	0.7
	Divorced	7	5.0
	Widowed	1	0.7
	Remarried	7	5.0
<u>Household Income</u>			
15,001-25,000		8	5.8
25,001-35,000		5	3.6
35,001-50,000		15	10.8
50,001-65,000		26	18.7
65,001-80,000		18	12.9
80,001-100,000		22	15.8
Over 100,000		45	32.4
<u>Individual Income</u>			
10,000-18,000		12	8.7
18,001-26,000		28	20.3
26,001-35,000		23	16.7
35,001-45,000		18	13.0
45,001-56,000		35	25.4
56,001-68,000		10	7.2
68,001-80,000		4	2.9
Over 80,000		8	5.8
Missing		1	
<u>Occupational Level or Type of Employment</u>			
Management/Manager		55	39.6
Professional/Supervisor		59	42.4
Office/Clerical		25	18.0
<u>Children in Family</u>			
1 child		62	44.6
2 children		61	43.9
3 children		13	9.4
4 children		3	2.2
Children with Special Needs		13	9.4
<u>Services for Special Needs</u>			
Physical & Developmental		17	12.2
Speech and Language		3	2.2

child currently involved in child care arrangements that were suggested by the Resource and Referral Service?" Of the 139 respondents, forty-five women with young children took advantage of the service (labeled users), and forty-eight women with young children did not take advantage of the service (labeled non-users), for a total response of 93. The remaining 46 did not need child care services at the time of this survey.

The results indicate an association among women who use employee sponsored child care services and who experience significantly lower levels of stress and higher levels of job satisfaction. Further analysis revealed that employee stress was associated with (a) *family characteristics* (number of children, children with special needs, parental responsibility for day to day arrangements for children, and whether the working mother has one or more children under the age of three); (b) *conflict characteristics* (job/family interference due to ill child, level of job/family interference, times late, times absent, times interrupted at work due to child care responsibilities); and (c) *use of child care program* (working mother's child was currently in a child care program recommended by resource and referral service). Acknowledging the likelihood of additional influences on employees stress level and job satisfaction family characteristics and job-family conflict characteristics were examined. Multivariate analyses were performed using a stepwise multiple regression analysis to examine the relationship of the predictor variables of (1) employee characteristics; (2) family characteristics; (3) job-family conflict characteristics; (4) recommended child care; and (5) child care satisfaction scale to the criterion variables of **employee stress** and **job satisfaction**. Only the following three predictor variables were found to be statistically significant (see Table 2): (1) level of job-family interference; (2) times late due to child care responsibility (see conflict characteristics); and (3) whether the child is currently in a child care program recommended by resource and referral.

Family characteristics explained 15% of the variance in the criterion variable employee stress level. Job-family conflict characteristics explained 38% of the variance and recommended child care explained 4% of the variance, as shown in Table 3.

TABLE 2

Significant Predictors of Employee Stress Level

	Beta
Level of Job Family Interference	.418**
Times Late Due to Child Care Responsibility	.264**
Whether Child is Currently in a Child Care Program Recommended by Resource and Referral	.232*

*p < .05

**p <.01

R^2 (total variance explained) = .564

TABLE 3

Employee Stress Level

	Variance Explained
Family Characteristics	15%
Job Family Conflicts Characteristics	38%
Recommended Child Care	4%

Job Satisfaction

Both significant predictor variables, job-family conflict characteristics and child care satisfaction scale were entered in a Stepwise Multiple Regression Analysis to the criterion variable of job satisfaction and both were found to be statistically significant (see Table 4).

Employee characteristics explained 13% of the variance in the criterion variable; job satisfaction and family characteristics explained 9% of the variance; job-family conflict characteristics accounted for 24% of the variance; recommended child care was 2% of the variance; and the child care satisfaction scale was 17% of the variance, as shown in Table 5.

TABLE 4

Significant Predictors of Job Satisfaction

	Beta
Job Family Conflicts Characteristics Level of Job Family Interference	.305**
Child Care Satisfaction Scale	.548**

**p <.01
R^2 (total variance explained) = .655

TABLE 5

Job Satisfaction

	Variance Explained
Employee Characteristics	13%
Family Characteristics	9%
Job Family Conflicts Characteristics	24%
Recommended Child Care	2%
Child Care Satisfaction Scale	17%

Stress and Job Satisfaction

The group of employees currently using the company's child care resource and referral program reported significantly lower levels of stress and significantly higher levels of job satisfaction than did the group which had developed their own child care arrangements.

DISCUSSION

The study yielded interesting results beyond those directly related to the initial hypothesis. High levels of overall satisfaction with child care arrangements were reported by 79 percent of women. In contrast to these positive perspectives, it is important to learn that 55 percent of this group continue to experience strong interference in balancing job and family responsibilities, for example, when a child is ill, or when a mother is traveling due to business responsibility. Eighty percent of the respondents worried about whether they should work less and spend more time with their families. Over 60 percent of the respondents described themselves as having the primary responsibility for the day to day arrangements for the care of their children, reporting that their spouse did not share the responsibility.

The results suggest that employee stress and feelings of job satisfaction are related to the type of child care arrangements chosen, to the level of satisfaction a working mother reports about her child care arrangements, and to the age and special needs of the child. Nevertheless, even with satisfaction with child care arrangements, women working full-time and attempting to combine the responsibilities of job and family experience interference between these two roles. They continue to ask, "Should I work less and spend more time with my family?"

CONCLUSION

This study has provided significant data that identifies important considerations for women within the work force, for the social work profession, and for the corporate community. The data clearly indicate that providing working mothers with information about child care programs as well as assistance in accessing such programs contribute to lessening the stress level for women who are attempting to balance work and family responsibilities. Moreover, working mothers with young or special needs children require specific child care information and arrangements, as their needs are going to be greater. The resource and referral service now provided by a growing number of companies has been available for only a short period of time. Within the next several years, a larger variety of companies may utilize this service which will permit more conclusive research on its effects.

The continuous role conflict experienced by women who work and have primary responsibility for the family has been identified with depression. The National Institutes of Mental Health (NIMH) has launched a major effort to study depression (McBride, 1988).

Research needs to focus on theoretical models aimed at explaining both how mental illness is caused by role overload/conflict and how it is prevented, limited, or modified by specific intervention. These models should not only be sensitive to the woman but should also be sensitive to the individual to family fit (McBride, 1990). Future research also should address such issues as quality child care standards, special needs services and care of ill children. Few professionals are better suited to accomplish the necessary research than are employee assistance professionals.

Employee Assistance professionals need to be knowledgeable and sensitive to the demands women face when balancing work and family obligations. Women employees should be encouraged to participate in exploring creative organizational solutions regarding child care issues. Possible solutions could include flex time, job sharing, and family leave. Furthermore, social workers in the role of EAP counselors should provide meetings at times workers can attend, for example, lunch time seminars. These meetings could provide support as well as resources to working women for identifying solutions for work related conflicts that interfere with balancing their lives. By associating with other women in similar situations, they will learn that their feelings of stress are shared by other women; that indeed they are not failing in their work roles or their family roles. Opportunities to share effective strategies to alleviate their stress and deal more effectively with conflicting work and family demands will be available. The experience could be very empowering, allowing women to come together to become agents of change within their own environments.

REFERENCES

Barnett, R. & Barach, G. (1985) "Women's involvement in multiple roles and psychological distress," *Journal of Personality and Social Psychology, 49,* 135-145.

Berg, W.E. (1980). "Effects of job satisfaction on practice decisions: A linear flowgraph analysis." *Social Work Research and Abstracts, 16,* 30-37.

Bohen, H.H., & Viveros-Lang, A. (1981). *Balancing Jobs and Family Life.* Philadelphia: Temple University Press.

Bohen, H.H., & Viveros-Lang, A. (1983). *Corporate Employment Policies Affect-*

ing Families and Children: The United States and Europe. New York: Aspen Institute for Humanistic Studies.

Bronfenbrenner, U. & Cochran, M. (1976). *Conceptual framework: Categories for assessing parental stresses and supports.* Mimeograph for Cornell Symposium, Cornell University.

Colletta, N.D. (1978). *Divorced Mothers at two income levels: Their systems and child-rearing practices.* Ph.D. Dissertation, Cornell University.

Emlen, A.C., & Koren, P.E. (1984). *Hard to Find and Difficult to Manage: The Effects of Child Care on the Workplace.* Portland, OR: Portland State University Press, p. 64.

Fernandez, J.P. (1975). *Black marriages in white corporations.* John Wiley & Sons: NY, NY.

Fernandez, J.P. (1986). *Child Care and Corporate Productivity: Resolving Family Work Conflicts.* Lexington, MA: Lexington Books.

Friedman, D.E. (1985). "Corporate Financial Assistance for Child Care," *The Conference Board*, Research Bulletin No. 177, 48-59.

Googins, B. & Burden, D. (1987). "Vulnerability of working parents: Balancing work and family roles," *Social Work*, 295-300.

Harrell, J. & Ridley, C. (1975). "Substitute child care, maternal employment, and the quality of mother-child interaction." *Journal of Marriage and the Family*, *37*(8), 556-564.

Herzberg, F. (1959). *Job Attitudes: Review of Research and Opinion.* Pittsburgh: Psychological Service of Pittsburgh, 342-351.

Hibbard, J. & Pope, C. (1987) "Employment characteristics and health status among men and women," *Women and Health*, *12*, 85-103.

Hoffman, L.W. (1979). "Maternal Employment," *American Psychologist*, 34.

Kamerman, S.B., & Kahn, A.J. (1987). *Child Care: Facing the Hard Choices.* Dover, MA: Auburn House Publishing Co.

Komarosky, M. (1977). *Blue-Collar Marriage.* New York: Random House.

Lennon, M. & Rosenfield, S. (1992) "Women and mental health: The interaction of job and family condition." *Journal of Health and Social Behavior*, *33*, 316-327.

McBride, A.B. (1989, August). Multiple roles, intimate relationships, and depression. Paper presented at the annual meeting of the American Psychological Association, Atlanta, GA.

McBride, A.B. (1990). "Mental health effects of women's multiple roles." *American Psychologist*, *45*(3), 381-383.

Pearlin, L.I. (1975). Sex Roles and Depression. In *Life-span developmental psychology: Narrative life crisis*, N. Dalton (Ed.). New York: Academic Press, 191-207.

Quinn, R.P., & Shepard, L.J. (1974). *The 1972-73 Quality of Employment Survey.* Ann Arbor, MI: University of Michigan Press.

Richardson, J.G. (1979). "Wife occupational superiority and marital troubles. An examination of the hypothesis." *Journal of Marriage and the Family*, *41*(2), 63-72.

Ridley, C.A. (1973). "Exploring the impact of work satisfaction and involvement on marital interactions when both partners are employed." *Journal of Marriage and the Family, 35*(5), 229-237.

Repetti, R. (1988) "Family and occupational roles and women's mental health," in *Women at work*, edited by R. M. Schwartz. Los Angeles: Institute of Industrial Relations Publications, University of California, 97-129.

Steers, R.M. & Porter, L.W. (1979). *Motivation and work behavior.* McGraw-Hill: NY, NY.

Employed Single Mothers: Balancing Job and Homelife

Judith C. Casey

Marcie Pitt-Catsouphes

SUMMARY. The recent attention on work and family issues has focused almost exclusively on dual earner couples and working married mothers while largely ignoring female headed single parent families. Given that single mothers have and will continue to have a significant presence in the work world, it is important to consider their priority needs. However, there is minimal empirical data about the work and home lives of working single mothers and little understanding of differences that exist between their experiences and those of other working mothers. This article offers a comprehensive description of the current experiences of employed single mothers and details new insights into their concerns and issues. EAP and corporate strategies that could reduce stress and enhance resiliency are discussed in order to maximize the role of EAPs in meeting the needs of this growing employee population.

Generally, corporations have not acknowledged the significant presence and participation of single mothers in the workplace. The recent attention on work and family issues has focused exclusively on dual earner couples and working married mothers while largely

Judith C. Casey, MSW, and Marcie Pitt-Catsouphes, MSP, are affiliated with the Center on Work and Family, Boston University, Boston, MA.

Address all correspondence to the authors at: Boston University Center on Work and Family, One University Road, Boston, MA 02215.

[Haworth co-indexing entry note]: "Employed Single Mothers: Balancing Job and Homelife." Casey, Judith C., and Marcie Pitt-Catsouphes. Co-published simultaneously in *Employee Assistance Quarterly* (The Haworth Press, Inc.) Vol. 9, No. 3/4, 1994, pp. 37-53; and: *Empowering Women in the Workplace: Perspectives, Innovations, and Techniques for Helping Professionals* (ed: Marta Lundy, and Beverly Younger) Harrington Park Press an imprint of The Haworth Press, Inc., 1994, pp. 37-53. Multiple copies of this article/chapter may be purchased from The Haworth Document Delivery Center [1-800-3-HAWORTH; 9:00 a.m. - 5:00 p.m. (EST)].

ignoring single parent families. The myth still prevails that single mothers are primarily welfare recipients who do not work outside of the home in significant numbers. On the contrary, single parents are very present in today's corporations with estimates that one third of all employees may be single parents at some point in their work career (Burden, 1986). EAPs are in a unique position to recognize the special needs of working single mothers and to advocate for programs and policies which respond to their concerns.

It is well-documented that the number of single parent families has increased dramatically in the last 20 years. Single parent families have tripled in number since 1970 with current estimates at 8.9 million families (Mulroy, 1988). In 1991, single parent households comprised 29% of all households with minor children (U.S. Bureau of the Census, 1992) which means that one in four children live in single parent households. Experts predict that one-half of all children born in 1980 will spend a portion of their childhood living in a single parent family (Glick & Norton, 1986).

It is important to remember that single parents are a heterogeneous group on various dimensions. Although more than ninety percent of single parent families are female headed, two-thirds of single parent mothers were previously married and were separated, divorced, widowed or abandoned by their husbands. The remaining one third have never been married.

A small percentage of single fathers are also raising their children alone, with 3% of U. S. children under age 18 living in single parent families headed by their father (Demo & Acock, 1988). This represents a 300% increase in the number of fathers raising children following separation and divorce since 1970 (U.S. Bureau of the Census, 1984). In addition, many fathers have joint custody of their children and/or assume primary care for their children during vacations and holidays.

Statistics consistently indicate that single parent households headed by women face particular financial difficulties with a median income 32% lower than married couples with children (U. S. Bureau of the Census, #458, 1992). Even though one-quarter of single parent families have incomes below the poverty level, the majority of female single mothers are in the labor force and employed full-time. In 1990, labor force participation rates were

69% for single mothers ranging from 44% for those with children under 2 years, 65% for those with children 2 to 5 years and 78% for those with children from ages 6-17 (Bureau of Labor Statistics, 1991). Fifty-four percent of African-American, never married women with children under 18 years old are working (Malson, 1986).

Clearly, these statistics indicate that employed single mothers have and will continue to have a significant presence in the work world. However, there is minimal empirical data about the work and home lives of working single mothers and what, if any, differences exist between their experiences and those of other working mothers. Although there is anecdotal information which suggests that employed single mothers are a particularly vulnerable group given their responsibility for the care of their children as well as the demands of their jobs, there is minimal empirical data which supports this contention.

This article represents an initial attempt to move beyond impressions and offer data about working single mothers. The major focus will be working single mothers since they represent the overwhelming majority of working single parents. Input from focus groups with working single parents, survey questions comparing working single mothers to dual earner mothers and information from corporate work-family managers about single parent employees will be presented in this article. The intent is to offer a comprehensive description of the current experiences of employed single mothers as well as to detail new insights into their concerns and issues. EAP and corporate strategies that could reduce stress and enhance resiliency will be detailed in order to maximize the role of EAPs in meeting the needs of this growing employee population.

BACKGROUND

The majority of studies focusing on single mothers have concentrated on those who are either outside of the workforce or only marginally affiliated with it, in spite of the fact that single mothers exhibit the same degree of labor force attachment as other mothers (Tilly and Albelda, 1992). Research initiatives that have explored the priority issues for working single mothers offer some insights into specific aspects of the work experience itself and work-family stress.

A few studies have compared the levels of work-family role conflict experienced by single parent employees with other populations. Burden (1986), for example, reported that employed single parent mothers, in comparison to other married working females or all types of male employees, were at risk for both *augmented job-family role strain* and decreased mental and physical well-being. However, a study conducted by Pleck found that single mothers reported *lower levels of work-family conflicts* in comparison to married working parents (Pleck, 1979). Cohen et al. (1990) did not find any evidence indicating that employment created additional role stress among single mothers.

The scarcest resource for employed single mothers is time. Research conducted by Sanik and Mauldin (1986) found that, in comparison to other family populations (e.g., dual earner families, unemployed one parent families), single parents have the least amount of time to devote to the total spectrum of non-work tasks including child care, household chores, recreation, personal time, and community involvement activities. One interesting result of this study is that the employed single parents did not devote significantly different amounts of time interacting with and providing emotional support to their children. Burden (1986) found that employed single mothers actually spent *less* time on home chores and child care in comparison to married female employees.

The workplace environment can be conceptualized as either a "stressor" or as a source of support. Perry-Jenkins and Gillman-Hanz (1992) did not find significant differences between the well-being of employed single mothers and mothers in dual parent families. Gorlick and Pomfret (1992) found that the employed single mothers in their study reported *higher self-esteem* in comparison to single mothers receiving public assistance; however, the researchers caution that these differences were "modest." In contrast, 53% of the single mothers receiving public assistance indicated that they felt hopeful about their own future "more so than usual," while only 37% of the employed single mothers indicated this level of optimism. These findings contrast other studies that suggest that single mothers' perceptions of their own abilities to effectively support themselves are correlated with life satisfaction and self-esteem (Mahler, 1989).

In spite of the challenges that face single parent employees, there is no research indicating that single parents derive different amounts of job satisfaction in comparison to other working parents. The findings from a few studies suggest that there is a relationship between the ease of combining work and family responsibilities and job satisfaction (Mahler, 1989). Burden (1986) reported that single mothers actually reported higher job satisfaction than other types of employees (e.g., single employees with no dependents, male employees), as well as did Bowen and Orthner (1986). Perry-Jenkins and Gillman-Hanz (1992) found that among single mothers, employment status and certain aspects of job satisfaction were associated with positive mental health outcomes.

Studies that have focused on the job performance of single parents have found no differences in either supervisors' ratings (Mahler, 1989) or in self-reports (Burden, 1986). In spite of wide-spread beliefs to the contrary, there do not appear to be any differences in the absenteeism rates of single parents in comparison to other working parents who have children of similar ages (Mahler, 1989; Burden, 1986).

This brief summary of existing research highlights that the current information about working single mothers is inconclusive and often contradictory. Although previous studies have provided some insights into the lives of single parent employees, many critical questions still remain unanswered. The next section represents an initial attempt to respond to these areas.

METHODS AND RESULTS

This section will provide data from three sources, obtained recently by the Center on Work and Family, about the experiences of working single parents. Qualitative insights, the first source, were derived from three focus groups conducted at local companies to determine how work and home life were affected by single parent status. The focus group of single parents, one-quarter of whom were men, were a diverse mix (age, job, income) of employees from various types of companies. The second source, a sub-study of a larger work and family survey compared working single mothers to dual earner mothers on questions related to balancing job and homelife. Third, results of a survey on single parent employees distributed to 71 companies, all demonstrating some level of commitment to work and family programs, will be reviewed.

Focus Groups

The major goal of the single parent focus groups was to gain insight into the overall experiences of working single parents. The primary areas explored in the focus groups included: (1) perceptions of how work life was affected by home life; (2) how family responsibilities interfered with overall job functioning; and, (3) whether they viewed themselves as similar or different from other working parents.

Working single parents universally stated that their work responsibilities interfered significantly with their family life. They described having to choose between doing a good job at work and being a good parent; this was seen as a no-win situation where they consistently felt like a failure in both spheres. Not only was there a scarcity of time for balancing job and home life demands, but there was even less time for personal needs or relationships. Many single parents described falling into bed exhausted at midnight without even minimal time for themselves. They reported rushing through every activity and constantly feeling pressured to keep on going and do more. Vacations, which can be a time to rejuvenate, were often used for children's appointments or to handle unexpected emergencies. Also, personal sick time or excused days off were often needed to care for sick children. As one mother noted, "I don't have enough sick days to get sick."

Most single parents were reluctant to discuss their single parent status or family concerns at the work place. Generally, the expectation was that this type of disclosure would affect their jobs in a negative manner. Ratings on performance reviews supported this belief, since some supervisors remarked they could have done more at work, if they were not parenting alone. One area of particular interest was underemployment and career aspirations. Single parents purposely selected jobs that could accommodate their single parent status and often deferred career aspirations to family needs.

Some single mothers noted that a double standard existed between male and female single parents. While women were chastised for wanting to participate in school activities, men were praised for these efforts. One women remarked, "When a single mother asks if she can go to her child's school play, she is seen as not committed to her job and often not allowed to go." On the contrary, a male single parent who asks the same question will be told, "Sure. It's just great that you are so interested in your children."

Participants also agreed that each company did set a tone about the legitimacy of balancing work and family issues, but every supervisor interpreted this differently. How your particular boss viewed work and family issues can be more critical than the company tone. However, even if supervisors were supportive, there was a lack of support from some co-workers who perceived flexibility for single mothers as inequitable.

When asked how their home life affects their work life, the overwhelming majority of single parents reported that they received minimal support from others and felt like they were "doing it all alone." Generally, they did not have back-up arrangements and felt like they had to beg others to help, since they were usually unable to reciprocate. Besides being drained from the concrete demands of their busy lives, they were emotionally overloaded, describing how difficult it was without a partner to share child related concerns and difficulties as well as positive events. They viewed their kids as emotionally needy, due to the dearth of available parental time, which adds to the burden experienced by these parents. This situation can be compounded by the presence of unresolved and difficult issues with the non-custodial parent which further strains family relationships. What this all added up to was an employee who arrived at work each day with two full-time jobs that they were attempting to manage on their own.

When asked which resources aided working single parents to meet their work and family demands, they noted how the age of their children affected their work and family balance. With every developmental stage, there are different needs and alternative arrangements which have to be developed and negotiated for each child. Before and after-school programs were considered to be helpful, but were not available in all towns. One women remarked, "I have my school-aged child in two private homes, one in the morning before school and one in the afternoon." Programs which respond to emergency situations (school closing, sick child) can provide needed back-up, but were limited in availability. Some parents have used technology to help them stay in contact with their children. Car phones and beepers (with a special code for "Bring home pizza!") were used to manage emergencies and keep in contact when the unexpected occurred.

Overall, schools were not viewed as supportive of the situation of working single parents. Parents were reluctant to disclose their single parent status to school personnel, since they were concerned that it would be seen as the explanation for any difficulties experienced by their children. Schools were not considered to be flexible or attuned to single parent needs when developing programs, policies or activities.

These working single parents considered themselves to be different than other working parents with less support, less personal time, more stress and greater difficulty balancing job and homelife. Given these unique needs, they requested programs and services specifically geared for them. They reported that they would not feel stigmatized by participation in such a group; some remarked that they already felt "different" in the corporate setting. Specific suggestions included regular, on-going support groups and other forums to share concerns. Participants revealed a need to feel connected and less vulnerable in the workplace. Often, these employees felt isolated and alone. Many remarked that they were glad to meet others in the same situation and some group members exchanged phone numbers at the end of the focus groups. Additionally, some participants wanted a mechanism to let their company know what their needs were as a group.

Employee Survey

The Center on Work and Family surveyed employees working at a high-tech firm to determine the salient work-family issues and employee preferences for services and benefits. An analysis was conducted comparing the experiences of 50 single mother employees to 140 female parent employees in dual earner households.

One of the significant findings was the differential in household incomes between these two groups of mothers. For example, although 22% of the single parents had household incomes under $25,000, only 1.5% of the mothers in dual earner households reported incomes at that level. Clearly, these differences in income limit the abilities of single mothers to purchase certain support services (such as extra sitters) that might help mitigate some work-family conflicts.

In this employee population, the single mothers were much less likely to hold supervisory positions. Only 2% of these mothers indicated that they were responsible for any direct reports in contrast to 16% of the dual earner female parents.

Another interesting finding among these respondents was the higher percentage of dual earner mothers who indicated that "most of their satisfaction comes from my job." Whereas two-thirds of the dual earner mothers agreed with this statement, less than half (46%) of the single mothers agreed.

One item included in the survey asked the respondents to compare the difficulty that they have balancing work and family responsibilities with their perceptions about how difficult this is for other families. The single mothers were much more likely to report that they had a more difficult time meeting both sets of responsibilities in comparison to other families. Thirty-five percent of the single mothers felt it was more difficult for them to achieve a work-family balance compared to only 10% of the dual earner mothers. This finding is very interesting when juxtaposed against the responses to the job-family role strain scale, where there were no significant differences between the role strain reported by the single mothers and the dual earner mothers.

There were several questions included in this study that addressed different aspects of the work experience. Contrary to the perception of some employers that single parents may be less committed than other employees to their jobs, there were no differences in the response patterns to questions about the importance of the job, overall satisfaction with their employment situation, self-ratings of productivity, and general levels of demands associated with job responsibilities. Between the two groups of mothers, there were no differences in the rates of absenteeism (due either to illness, dependent care responsibilities or "other"). Finally, the results suggest that the single and dual earner mothers in this study had similar perceptions about the extent to which their dependent care responsibilities affected their participation in work-related activities such as training, attending conferences, working overtime, traveling and considering promotions.

The findings of this survey indicate that many single mother employees share the same work-related experiences with mothers from dual earner families. However, wherever differences surfaced, single mothers were always in a more challenged position.

Corporate Survey

The Center on Work and Family conducted an exploratory study to gather information about: (1) how much information employers have about their single parent population; (2) company perceptions of the needs of single parent employees; and (3) the availability of family-friendly policies and programs that could assist single parent employees to balance their work and family responsibilities. The majority of the participant companies (85%) were affiliated with corporate membership groups established by the Center to support companies' efforts to develop work-family programs. Forty-eight surveys (or 68%) were completed and returned to the Center.

There was a significant variation in the size of the workforce of these companies, ranging from 200-230,000, with a median employee population of 18,000. Although the purposive sample did not result in a representative group of companies, the participant companies did offer perspectives from a number of different industries ranging from service companies to pharmaceuticals to insurance and financial organizations.

A profile of key policies and programs illustrates the commitment these organizations have made to work-family issues. Nearly all of these companies (94%) had some type of counseling services available to employees. Other work-family benefits included pretax dependent care assistance programs (92%), flexible hours (88%), job sharing (75%) and child care referral services (81%).

One of the survey items asked the companies whether they had any statistical information about their single parent employees. Only one-fourth of the companies indicated that they did have this type of information and only half of these (12.5% of all respondents) had collected information about the needs of their single parents employees (e.g., as part of a work-family needs assessment). Estimates of the size of the single parent employee population ranged from a low of 1% to a high of 35% with the median range being 7.5% to 10%.

It is possible that the relatively low profile of single parents at the workplace has affected the extent to which companies make an effort to determine their unique work experiences. Only 22% of the companies reported that they "sometimes" or "often" specifically invite single parent employees to participate in employee committees so that they can represent this sub-population.

There was no clear consensus among the survey respondents concerning whether single parents have work-family needs that are different from other working parents. In fact, there was a fairly even split among the companies relative to this issue; approximately half (54%) of the organizations "disagreed" with the statement that single parents have essentially the same needs as other parent employees.

DISCUSSION

The findings of these three studies suggest that there are several workplace issues pertinent to single parent employees.

1. *As a group, single parents have mustered together the resources necessary for them to meet both their work and their family responsibilities.* This is the "good news." On several key measurements, such as job performance indicators and most aspects of job-family strain, there are few if any differences between the experiences of single mothers and dual earner mothers. In spite of the challenges that these women face, they seem to have fulfilled critical work and parenting tasks. This profile of the working single mother who is able to function effectively as a worker and a parent is a testimony to the commitment of these women.

2. *The majority of single parents feel stretched to the limit in terms of time, energy and personal finances.* Although many single parents have devised a host of strategies so that they can manage the work and family aspects of their lives, they pay a price for this effort. The extraordinary demands that are placed on working single

mothers may make their lives feel less like a "balancing act" and more like a marathon. Single parents have a common experience in having absolutely reached their limits in terms of what they can do at work and at home, unless they are offered some additional supports beyond those already available to them.

3. *Single parents portray a work and family life that is isolated and virtually disconnected from formal and informal supports.* Isolation is an ever-present experience for many single parents.

- Only a minority of *communities* provide before and after school programs that can be vital to working single parents. Beyond these extended child care programs, most single parents are unfamiliar with other services that could meet their work-family needs.
- Although many companies have taken important steps to strengthen the family-friendly policies and programs offered at the *workplace,* most employers have established only a limited range of work-family options. Furthermore, the existing programs and policies may not be extensive enough to make an appreciable difference in the lives of these workers. For example, many companies report that they have flextime policies, but these are often limited to one-hour "windows" at the beginning or the end of the day. For some single mothers, this flexibility can help but it may not be sufficient to really make a difference in their ability to juggle work and family schedules. The effectiveness of employer-sponsored initiatives may also depend on the informal workplace systems. Very often, the relationships which the single mother has with her supervisor and co-workers is a significant factor influencing whether the single parent employee perceives the work environment to be supportive.
- Although single parents often rely on *friends and family*, they are often not available to offer support on an on-going basis. Grandparents, for instance, may be working themselves or live in a location that is some distance from the single parent's household. It is important to recognize the obvious: the single mother may be the only adult available to respond to the family's needs.

4. *Most companies have scant information about the single parents who work for them.* Clearly, it is difficult for companies to design policies and programs that are sensitive to the work-family experiences of single parents if they do not have even basic demographic data that describes "who" these employees are and "how many" of them fill "what types of positions" within the company. If companies were able to examine the utilization of work-family benefits for specific sub-population users, they would be in a better position to determine whether particular strategies are actually being used by proportionate numbers of single parents in contrast to other parents.

5. *Among the work-family experts who develop and administer key employee programs, there is a significant divergence of opinion about the work experiences and key work-related challenges facing single parent workers.* There does not seem to be any consensus among work-family program coordinators concerning whether the needs of single parents are the same as other working parents.

6. *In spite of the lack of empirical data, there does seem to be an awareness among work-family coordinators that three types of employer-supported initiatives would be helpful to working single parent families.* Increasingly, employers have begun to appreciate that it is essential for single parents to have access to quality, affordable child care in order for them to fulfill their basic work and family responsibilities. In addition, because single parents often have to assume the full burden for child care, a range of flexibility options can make the difference between achieving a balance between work and family versus feeling that these two sets of responsibilities are bound to interfere with one another almost continually. Employee assistance programs can be instrumental in helping their companies to address these issues, so that the workplace is a more supportive environment for single parents.

IMPLICATIONS FOR EAPs

EAPs can be supportive to working single mothers by being more responsive to this population and by using their position within the corporation and larger community to facilitate the job and home life balance for working single mothers. It is suggested that

EAPs determine the exact number of single parent employees in their company and then take steps to understand their unique concerns and needs. It is critical to remember that working single mothers are a heterogeneous group along a range of dimensions, including aspects of family structure (marital status, custody arrangements) as well as the developmental stage of the family. Of special interest would be whether the corporate culture is supportive of working mothers in general and working single mothers in particular.

EAPs can intervene on three major levels with working single mothers–assistance with individual coping, increased utilization of formal and informal supports and access to structural supports (Shin et al., 1989). EAPs can begin by evaluating whether their programs are responsive to the needs of working single mothers. Questions to ask include whether working single mothers have access to the EAP and have utilized this benefit in representative numbers. It can't be assumed that single mothers who have used EAP services in the past are representative of the total employee population of single mothers. A review of recent caseload statistics could determine whether the EAP is seeing single mothers and if so, for what presenting problems. If there are not a significant number of working single mothers who currently use EAP services, outreach activities could be implemented to encourage both involvement and an opportunity to view EAP services as a viable option for assistance with personal difficulties.

Short-term counseling and referral may help single mothers to develop new strategies for resolving specific issues. However, attention should be paid to barriers that might interfere with single mother's utilization of EAP services. The survey data indicated that 32% of single parents did not feel comfortable talking to their company EAP about their work and family conflicts. Given that single mothers experience such pressure to "do it all," they may be reluctant to use EAP, since it could be perceived as another example of how they are a failure. It may be more acceptable for them to request help with a child's problem or a work difficulty, than to go to the EAP and say, "I just can't do this all by myself anymore." Another possible barrier is EAP staff that are not attuned to the concerns of working single mothers.

EAPs can develop work-based programs and services to increase the development of formal and informal supports among working single mothers. Some possibilities for EA programs include support groups, lunch time seminars, discussion groups and assistance with concrete services (child care, legal, financial). Any activity or program which could reduce isolation and provide a forum for sharing concerns with others in the same situation would be most helpful as social supports have been found to be positively correlated with the mental health of single parents (Hanson, 1986; Lindblad-Goldberg, 1987). EAPs can also assist working single mothers to develop work and home-based support networks which can fill in the gaps for those single mothers currently without supportive family, friends and co-workers.

Currently, some companies have implemented programs specifically for their single parent employees. These include lunchtime seminars, support groups and discussion groups. One company has expanded the concept of diversity to include variations in family structure and lifestyles, which includes single parents. This allows the company to develop a sensitivity to the family lives of all its employees, rather than focus on a certain group.

EAPs can improve access to structural supports by making referrals to appropriate community based agencies and services. However, it is important to determine whether the policies and programs of referral sources are sensitive to the needs of working single mothers. This might include sensitive staff, babysitting, flexible hours and a fee structure that is based on income level. Gorlick and Pomfret (1992) found that informational supports played a critical role in the lives of single mothers.

EAPs should also examine how they can encourage other company departments to consider single mothers in their planning and programs. One possible area where EAPs could have an impact would be the benefits departments where attention could be paid to whether existing and future benefits are single parent friendly. A work and family manager, if available, could be an advocate for jointly pursuing single mother's concerns in the corporation. The personnel department could be encouraged to assist single mothers to pursue career advancement, with flexibility incorporated to accommodate their single parent status. Vocational counseling, with an understanding of the dilemmas faced by working single mothers, might open new doors to possibilities previously seen as unworkable. The training department could be instrumental in educating corporate staff about work and family balance issues for working single parents. The EAP is encouraged to look for opportunities where their company can be reminded to direct attention to working single parents.

EAPs can also explore how they can motivate the larger community to be more responsive to working single mothers. According to our focus group participants, schools and existing community resources were not seen as supportive and in fact were considered for the most part to hinder rather than help working single mothers. Corporate community partnerships that could encourage joint ventures to advocate for and address the deficiencies noted by single mothers would be a giant step toward making some concrete differences in the lives of these working single mothers.

REFERENCES

Bowen, G.L. and Orthner, D.K. (1986). Single parents in the U.S. air force. *Family Relations*, 35(1), 45-52.

Burden, D. (1986). Single parents and the work setting: the impact of multiple job and homelife responsibilities. *Family Relations*, 35(1), 37-43.

Bureau of Labor Statistics. (1991). Working women: a chartbook. Washington, D.C.: U.S. Department of Labor. #2385.

Cohen, P., Johnson, J., Lewis, S.A. and Brook, J.S. (1990). Single parenthood and employment-double jeopardy? *Stress Between Work and Family*, edited by John Echkenrode and Susan Gore. New York: Plenum Press. 117-132.

Demo, D.H. and Acock, A.C. (1988). The impact of divorce on children. *Journal of Marriage and the Family*, 50, 619-648.

Gorlick, C.A. and Pomfret, D.A. (1992). Two approaches to understanding the impact of employment status on stress among single mothers. Paper presented at the 54th Annual Meeting of the National Council on Family Relations.

Hanson, S. (1986). Single parent families. *Family Relations*, 35(1) 3-8.

Lindblad-Goldberg, M. (1987). The assessment of social networks in black, low-income single parent families. *Family Therapy Collections*, 23, 39-46.

Mahler, S. (1989). How working single parents manage their two major roles. *Journal of Employment Counseling*, 26, 178-185.

Malson, M. R. (1986). Understanding black single parent families: stresses and strengths. Wellesley, Massachusetts: Wellesley College Stone Center for Developmental Services and Studies.

McLanahan, S. (1985). Single mothers and psychological well-being: a test of the stress and vulnerability hypotheses. *Research in Community and Mental Health*, 5, 253-266.

Mulroy, B. (1988) *Women as Single Parents: Confronting Institutional Barriers in the Court, the Workplace and the Housing Market*. Dover, MA: Auburn House.

Norton, A.J. and Glick, P.C. (1986) One parent families: a social and economic profile. *Family Relations*, 35 (1), 9-17.

Perry-Jenkins, M. and Gillman-Hanz, S. (1992). All in the family: processes linking work, parents' well-being, and children's well-being in single parents and two-parent families. Urbana, Illinois: University of Illinois.

Pleck, J.H. (1979). Work-family conflict; a national assessment. Washington, DC: U.S. Department of Labor.

Sanik, M.M. and Mauldin, T. (1986). Single versus two parent families: a comparison of mothers' time. *Family Relations*, 35(1), 53-56.

Shin, M., Wong, N.W., Simko, P.A. and Ortiz-Torres, B. (1989). Promoting the well-being of working parents: coping, social support and flexible job schedules. *American Journal of Community Psychology* 17(1), 31-55.

Tilly, C. and Albelda, R. (1992). It'll take more than a miracle: income in single-mother families in Massachusetts, 1979-1987. Boston, MA: The John W. McCormack Institute of Public Affairs at University of Massachusetts at Boston.

U.S. Bureau of the Census. (1992). Income, poverty and wealth in the United States: a chart book. Series P-60 #179. *Current Population Reports* Washington, D.C.: U.S. Government Printing Office.

U.S. Bureau of the Census. (1992). Household and family characteristics. Series P-20 #458. *Current Population Reports* Washington, D.C.: U.S. Government Printing Office.

U.S. Bureau of the Census. (1984). Household and family characteristics. Series P-20, # 388. *Current Population Reports* Washington, D.C.: U.S. Government Printing Office.

Wescot, M.E. and Dries, R. (1990). Has family therapy adapted to the single parent family? *The American Journal of Family Therapy*, 18(4). 363-372.

Worell, J. (1988). Single mothers: from problems to policies. *Women & Therapy*, 7(4) edited by Ellen Cole and Esther D. Rothblum. 3-14.

Interference Between Work and Family:
A Status Report on Dual-Career
and Dual-Earner Mothers and Fathers

Linda Duxbury
Christopher Higgins

SUMMARY. This study examined differences by gender and job type in levels of role overload, interference from work to family, interference from family to work, and perceived stress for parents with pre-school children. The results indicate that mothers of pre-schoolers experience more problems balancing work and family demands than fathers, regardless of whether they are in career or earner positions. The dual-career situation is less problematic than the dual-earner situation. Career parents appear to have more control over both work and family domains. Such an increase in control facilitates the ability to balance work and family. The results of this study suggest that employers who are interested in helping their employees balance work and family demands should investigate different mechanisms by which they can increase employees' control over the work and family interface. Interventions such as on-site day care,

Linda Duxbury is Imperial Life Professor, School of Business, Carleton University, Ottawa, Canada K1S 5B6. Christopher Higgins is Imperial Life Professor, Western Business School, University of Western Ontario, London, Canada N6A 3K7.

This research was supported by grants from the Social Sciences and Humanities Research Council of Canada, Health and Welfare Canada, and the National Centre for Management Research and Development.

[Haworth co-indexing entry note]: "Interference Between Work and Family: A Status Report on Dual-Career and Dual-Earner Mothers and Fathers." Duxbury, Linda, and Christopher Higgins. Co-published simultaneously in *Employee Assistance Quarterly* (The Haworth Press, Inc.) Vol. 9, No. 3/4, 1994, pp. 55-80; and: *Empowering Women in the Workplace: Perspectives, Innovations, and Techniques for Helping Professionals* (ed: Marta Lundy, and Beverly Younger) Harrington Park Press an imprint of The Haworth Press, Inc., 1994, pp. 55-80. Multiple copies of this article/chapter may be purchased from The Haworth Document Delivery Center [1-800-3-HAWORTH; 9:00 a.m. - 5:00 p.m. (EST)].

time management courses, flexible work arrangements, sick-child care, and parenting courses all offer promise in this regard.

In the past 20 years there has been an enormous influx of women into the work force. According to recent statistics there are now more: (1) dual-income families, (2) working mothers heading single-parent families, (3) women working throughout the various stages of their lives, (4) working mothers, particularly mothers of young children, and, (5) working women caring for elderly parents or relatives (Edmonds, Cote-O'Hara & MacKenzie, 1990; Galinsky, Friedman, & Hernandez, 1991). The traditional family model with "Mom" at home and "Dad" at work is no longer a viable option for the majority of today's families.

These changes in workforce demographics have created a new emphasis on the balance between work life and family life. For millions of North Americans mothers, juggling the myriad of activities involved in being a working parent–keeping a home, raising children or caring for an elderly dependent–has become extremely difficult. If both mother and father are working, as was the case in 65% of Canadian families in 1991, someone still has to find time to make lunches, attend doctor appointments, shop for groceries, cook and clean. This someone is usually the mother.

A number of studies have reported that working mothers have more difficulties than fathers in balancing work and family demands (Duxbury & Higgins, 1991; Gupta & Jenkins, 1985; Gutek, Repetti and Silver, 1988; Higgins, Duxbury & Lee, 1993; Jick & Mitz, 1985; Piotrkowski, Rapaport, & Rapaport, 1987). Women don't stop being parents, spouses, friends or responsible community members when they perform paid employment outside the home. Neither the advent of labour saving devices, nor the acceptance of women into the labour force, has eliminated the need for most working women to wear two hats; paid employee and mother.

The data are quite clear. Women shoulder most of the family responsibilities while putting in at least eight hours a day in the labour force (Cowan & Cowan, 1988; Higgins, Duxbury & Lee, 1993; Hochschild, 1989; Vanderkolk & Armstrong, 1991). While recent studies indicate that the vast majority of husbands and wives believe that when the wife is employed, the husband should do more of the household; most research indicates that a persistent discrepancy exists between beliefs about division of household labour and actual domestic behaviour (Berardo, Shehan & Leslie, 1987; Rexroat & Shehan 1987). A recent study by Vanderkolk and Armstrong (1991) found that 70% of the total time spent on household chores was contributed by women, 15% by men, and the remainder by other members of the household. This disproportionate burden meant that mothers had 25% less leisure time than fathers.

Many mothers are paying a price for this "second shift." The Canadian Conference Board (MacBride-King & Paris, 1989) indicates that 80% of Canadian employees experience some degree of stress or anxiety related to the attempt to balance the conflicting demands of work and family. In support of this, Duxbury, Higgins and Lee (1993) found that over 60% of mothers of pre-school children experienced high levels of stress and work-family conflict.

The main objective of this research is to empirically investigate how job type (i.e., career versus earner) and gender affect working parents ability to balance competing work and family demands and cope with perceived stress. Specifically this study examines differences by gender and job type in: (1) role overload, (2) interference from work to family, (3) interference from family to work, and (4) perceived stress for parents with pre-school children (i.e., five years of age or less). The findings presented lead to suggestions and recommendations having implications for family practitioners, educators and employers.

LITERATURE REVIEW

In the following section we review the relevant literature on the dependent (i.e., work-family conflict, perceived stress) and independent variables (i.e., job type, gender) used in this research.

Dependent Variables

Work-family Conflict: Work-family conflict occurs when an individual has to perform multiple roles: worker, spouse and, in many cases, parent (Greenhaus & Beutell, 1985). Each of these roles imposes demands requiring time, energy and commitment to perform the role adequately. The cumulative demands of multiple roles can result in role strain of two types: overload and interference. Overload exists when the total demands on time and energy associated with the prescribed activities of multiple roles are too great to perform the roles adequately or comfortably. Interference occurs when conflicting demands make it difficult to fulfil the requirements of multiple roles. This commonly occurs because many work and family activities must be performed during the same time periods in different physical locations (Greenhaus & Beutell, 1985).

Gutek, Searle and Kelpa (1991) have expanded the concept of role interference. They define interference as having two components: family interference with work, and work interference with family. In the first case, interference occurs when family-role responsibilities hinder performance at work (i.e., a child's illness prevents attendance at work). In the second case, problems arise when work-role activities impede performance of family responsibilities (i.e., long hours in paid work prevent the performance of duties at home).

Both types of interference have been studied extensively, but primarily by different researchers (Gutek et al., 1991). Developmental and family psychologists and work-family sociologists tend to focus on the effects of work on family life (e.g., Aldous, 1969; Piotrkowski et al., 1987; Voydanoff, 1988). The effects of family life on work, on the other hand, are addressed by organizational-behaviour researchers (e.g., Cooke and Rousseau, 1984; Galinsky et al., 1991; Gutek et al., 1988; Herman & Gyllstrom, 1977).

In this paper we build on Gutek, Searle and Kelpa's (1991) research by defining work-family conflict as being made up of three components: role overload, interference from work to family, and interference from family to work. It is expected that by examining the higher-level, work-family conflict construct in terms of these three main components, we will be better able to explain gender and job type differences.

Perceived Stress: Work-family management problems facing dual-career and dual-earner parents may be manifested in symptoms of stress. Stress can be produced by stressors that arise in the work domain, the family domain, and at the interface of the work and family domains. Stress has been found to be related to various psychological symptoms, including job dissatisfaction, anxiety, and depression. It has also been related to health consequences such as high blood pressure, increased heart rate, gastrointestinal disorders and cardiovascular disease (Greenhaus & Parasuraman, 1986). The degree of stress experienced may be mediated by personal characteristics such as high self-esteem and an internal locus of control, which affect the way people interpret the environment (Greenhaus & Parasuraman, 1986). Effective coping and the utilization of social support from the work or family domain can also reduce perceived stress and can directly improve well being (Brief, Schuler, & Van Sell, 1981).

The scarcity hypothesis (Barnett & Baruch, 1987) postulates that the more roles a woman occupies, the less energy she will have, the more stress she will experience, and the more negatively her well-being will be affected. This hypothesis rests on two premises: (1) that individuals have a limited amount of energy; and, (2) that both work and family are greedy, demanding all of a woman's devotion. Edmonds et al. (1990) suggest that the pressures of managing multiple roles are greatest, and the psychological benefits from employment are least, under conditions of heavy family responsibilities.

The literature suggests three reasons why mothers are more likely than fathers to experience stress from conflicting work and family demands. Women are more likely than men: (1) to put family demands before personal needs (Boden & Mitelman, 1983; Hochschild, 1989; Jick & Mitz, 1985); (2) to feel guilty and stressed if they perceive that their role as provider takes away from their time as nurturer (Boden & Mitelman, 1983); and, (3) to exhibit greater concern and stress if they feel that they are neglecting their partners.

Independent Variables

Job Type: Individuals who hold career positions (defined in this analysis as individuals in managerial and professional jobs with high work involvement) are generally believed to be highly committed to their work roles. In most instances, career positions require higher levels of effort and energy for success (Rapaport & Rapaport, 1976). Individuals who hold non-career positions (defined in this analysis as technical, clerical, administrative, retail and production jobs with low work involvement) are generally believed to be less committed to their work roles. In most instances, non-career positions require lower levels of effort and energy and are non-developmental in nature.

Research evidence suggests that while work role demands are significantly greater for individuals in career positions, the increased income available to this group and the more flexible nature of their work may make them better able to manage the work-family interface.

Gender: There are four theoretical frameworks that can be used to help understand gender differences in work-family conflict and perceived stress. Each of these is reviewed below.

The *rational view* suggests that the amount of work-family conflict and stress one perceives rises in proportion to the number of hours one expends in both the work and family domain (Greenhaus, Bedeian & Mossholder, 1987; Keith & Schafer, 1980; Staines et al., 1978). According to this view, the more hours a person spends in work activities, the more he or she should experience interference from work to family. The more time spent in family activities (i.e., home chores and child care), on the other hand, the more he or she should experience interference from family to work. The rational view also predicts that the total amount of time spent performing work and family roles is positively associated with role overload (Greenhaus & Beutell, 1985; Gutek et al., 1991).

The sex-role expectations perspective suggests that gender-role expectations will affect men's and women's perceptions of work-family conflict and stress differently (Gutek et al., 1991; Pleck, 1979). This position is based on the fact that socio-cultural role expectations (i.e., the breadwinner role for men, family responsibility and home maintenance for women) have not changed appreciably in the past 30 years despite the large influx of mothers into the paid labor force (Galinsky et al., 1991; Hochschild, 1989; Schwartz, 1989).

According to the sex-role expectations perspective, women ought to report higher levels of interference from work to family than men, even when the number of hours spent in paid work is approximately the same. Men, on the other hand, should report higher levels of interference from family to work than women, even when the number of hours spent in home chores and child care is approximately the same.

For men, working many hours to provide a stable income for the family is part of the "good provider role" (Gutek et al., 1991). Men see their paid work as a major contribution to their family, despite the fact that their paid work represents time away from their family. The sex-role expectations theory suggests that men will be less likely to perceive that this time spent in work interferes with their family, because paid employment has traditionally been the way in which men participate in the family (Gutek et al., 1991).

In contrast, family work has not traditionally been considered to be part of the male domain (i.e., fathers "help out" at home). The sex-role expectation perspective suggests that men who spend even relatively few hours in family work may perceive that time to be an imposition on their work time. In other words, men will be more likely than women to perceive that their family interferes with their work.

Women, on the other hand, are still expected to place family demands first. Despite the rapid movement of women into the paid labour force, the care of husband, children and household is still seen by many as the woman's domain. In addition, women are still judged by society in terms of their ability to provide a "stable home situation" rather than by their financial contribution to the family (Gutek et al., 1991). These socio-cultural expectations suggest that women will not be as sensitive as men to interference from family to work. Because a woman feels responsible for family affairs, however, sex-role expectations theory suggests that the more hours she spends in paid work, the more she will perceive that work is interfering with her family obligations.

A third framework, *simultaneous versus sequential role demands* is drawn from Pleck's (1977) asymmetrical role boundaries theory and Hall's (1972) work on simultaneous versus sequential role demands. According to Pleck (1977) and Hall (1972), interference from family to work should be a greater source of work-family conflict for women, while interference from work to family should be a greater source of work-family conflict for men. They base this prediction on the fact that women have been found to be more likely than men to allow the demands of the family role to intrude into the work role (Pleck, 1984; Voydanoff, 1987). This vulnerability of the female work role to family demands should be a major source of interference from family to work, since the sex-role norm that women take responsibility for the family conflicts with the norms of the job role (Pleck, 1984). For men, the opposite situation is believed to occur, as men have been found to be more likely to permit the demands of the work role to intrude into the family role (Pleck, 1984; Voydanoff, 1987). As many husbands literally "take work home" with them or use family time to recuperate from the conflicts they face in their work role, they may experience increased interference from work to family.

The job strain model developed by Karasek (1979) provides a fourth framework with which to predict gender differences in work and family conflict and perceived stress. Karasek's model focuses on identifying the objective conditions conducive to perceived stress. He identifies two key operating forces: role demands and control. His job strain model asserts that jobs with similar demands or expectations may differ substantially by the degree of conflict or stress, which is generated by virtue of the level of control an individual has over the stressful situation (LaCroix & Haynes, 1987). Karasek's (1979) model suggests that the amount of work-family conflict and stress perceived by an employee will be associated with the amount of control that they feel that they have over work and family roles. Applying his concepts to this study, gender differences in control over work and family role demands will be considered.

The literature indicates that men have more control over the distribution of their time which, in turn, makes it easier for them to satisfy both work and family expectations. Traditionally, men have perceived that they can fulfil their family role expectations simply by being a good provider, without having to meet many additional demands within the home (Barnett & Baruch, 1987). Thus, time spent satisfying work expectations is perceived by men as also satisfying family expectations. In short, although work and family demands may compete for a man's time, they are experienced as mutually supportive (Barnett & Baruch, 1987).

Women, on the other hand, do not have mutually supportive work and family roles (Barnett & Baruch, 1987). Central to the traditional roles of wife and mother is the obligation to be available to meet the needs of the family. Career women are unable to take time away from the work role to satisfy family expectations, as organizations base expectations in terms of position rather than gender. Women, therefore, do not have the same control over the distribution of their time as men since the time spent satisfying work or family expectations is mutually exclusive. This lack of control (given similar expectations) should lead to a greater perception of interference from work to family and from family to work for women. It should also be associated with increased levels of stress for women.

Hypotheses

The research literature reviewed above gives rise to the following hypotheses:

1. Mothers will experience significantly more role overload than fathers, independent of job type.
2. Career parents will experience more role overload than earner parents, independent of gender.
3. Mothers will experience significantly more interference from work to family than fathers, independent of job type.
4. Career parents will experience more interference from work to family than earner parents, independent of gender.
5. Mothers will experience significantly more interference from family to work than fathers, independent of job type.
6. Career parents will experience more interference from family to work than earner parents, independent of gender.
7. Mothers will experience more perceived stress than fathers, independent of job type.
8. Earner parents will experience more perceived stress than career parents, independent of gender.

METHOD

The Sample

The data presented in this paper come from a recently completed Canadian study on balancing work and family. To date, 20,836 survey responses have been collected (response rate of 56%). The respondents to the survey were from two sources: a random sample of all Canadian federal public sector employees working in the National Capital region (n = 6,287) and a cross-section of private sector employees from large, geographically-diverse organizations (n = 14,549). The responses come from employees working in 7 government departments and 37 private sector organizations. The geographical distribution is large, with the respondents living in 408 different Canadian population centres.

Many individual and organizational factors have an impact on work-family conflict and perceived stress. To minimize the influence of non-measured confounds, and to make the population as homogeneous as possible, the sample was limited to males and females who met the following criteria. They all had to: (1) have full-time (i.e., greater than 37 hours per week) paid employment outside the home; (2) be parents of children who were five years of age or younger and living at home one-hundred percent of the time; (3) be married or living with a significant other; and (4) be members of either a dual-career or a dual-earner couple.

The employment status of the respondent and the respondent's spouse and their work involvement score (Lodahl & Kehner, 1965) were used to categorize the sample with respect to family type. The work involvement scale was a three-item measure using a five point Likert scale with high scores indicating strong work involvement. Dual-career couples were operationalized as those couples in which both partners were managers or professionals with high work involvement scores (i.e., scores greater than 3.5). Dual-earner couples were operationalized as couples in which both partners were in clerical, administrative, technical, retail or production positions with low work involvement scores (i.e., scores less than 2.5).

Altogether, 1,138 respondents met our criteria (202 dual-career fathers, 169 dual-career mothers, 254 dual-earner fathers, and 513 dual-earner mothers).

The Instrument

Data were collected using a 21 page survey instrument that measured 56 constructs. Most of the items in the questionnaire were collected for other research purposes and are not reported here. Those that are relevant are discussed below.

Work-family conflict (role overload, interference from work to family, interference from family to work) was operationalized using the work-family role strain instrument developed by Bohen and Viveros-Long (1981). This scale asks respondents to indicate, using a five point Likert scale, the extent to which they agree or disagree with a number of statements. High scores indicate greater agreement and, hence, higher role overload and interference.

Individuals with mean scores on the scales of 3.5 or greater were considered in this analysis to be experiencing "high" levels of overload or interference, while individuals with scores of 2.5 or lower were classified as having "low" work-family conflict. This division was arbitrary.

The Perceived Stress Scale (PSS; Cohen, Kamarck & Mermelstein, 1983) was used in this study to measure levels of stress. Perceived stress scores can only be interpreted in light of normal value ranges for the general population. Using these normal values, respondents who had PSS scores of 2.8 or higher were considered to be experiencing "high" levels of stress, while individuals with PSS scores of 1.5 or lower were deemed to have "low" stress (Cohen, Kamarck & Mermelstein, 1983).

Time in work and family roles was obtained by asking the respondent, "On your last regular work day (and non-work day), approximately how many hours did you spend in the following activities: (1) working at the office; (2) working at home (job-related); (3) in home chores and errands; (4) in activities with your children; and (5) in self-related activities (i.e., recreation alone or with spouse)."

Responsibility for child care was assessed by asking the respondent, "Who in your family has the main responsibility for the day to day arrangements for the care of the children?" A five point Likert format was used where 1 indicated "I Have," 3 indicated "We share equally" and 5 indicated "Spouse Has."

Characteristics of the Sample

The demographic differences between the dual-career and dual-earner couples in the sample are consistent with the fact that they belong to quite different socio-economic groups. The dual-career men and women have more formal education (73% of dual-career men, 69% of dual-career women, 19% of dual-earner men, and 8% of dual-earner women have a university education) and earn more money (29% of dual-career men, 18% of dual-career women, 2% of dual-earner men, and 0.2% of dual-earner women make more than $60,000 per year). Within job type, men have significantly more education and earn more money than women.

The data indicate that the personal and family characteristics of the respondents in the study are quite similar. The average number of children (1.5 for dual-career fathers, 1.3 for dual-career mothers, 1.4 for dual-earner fathers, 1.3 for dual-earner mothers); the average age of children (2.4 years for dual-career fathers, 2.3 years for dual-career mothers, 2.4 years for dual-earner fathers, 2.5 years for dual-earner mothers); and the average age of the respondents (33.0 years for dual-career fathers, 32.6 years for dual-career mothers, 31.8 years for dual-earner fathers, 30.0 years for dual-earner mothers) was independent of gender or job type. This homogeneity is consistent with the way in which the sample was selected (i.e., we selected respondents who had pre-school children only).

Responsibility for child care data demonstrate that mothers, regardless of job type, were significantly more likely than fathers to *indicate* that they have primary responsibility for child care (2.8% of dual-career fathers, 65.6% of dual-career mothers, 3.8% of dual-earner fathers, and 67.3% of dual-earner mothers indicated that they had primary responsibility for child care).

Time in Work and Family Roles

To help interpret the results presented in the next section, it is useful to review the amount of time spent in work and family roles for our respondents. These time data are given in Table 1.

The time in paid employment data indicate that: (1) career employees spend more time per day in paid employment than their earner counterparts independent of gender; (2) dual-career fathers spend significantly more time in paid employment than dual-career mothers; and (3) there is no gender difference in time spent in paid employment for dual-earner parents.

The time spent in home chores supports previous research in that

TABLE 1

Time in Work and Family Roles: Work Day

Hours per Day in:	Dual-career Parents				Dual-earner Parents			
	Men		Women		Men		Women	
	Mean	S.D.	Mean	S.D	Mean	S.D.	Mean	S.D.
Paid Employment	9.3	1.5	8.9	1.0	8.3	2.2	8.2	0.9
Home Chores	1.6	1.0	2.2	1.3	2.0	1.1	2.7	1.4
Child care	1.9	0.9	2.3	1.0	2.1	1.2	2.3	1.2
Self-related Activities	1.7	1.2	1.2	0.9	1.9	1.5	1.3	1.1

it indicates that mothers spend significantly more time in home chores than fathers, regardless of job type. Job type does, however, have a significant impact on the amount of time spent in home chores. Both mothers and fathers in career positions spent significantly less time working around the home than their earner counterparts (i.e., dual-earner mothers spend the most time in home chores, dual-career fathers spend the least). This is consistent with the fact that career parents have more money with which to pay others to do home chores than do parents in non-career positions.

Child care data show a slightly different pattern. Mothers spend more time in child care than fathers regardless of job type. For mothers, the type of job held does not have an impact on the amount of time spent in child care. Dual-career fathers, on the other hand, spend significantly less time in child care than dual-earner fathers.

Fathers spend significantly more time in self-related activities (i.e., leisure) than mothers. Job type does not have an impact on the amount of time spent in leisure for mothers. Dual-earner fathers spend significantly more time in leisure than do dual-career fathers.

Summary data show that mothers of pre-schoolers devote significantly more time per day to work and family roles than fathers. It is interesting to note that despite the differences noted above, there are no significant differences between dual-career and dual-earner mothers with respect to the total amount of time devoted per day to work and family. While dual-earner mothers spend less time in paid employment than their dual-career counterparts, they allocate more time to home chores than they do to leisure.

Dual-career fathers spend more time in work and family role responsibilities than their dual-earner counterparts. In this case, the difference is due to the significantly higher number of hours in paid employment.

Data Analysis

MANOVAS with follow-up univariate F tests and Bonferroni adjustments were used to test the significance of: (1) gender differences (within job type), and (2) job type differences (within gender). Detailed results of the statistical tests are not shown.

RESULTS

Role Overload

The data (see Table 2) support hypothesis 1 and partially support hypothesis 2. Mothers experience significantly more role overload than fathers regardless of job type. Dual-career fathers experience significantly more role overload than dual-earner fathers. Job type does not, however, have a significant impact on the amount of role overload experienced by mothers.

Interference from Work to Family

In support of hypothesis 3, mothers of pre-schoolers experience significantly more interference from work to family than fathers, regardless of job type. Contrary to hypothesis 4, dual-earner mothers experienced significantly more interference from work to family than dual-career mothers. Job type did not have a significant impact on the amount of interference from work to family experienced by fathers.

Interference from Family to Work

Hypothesis 5 is supported. Mothers of pre-schoolers experience significantly more interference from family to work than fathers, regardless of job type. Hypothesis 6 is not supported by the data, however, as job type does not have a significant impact on the amount of interference from family to work experienced by mothers or fathers.

Perceived Stress

In support of hypotheses 7 and 8, mothers perceive significantly more stress than fathers, independent of job type. Earner parents perceive significantly more stress than career parents, regardless of gender.

DISCUSSION

Role Overload

The role overload data support the rational view of work-family conflict: the more time spent in work and family roles, the greater

TABLE 2
Work-family Conflict and Stress by Gender and Job Type

	Dual-career Parents				Dual-earner Parents				Gender Differences	Job Type Differences
	Men		Women		Men		Women			
	Mean	S.D.	Mean	S.D	Mean	S.D.	Mean	S.D.		
Role Overload	3.46	0.81	3.80	0.76	3.35	0.80	3.80	0.79	YES	PARTIAL
Interference: Work to Family	3.08	0.75	3.22	0.76	3.07	0.75	3.37	0.76	YES	NO
Interference: Family to Work	2.71	0.78	3.04	0.74	2.64	0.71	3.00	0.77	YES	NO

the perception of role overload. The significantly higher levels of role overload reported by women in this study are not surprising given the fact that mothers spend significantly more time in work and family roles than fathers. The fact that dual-career fathers experience more role overload than dual-earner fathers is consistent with the fact that career fathers spend more time in work than their dual-earner counterparts.

The lack of a career/earner difference in role overload for women is very interesting. The data suggest that career mothers cope with greater work demands by decreasing the amount of time that they spend in home chores (not in child care). While dual-earner women spend less time in paid employment than their dual-career counterparts, the total time given to work and family is virtually identical for the two groups. As noted previously, extra time is allocated to home chores rather than to leisure.

Interference from Work to Family

Mothers experience more interference from work to family than fathers. Dual-earner mothers report more interference than career mothers. Job type has no impact on the interference from work to family reported by fathers.

These data refute the rational view of work-family conflict (i.e., dual-career mothers spend more time in paid employment than dual-earner mothers but report less interference; dual-career fathers spend the most time in paid employment but report the same levels of interference as dual-earner fathers who spend the least amount of time in paid employment). The fact that mothers have more spill-over of interference from work to family than fathers also refutes Pleck's (1977) asymmetrical role boundaries theory and Hall's (1972) work on simultaneous versus sequential role demands.

Sex-role expectation theory could explain why dual-career fathers are able to spend more time in paid employment than their female counterparts yet experience less interference between work and family. The fact that career mothers spend more time in paid employment than earner mothers yet report less interference from work to family indicates, however, that this theory does not adequately explain interference from work to family for mothers.

Karasek's model seems to do the best job of explaining the data on interference from work to family for mothers. Career women have more control over their work environment than women in non-career positions (Higgins et al., 1992). They have more flexibility over when and where they work. The increased income available to this group, and their greater access to material resources and paid support, also suggests that they are better able to manage the work-family interface. Karasek's model would suggest that it is this higher level of control over work and family demands that allows career mothers to minimize the spillover of interference from work to family.

Interference from Family to Work

Mothers experience more interference from family to work than fathers. Job type has no impact on this perception. This finding can be partially explained by the rational view of work-family conflict. The fact that mothers spend more time in family activities than fathers is consistent with the fact that they are more likely to perceive that family-role responsibilities interfere with work. It is also consistent with the idea of sex-role norms that women take responsibility for the family.

The rational view does not, however, completely explain what is going on for women. While dual-career mothers spend less time in family roles than dual-earner mothers, there is no significant difference between the two groups with respect to the level of interference perceived. It may be that time spent in child care (not time in child care and home chores) is the critical variable for explaining interference from family to work for mothers. Job type had no impact on time spent in child care for mothers of pre-school children.

The data do not support the sex-role perspective on work-family conflict as mothers experienced more, not less, interference from family to work. It may be that while mothers are judged by society on their ability to provide a good family environment, the fact that they are also judged by their employer with respect to their ability to get work done may be more important to their perception of conflict between work and family. Higher levels of responsibility at home conflict with their ability to put work first and compete with colleagues who have fewer responsibilities at home.

Fathers, on the other hand, have fewer responsibilities at home. In their case, the reduced interference from family to work probably reflects the reality of the situation (i.e., fathers actually have less interference from family to work than mothers).

Karasek's model can be used to explain gender differences in interference from family to work. Both groups of mothers in this sample had more responsibilities at home than fathers and thus less control. It is not unreasonable to expect that these family demands make it more difficult for mothers than fathers to keep family demands from intruding on work.

It is interesting to note that while career mothers perceive that they have a greater degree of control over their work environment than earner mothers they are no more able to control family demands than their earner counterparts. This finding suggests that mothers, as well as families and society, have been socialized to expect mothers to take primary responsibility for child care (i.e., daycare, schools, and children tend to call mother not father to deal with an emergency). Having a higher level job does not appear to protect women from this type of socialization.

Perceived Stress

Mothers perceive significantly more stress than fathers. This gender difference in perceived stress is consistent with the work-family conflict data presented earlier. It is also consistent with the fact that mothers have less time for leisure, which has been found to be an effective way to cope with stress (Brief, Schuler, & Van Sell, 1981).

The fact that dual-career mothers and fathers spend more time in work and family than their dual-earner counterparts but perceive significantly less stress suggests that the dual-career lifestyle provides parents with healthier ways to cope with stress than does the dual-earner lifestyle. The differences in stress experienced by these two groups can be explained using Karasek's model. The data indicate that dual-career mothers and fathers have a greater ability to control the work and family interface (Higgins et al., 1992). The nature of their jobs gives them more control over their work and a greater ability to control when and where work is to be done. Their higher income levels also give them more control over their family roles, as they are more able to purchase services to help them cope with family demands.

Evaluation of the Models

Table 3 provides an evaluation of the four models commonly used in the research literature to predict gender differences in work-family conflict and stress. In each case, gender and job type differences predicted from the models are compared to the empirical findings obtained in this study.

The data show that both the rational model and the job strain model do a reasonable job of explaining why mothers experience more role overload, interference from family to work and stress than fathers. It would appear that the main reason mothers have more problems balancing work and family than fathers is because they have more to do at home. Women have taken on the paid employment role but have not substantively decreased the amount of time spent in child care and, in the case of non-professional women, in home chores. In other words, a substantive proportion of the gender differences observed in work-family conflict and stress may simply be due to the fact women have more demands on their time than men. These findings indicate that one way counsellors can help mothers balance work and family demands is to show them how they can reduce their family demands.

Only one model, Karasek's (1979) Job Strain Model, is able to explain why dual-career women are better able to manage work and family than their dual-earner counterparts. Career mothers spend more hours in paid employment than their dual-earner counterparts, yet report less interference from work to family and less stress. They spend the same amount of time in child care as earner mothers but experience less interference from family to work. These findings suggest that a second set of strategies aimed at assisting mothers in managing the work-family interface would focus on increasing their control over work and family demands. Increased control would likely require that organizational decision-makers champion the implementation of new family-friendly work policies and benefits such as flex-time, part-time work and telework.

TABLE 3

Evaluation of Theories

THEORY	ROLE OVERLOAD	INTERFERENCE: WORK TO FAMILY	INTERFERENCE: FAMILY TO WORK	PERCEIVED STRESS
Rational Model	Supported (Women > men)	Not Supported Earner mothers > career mothers	Supported (Women > men)	Supported (Women > men)
Sex Role Expectations Model	No prediction	Supported (Women > men) Not Supported (Career women < earner women)	Not Supported (women > men)	No prediction
Simultaneous Versus Sequential Role Model	Supported (Women > men) Not Supported (Career women < earner women)	Not Supported (Women > men)	Supported (Women > men)	Supported (Women > men) Not Supported (Career women < earner women)
Job Strain Model	Supported (women > men)	Supported (women > men) (career women < earner women)	Supported (women > men) (career women < earner women)	Supported (women > men) (career women < earner women)

CONCLUSIONS

Virtually all the parents surveyed reported high levels of role overload. More than half of the mothers, and almost half of the fathers, had high levels of stress. Approximately one-third of the mothers, and one-quarter of the fathers, reported high levels of interference from work to family. One-quarter of the mothers had high levels of interference from family to work. When taken together, these data suggest that a significant proportion of the working-parent population in North America is having problems balancing work and family. They have more to do than time permits. Rigid work schedules and high work demands are making it difficult for them to fulfil family responsibilities.

It appears that work demands are being satisfied at the expense of the individual and the family, and that many parents are experiencing conflict from the choices that they are having to make. The work force has changed dramatically in the past three decades, but our data indicate that employers have not changed management styles and do not expect they will have to accommodate the work/family needs of their new work force (Duxbury & Higgins, 1991). This lack of fit between work and family has contributed to dangerously high stress levels for today's working parents, especially working mothers.

Mothers of pre-schoolers experience more problems balancing work and family demands than fathers, regardless of family type. The time and responsibility for child care data indicate that mothers have added the work role with no concomitant decrease in family-role responsibilities, operating under the assumption that they can, should, or must do it all. Such behavior is highly stressful.

The dual-career situation is less problematic than the dual-earner situation. Career parents appear to have more control over both work and family domains, facilitating the ability to balance work and family. It also suggests that employers who are interested in helping their employees balance work and family demands should investigate different mechanisms by which they can increase employees' control over the work and family interface.

The results of this analysis also indicate there are real advantages in viewing work-family conflict as the embodiment of three different components (role overload, interference from work to family, and interference from family to work) rather than as a higher-level construct. The extent to which each component of work-family conflict is problematic appears to be dependent upon both gender and job type. This would suggest that gender-specific work-family conflict interventions should be provided on the basis of employee needs. For example, organizations who employ a large number of dual-earner mothers should offer programs to help their employees cope with role overload and interference from work to family. Organizations with a higher proportion of dual-career mothers, on the other hand, should address role overload issues.

Implications for Practitioners

The findings suggest that to help mothers balance work and family demands one must: (1) help them reduce the total number of demands on their time, and (2) give them more control over the work and family interface. Employee Assistance counsellors should work at the individual level with mothers to show mothers how they could reduce the demands on their time. The primary responsibility of organizational and government decision-makers, on the other hand, would be to implement family supportive policies and benefits which would give mothers (especially those in non-professional positions) more control over the work and family interface. EAP practitioners could facilitate this process by demonstrating how family benefits make good sense from a business perspective.

EAP practitioners can assist working mothers in coping with competing work and family demands by helping them: (1) develop a new perspective on family-role responsibilities; (2) develop skills which can help them manage work and family and show them how these skills can be transferred to the home environment; and (3) take action at work and at home. EAP counsellors can help in this regard by offering assertiveness training courses, courses that build up self esteem and confidence, and self-awareness seminars. They can also set up female support groups to increase awareness of how others are handling work and family situations. Such an awareness will allow mothers to negotiate the division of family tasks from a position of strength, not defensiveness.

Most working mothers have acquired work-place skills which can enhance their ability to balance work and family. However, to utilize these skills, they must develop a perspective that is conducive to applying such skills as time management, planning, resource allocation, setting of goals and priorities to the family domain. EAP practitioners can help mothers transfer these skills by providing role playing opportunities and offering courses which show how these skills can be used in non-work settings.

In conclusion, it appears that demographic changes have outpaced political, social and organizational supports for dual-income families. Employers need to recognize that employees who are stressed and overloaded at home are less productive workers. EAP programs could help this process by sponsoring work-place policies which would help employees manage their family time and their stress (i.e, flextime, part-time work with pro-rated benefits, on-site exercise programs, after-school programs, family leave days, work at home, on-site day care). It is not inconceivable that forward-thinking organizations who offer such programs would ultimately be able to recruit and retain the best employees available.

REFERENCES

Aldous, S. (1969). Occupational Characteristics and Male Role Performance in the Family, *Journal of Marriage and the Family, 31*, 707-712

Barnett, R. C. & Baruch, G. K. (1987). Social roles, gender and psychological distress. In R. C. Barnett, L. Biener & G. K. Baruch (Eds.), *Gender and Stress* (pp. 122-143). New York, NY: The Free Press.

Beutell, N. & Greenhaus, J. (1982). Interrole Conflict Among Married Women: The Influence of Husband and Wife Characteristics on Conflict and Coping Behavior, *Journal of Applied Psychology, 21*, 99-110.

Beutell, N. & Greenhaus, J. (1983). Integration of Home and Non-home roles: Women's Conflict Behavior, *Journal of Applied Psychology, 68*, 43.48

Bohen H., Viveros-Long, A. (1981). *Balancing jobs and family life*, Temple University Press.

Brief, A. P., Schuler, R. S., & Van Sell, M. (1981). *Managing job stress*, Boston, MA: Little Brown.

Cohen, S., Kamarck, T., & Mermelstein, R., (1983). A Global Measure of Perceived Stress, *Journal of Health and Social Behaviour, 24*, 385-396.

Cooke, R., & Rousseau, D. (1984). Stress and strain from family roles and work-role expectations. *Journal of Applied Psychology, 69*, 252-260.

Cowan, C. & Cowan, P. (1988). Who Does What When Partners Become Parents: Implications for Men, Women, and Marriage, *Marriage and Family Review, 12*, 105-131.

Duxbury, L. & Higgins, C. (1991). Gender Differences in Work-Family Conflict, *Journal of Applied Psychology, 76*, 60-74.

Edmonds, J., Cote-O'Hara, J. & MacKenzie, E. (1990) *Beneath the Veneer*, Supply and Services, Ottawa, Canada.

Galinsky, E., Friedman, D., & Hernandez, C., (1991). *The Corporate Reference Guide to Work Family Programs.* Families and Work Institute, New York, New York.

Greenhaus, J., Bedeian, A., and Mossholder, K. (1987). Work Experiences, Job Performance, and Feeling of Personal and Family Well-Being, *Journal of Vocational Behavior, 31*, 200-215.

Greenhaus, J., & Beutell N. (1985). Sources of conflict between work and family roles. *Academy of Management Review, 10*, 76-88.

Greenhaus, J., & Parasuraman, S. (1986). A work-nonwork interactive perspective of stress and its consequences. *Journal of Organizational Behavior Management, 8*, 37-60.

Gupta, N., & Jenkins, D. (1985). Stress, stressors, strains, and strategies. In T. A. Beehr, & R. S. Bhagat (Eds.), *Human stress and cognition in organizations* (141-176). New York, NY: John Wiley & Sons.

Gutek, B., Nakamura, C. and Nieva, V. (1981). The Interdependence of Work and Family Roles, *Journal of Occupational Behavior, 2*, 1-16.

Gutek, B., Repetti, R., & Silver, D. (1988). Nonwork roles and stress at work. In C. Cooper, & R. Payne (Eds.), *Causes, coping and consequences of stress at work* (41-174). New York, NY: John Wiley & Sons.

Gutek, B., Searle, S. and Kelpa, L. (1991). Rational Versus Gender Role Explanations for Work-Family Conflict, *Journal of Applied Psychology, 76*, 560-568.

Hall, D., (1972). A model of coping with role conflict: The role behavior of college educated women. *Administrative Sciences Quarterly, 17*, 471-486.

Herman, J.B., & Gyllstrom, K.K. (1977). Working men and women: Inter- and intra-role conflict. *Psychology of Women Quarterly, 1*, 319-333.

Higgins, C., Duxbury, L, Lee, C. and Mills, S. (1992). An Examination of Work-time and Work-location Flexibility, *Optimum, 23*, 29-38.

Higgins, C., Duxbury, L. & Lee, C. (1993). *Balancing Work and Family: A Study of the Canadian Private Sector*, National Centre for Research, Management and Development, University of Western Ontario, London.

Hochschild, A. (1989). *The Second Shift*, New York, NY: Viking.

Jick, T., & Mitz, L. (1985). Sex differences in work stress. *Academy of Management Review, 10*, 408-420.

Kanter, R. (1977). *Work and family in the United States: A critical review and agenda for research and policy.* New York, NY: Sage Publications.

Karasek, R. (1979). Job demands, job decision latitude and mental strain: Implications for job redesign. *Administrative Science Quarterly, 24*, 2, 285-307.

Keith, P., & Schafer, R. (1980). Role strain and depression in two-job families. *Family Relations, 29*, 483-488.

LaCroix, A. & Haynes, S. (1987). Gender differences in the health effects of workplace roles. In R. C. Barnett, L. Biener & G. K. Baruch (Eds.), *Gender and Stress* (pp. 96-121). New York, NY: The Free Press.

Lewis, S., & Cooper, C. (1988). Stress in dual-earner families. In B. Gutek, A. Stromber, & L. Larwood (Eds.), *Women and Work, Volume 3* (pp. 139-169). New York, NY: Sage Publications.

Lodahl, T. M., & Kehner, N. (1965). The definition and measurement of job involvement. *Journal of Applied Psychology, 49,* 24-33.

Piotrkowski, C. S., Rapaport, R. N., & Rapaport, R. (1987). Families and work. In M. Sussman, & S. Steinmetz (Eds.), *Handbook of marriage and the family* (pp. 251-283). New York, NY: Plenum Press.

Pleck, J. (1977). The work family role system. *Social Problems, 24,* 417-428.

Pleck, J. (1979). *Work-family conflict: A national assessment.* Presented at the Annual Meeting of the Society for the Study of Social Problems, Boston, MA.

Pleck, J. (1984). The work-family role system, work and family: Changing roles of men and women. In P. Voydanoff, (Ed.). *Work and family* (1st ed.). Palo Alto, CA: Mayfield.

Pleck, J. (1985). *Working wives/working husbands.* Beverly Hills, CA: Sage Publications.

Rapaport, R., & Rapaport, R. N. (1976). *Dual-career families re-examined.* New York, NY: Harper-Row.

Repetti, R. (1987). Linkages between work and family roles. In S. Oskamp (Ed.), *Family processes and problems: Social psychological aspects* (pp.98-127). Beverly Hills, CA: Sage.

Schwartz, F. (1989). Management Women and the New Facts of Life, *Harvard Business Review,* (Jan.-Feb.), 65-76.

Staines, G., Pleck, J., Shepard, L., & O'Connor, (1978). Wives' employment status and marital adjustment: Yet another look. *Psychology of Women Quarterly, 3,* 90-120.

Vanderkolk, B. & Young, A. (1991). *The Work and Family Revolution,* New York, NY: Facts on File.

Voydanoff, P., (1987). *Work and family life.* Newbury Park, CA: Sage Publications Inc.

Voydanoff, P. (1988). Work Role Characteristics, Family Structure Demands, and Work/Family Conflict, *Journal of Marriage and the Family, 50,* 749-761.

Older Women in the Workplace and Implications for Retirement: EAP Can Make a Difference

Kathleen Perkins

SUMMARY. More women are in the work place than ever before. Job opportunities continue to open up for women, especially in non-traditional professions, for example, medicine, law, administration. While these facts seem optimistic, for today and many years to come, an alarmingly vast number of women are living in post-retirement poverty. The poverty is due in part because women of all races remain over-represented in lower paying occupations and industries, a phenomenon which directly affects retirement. Employee assistance programs have a particularly unique opportunity to assist women in helping to eradicate inequities in the marketplace and in averting post-retirement poverty.

More women are in the workplace than ever before. Job opportunities continue to open up for women, especially in "non-traditional" professions, for example, medicine, law, administration. While these facts are optimistic, there exists an alarmingly vast number of

Kathleen Perkins, DSW, is Assistant Professor, School of Social Work, Louisiana State University, Baton Rouge, LA.

Please address all correspondence to the author at: School of Social Work, Louisiana State University, Baton Rouge, LA.

[Haworth co-indexing entry note]: "Older Women in the Workplace and Implications for Retirement: EAP Can Make a Difference." Perkins, Kathleen. Co-published simultaneously in *Employee Assistance Quarterly* (The Haworth Press, Inc.) Vol. 9, No. 3/4, 1994, pp. 81-97; and: *Empowering Women in the Workplace: Perspectives, Innovations, and Techniques for Helping Professionals* (ed: Marta Lundy, and Beverly Younger) Harrington Park Press an imprint of The Haworth Press, Inc., 1994, pp. 81-97. Multiple copies of this article/chapter may be purchased from The Haworth Document Delivery Center [1-800-3-HAWORTH; 9:00 a.m. - 5:00 p.m. (EST)].

women living in post-retirement poverty (Perkins, 1993b). Employee Assistance Programs have a particularly unique opportunity to assist women in averting the post-retirement poverty risk that has already befallen thousands.

Work force participation is an economic predictor for women's retirement, with labor market inequities continuing throughout employment into retirement. Evidence of this inequity exists when 77% of all employed women are working in low pay occupations and industries (National Commission on Working Women, 1986). This trend is expected to extend into the next century. Women in lower paying jobs are typically considered working-class; are defined as semi-skilled and unskilled, and hold traditional, sex segregated, low paying jobs that have become referred to as pink-collar, for example, bookkeeper, beautician, secretary, nursing aide, clerical, food preparation and services, retail sales, housekeeping, and child-care worker (Perkins 1993, a; Walshok, 1981).

This pink-collar working domain is particularly staffed by African-American women, over half of whom are employed in clerical and service occupations (Watson, 1989). African-American women also have a higher incidence of being the head of a household and have more discontinuous, sporadic work patterns, more market discrimination, and greater physical disabilities than their white counterparts (Brown, 1988: Gibson, 1983b, 1987; Jackson & Gibson, 1985).

Many factors come into play when examining the inequities of women in the workplace. Racism and ageism interact to produce gender-specific inequities in the workplace, with gender no longer the exclusive explanation. Other factors which work to intensify female employment include changing sex-role socialization, postponing marriage to a later age, reduction in fertility, escalating divorce rates, and rising monthly payments for houses (England & Farkas, 1986). This article will discuss three ways that Employee Assistance programs can assume a major role in helping to eradicate some of these inequities that have beleaguered older women in the workplace for far too long: (1) provide retirement education for women; (2) work within the employment systems to advocate for better salaries and retirement benefits for older women as well as grappling with discrimination; and (3) offer training/retraining for those who need to remain employed.

HISTORICAL OVERVIEW OF WOMEN'S WORK FORCE PARTICIPATION

World War II brought undreamed of opportunities for women in jobs previously labeled "men only." Many of these women were married and over thirty-five, whereas their prewar working sisters had been young, single, and poor. Employment for women increased during the 1950s at a rate four times faster than for men, and in 1960, twice as many women were on the job than in 1945. There has been a steady increase of women in the workplace over the last four decades, and the trend is continuing. The thrust of the growth in the numbers of working women occurred during the postwar period when a greater labor demand existed for female-related jobs as opposed to the traditional male jobs. This growth resulted from the decline in agricultural and manufacturing industries, and from increased employment in the service industries, health, insurance, retail sales, and service occupations, waitresses, sales clerks, nurses, and secretaries (England & Farkas, 1986). With the increase in demand, the supply was tapped. This led to a new market equilibrium bringing more workers into the market by offering a higher wage. Women's wages did not go up per se, however, their absolute inflation-adjusted wages did go up in the 1950s and 1960s. In many ways, this "increase" could be considered a false enticement by the labor market (Perkins, 1993b).

By 1970, more than 50% of all women from thirty-five to fifty-four held jobs outside the home. Although there has been a major shift in women's occupations between 1940 and 1981, from service jobs to white-collar occupations, women remain over-represented in lower paying occupations, and industries where they receive virtually no on-the-job training (see Perkins, 1991).

Women's life experience in the work force, especially their low earning power, has far-reaching effects on the psychological, physical, social, and economic well-being in old age. African-American women and immigrants were the pioneers of work, followed by young single women, then mature women/wives (Levitan, Mangum, & Marshall, 1976). By the turn of the 20th century, 9.1% of women over 65 were considered breadwinners, as compared to 40% for those aged 45-64 (Synder, Miller, Hollenshead, & Ketchin, 1984).

Women seek feelings of competence, of making a contribution, of being necessary and productive, and of being in control of time and energy in their work lives (Walshok, 1981). For women as well as men, earnings are crucial to personal support and to support families (Levitan et al., 1976; Report on Status of Midlife and Older Women, 1986). A major reason for the increase in women's employment over the last four decades is economic necessity associated with an increasing number of female-headed households (England & Farkas, 1986). The differences, however, are significant with regard to earnings and occupations (England & Farkas, 1986; Faludi, 1991).

Women's salaries are not commensurate with those of men, rather, earnings are substantially less (Report on Status of Midlife and Older Women, 1986). Women have earned an average of $0.64 for every $1.00 earned by men consistently since 1950 (Smith & Ward, 1984; Faludi, 1991). This gap has closed slightly (about 10%) in the past decade, not due to salary increases for women, but due to the decline in men's salaries (Cory, 1993). In 1984 women working full-time year-round had median annual earnings of $14,780, about $8,438 less than the median for employed men (ibid., 1993).

The role of the employer in promoting job segregation is manifested in hiring, placement, and promotion decisions and in organizational characteristics, e.g., for example, structured mobility ladders, all practices that connote discrimination.

Work Place Discrimination

There are two types of employment discrimination. The first is job discrimination by employers, a major catalyst for job segregation by sex and race. The second reason is the practice of allowing workers with equal productivity to earn different wages, motivated by economics. Occupational mobility, on-the-job-training, and union membership are additional areas where discrimination exists for women (Perkins, 1993b).

The predominant reason for women's low earnings is job segregation by sex (England & Farkas, 1986; Reskin & Hartmann, 1986).

Job segregation is an accepted and basic feature of the world of work (Reskin & Hartmann, 1986). Social scientists look to sex role socialization and economists to human capital theory to explain sextypical job choices (Becker, 1975).

Female-dominated occupations characteristically have shorter career ladders, meaning women often "max-out" on employment ladders within a few years. Women in traditionally male-identified occupations are often assigned jobs that offer fewer opportunities for promotion, e.g., personnel administration rather than sales (Martin, 1980). Structured mobility ladders, both at the entry level and within the employment structure, perpetuate job segregation by sex and consequently, produce discrimination in the workplace. Women receive less on-the-job-training than men or are given jobs with shorter training periods (Reskin & Hartmann, 1986), leading to higher rates of placement layoff and turnover. In human capital theory, this makes female employees less valuable to employers and more likely to be fired or not hired; their human capital potential is decreased (Perkins, 1993b).

Jobs and training programs still exist that impose explicit limitations based on age (Shaw, 1985). Apprenticeship programs are exempt from the provisions of the Age Discrimination in Employment Act. Formal age limits on some scholarships and fellowships also exist. Informal limits characterize many jobs offering on-the-job-training and advancement (Shaw, 1985).

In the past, unions barred women from membership, and in effect, from higher paying jobs. Lack of unionization by female employees has been a disadvantage, barring them from union-sponsored pension plans thus lowering their human capital investment (Perkins, 1993b).

Race and Gender Differences in the Work Force

Black women have a narrower sex-wage differential than white women due to the interaction of race and sex discrimination in hiring and promotion (Madden, 1985). Bergmann (1971) suggests that discrimination can cause wage differentials among equally skilled occupations, and that wage differentials by race may be maintained through occupational segregation rather than overt wage discrimination. Further, Bergmann (1971) maintains that the discrimination coefficient differs among occupations because of status considerations; employers prefer to hire whites over blacks.

An examination of differences in work histories among black and white, male and female adult workers found black women's work histories to be less continuous than those of black and white males. Black women worked fewer years after leaving school, worked fewer years full-time, had more frequent and longer work interruptions, with shorter tenure in a single job. Black women's work histories were less continuous than men's but more continuous than white women (Gibson, 1983a). Also, the incidence of physical disability is higher among older working-class black women (Gibson, 1983a, 1986; Jackson & Gibson, 1985). Disability limits labor force participation (Malveaux, 1980) and is an important predicate of work and retirement patterns and benefits (Gibson, 1983a, 1987).

Low level occupations, discontinuous work histories, physical disabilities, market discrimination, and early retirement contribute to depreciation of the working-class black woman's earning power, or her "human capital potential." Working-class black women accumulate less human capital through work experience (although their participation in the labor market over many years is greater than white women's years), and they are unable to fully participate in human capital investment. Human capital appreciation also reflects the investment of time and money in schooling and job training, neither of which are available to many black women participating in the labor force (Perkins, 1993,b).

POVERTY AND OLDER WOMEN

Females account for 63% of all elderly people, over 73% of the elderly poor and 82% of poor elderly living alone, making poverty exceptionally high among older women (Commonwealth Fund Commission, 1987). The poorest category among all the elderly group is black women. Five out of eight (64.9%) aged black females had an annual income below $5,000 in 1985, and one out of six (17%) had less than $3,000 (Gould, 1989).

Drastic decreases in income characterizes retirement for women. For most older women, Social Security is their only income. The lack of an adequate pension is a major contributor to low retirement income (Gibson, 1983a,b; Report of Status of Midlife and Older Women, 1986; Shaw, 1985). Black elderly women in general receive lower social security benefits than white older women and are only half as likely as their white counterparts to receive a private pension (Gould, 1989).

Marital status, living arrangements, and physical health are other factors that have an influence on how older women live. Marital status impacts the financial condition of every woman, and necessarily impacts on the type of housing that each can afford. Black women are more likely than white women to have never-married, or if married, to be separated or divorced, and they have a greater likelihood of being widowed (Brown, 1988; Gould, 1989). Both white and black older women face problems with housing. Many are unable to find housing that is suitable and affordable and consequently often remain in neighborhoods and structures inappropriate for their changing needs (Sheehan, 1986).

Affordable health care is a critical problem when women are unemployed, are ineligible for Medicare and Medicaid, or employed in jobs without health care benefits, especially since women are highly dependent on marital and employment status. Most married women, in or out of the labor force, have private health insurance, but 40% of divorced women and 27% of widows who are not employed have no such benefits (Perkins, 1992; Report on Status of Midlife and Older Women, 1986). This means that four to five million older women spend much of their social security payments for health care (Stone, 1986).

The role of primary caregiver has a significant impact on women and their participation in the labor force. Approximately 2.2 million people provide unpaid care to frail elderly at home. Of those, 72% are women and over half are 45 years and older, with an average age of 57 (Stone, Cafferata & Sangl, 1986). More men are assuming greater caregiving roles than ever before, but the unpaid caregivers are overwhelmingly female. While women originally assumed the caregiving role because they were at home, their influx into the workplace has not significantly diminished their caregiving role; they simply do both (Jackson, 1989). More than 8% of these women caregivers quit work; of those who continue to work, more than 20% reduce hours or take time off without pay (Stone et al., 1986).

In reality, poverty is the same among older and younger women. While the poverty level of older women, quantified in dollars and cents, equates to the poverty of younger women, there is one glaring difference. Retired poor women have spent a work-life trying to eradicate their plight. The possibility of poverty is ever-present for many retired women who have not contemplated it before. Today young and middle-age women have an advantage over older women. There is time for them to improve their economic status resulting in a much better chance of their older years offering more economic security than hardship (Malveaux, 1992; Perkins, 1993b).

RETIREMENT FOR WOMEN

A woman's decision to retire can be voluntary, based on the attainment of economic and psychological goals and/or based on a mutual agreement with her spouse; or it may be forced, because of extended periods of unemployment (e.g., discouraged worker), lack of employment opportunities, gender and race discrimination, family responsibilities, or health problems (Belgrave, 1988; Brown, 1988; Gibson, 1983b). Because of the lack of economic resources available to women in retirement, many low-salaried older women workers choose to continue to work as long as they can (Perkins, 1993a). For these women, retirement is a luxury they may not be able to afford. Unfortunately, many women enter retirement prematurely and involuntarily, before they are financially ready, forcing them to re-enter the job market after retirement. Most re-entry jobs resemble the low paying, sex-segregated jobs they were forced to retire from (Perkins, 1991).

Retirement involves three major periods–pre-retirement, transition, and post-retirement. The pre-retirement period requires looking ahead to a future life; it is a period during which decisions about whether and when to retire are made (Atchley, 1982a). If economic security in retirement is to be realized, it is during the pre-retirement period that planning must occur (Hayes & Deren, 1990).

Pre-Retirement Planning for Women

Women plan less frequently for retirement than men (Atchley, 1982b; McKenna & Nickols, 1986; Perkins, 1993a). Middle-aged, white collar working women (Colye, 1986), black women (Gibson, 1987; Jackson & Gibson, 1985; Perkins, 1993a) and women over the age of 50 (American Association of Retired Persons, 1986; Hayes & Deren, 1990) are exposed to little retirement preparation. The reasons for the lack of information are more institutional and societal than the fault of the women themselves. The institutional barriers of the past relative to accessing retirement education still exist today, for example, this education is not offered in the employment setting; union membership is a prerequisite for the educational opportunity, and/or the programs, when offered, are limited in nature.

In addition to the lack of access to retirement education, other factors contribute to the absence of retirement planning. The fear of aging, and the consequences of the traditional roles for women in society, which emphasizes inferiority, dependency, and passivity contribute to women's impoverished circumstances (Dowling, 1981; Sontag, 1972). The devaluation of women, and the double jeopardy imposed by sexism and ageism, can be traced over many centuries (Yolam, 1981). The necessary education to promote a more economically secure retirement for women must be dispersed not only to women, but more importantly to employers and to policy makers.

ADVOCACY ROLE OF EAP AND OLDER WOMEN IN THE LABOR MARKET

Innovations for Older Workers in the Marketplace

There are two benefits for older workers to remain in the labor force: economic security in retirement, and their economic contribution to the dependency ratio. There are many innovative ways that both can happen. It has already been established that vast numbers of older women must remain in the work force out of economic necessity. On the broader societal level, older women are an important resource and their economic contribution is significant. By 2020, the number of people 65 and over will exceed those under 25 (U.S. Bureau Census, 1980). Pressure on the Social Security system and burdens on the young are, as yet, difficult to assess, although an alarming increase in per-worker cost to support the non-working aged seems likely by the turn of the century. The dependency ratio has steadily increased for the last 50 years and will rise dramatically as "baby boomers" reach 65. In 1930, 7.54 workers supported each retiree above the age of 65. By 1976 the ratio was 4.23, and for 1990, the predicted ratio of workers to retirees is 3.89 (Polachek, 1980).

In addition to economic hardships imposed by forced retirement, older women, like older men, have to deal with the psychological effects of joblessness. Older women work because they need money and they have a desire to do something productive, to have social contact, to be challenged and to achieve, and to gain recognition and personal satisfaction (Reddick, 1985; Walshok, 1981). Women's work not only determines income and social status, but it also provides associations and relationships and determines lifestyles and goals (Kuhn, 1985). Work-centered women broaden their interests as they grow older and become more satisfied with their lives (Jacobson, 1975; Livson, 1976; Mass & Kuyper, 1975). Women in their 50's who were ambitious and unconventional have improved health (Jacobson, 1975). This suggests that active involvement in work coupled with outside interests in later years may help to reduce psychological and physical problems (Perkins, 1992). However, retirement needs to be flexible and optional. For those who need to work, the work must be dignified and healthy as well as providing flexible hours (Kuhn, 1985; Perkins, 1992). Many employers have begun to put innovative alternatives into practice, providing excellent models which others can follow. EAPs have the opportunity to promote the already existing models or to create some of their own. Some useful examples include:

1. Banks. With a life-time of managing their money, older workers excel as tellers and customer-service representatives. The Bank of America in Los Angeles provides two weeks of training and typically pays $7 to $10 an hour (Silver, 1990, p. 76).

2. Hotels. In 1985, two Days Inns found that the average employee quit after three months; this was accompanied by an absentee rate of 30%. Days Inn tapped the over-55 labor market and, today in nearly a third of the centers, 450 employees are 55 or older. Their average tenure is three years; the absentee rate is 3%; the average salary is $6.50 an hour (Silver, 1990, p. 76).

3. Hardware stores. Roaming a hardware store in search of the right widget to fix the toilet. A mature face suggests years of fix-up experience, a lesson learned by home-improvement chains like Builders Emporium, where 15% of the 6,200 employees are over age 55, as well as Hechinger and Home Depot. A typical salary in a California Builders Emporium is $7.35 per hour (Silver, 1990, p. 76).

Most older women need retraining in order to step into the dignified and healthy jobs that will help sustain them financially. Few programs specifically provide retraining for older adults, except for the program Senior Community Services Employment (SCSE), which is funded by the Older Americans Act of 1965. This program provides part-time subsidized employment opportunities for older adults, making a difference both in income and quality of life (Mor-Barak & Tynan, 1993).

There are other programs that draw on public and community resources, and, to some extent, private industry. These programs for older workers typically fall into two categories, one facilitating linkages between older adults and potential employers, the other accommodating the needs of older adults in the work place through job modification, job training, and senior care. For a full description of these programs, see Mor-Barak and Tynan (1993).

Income Adjustment for Retirement

Most people wish to live at least as well in retirement as they have throughout their work lives. One measure for estimating income requirements in retirement, called the "replacement rate," determines the ratio of post-retirement income, for example, Social Security, pensions, interest and dividends, to pre-retirement income. Because of the reduction in many work-related expenses after retirement, a 100% replacement rate is usually not necessary. To be adequate, retirement income replacement rates should range from approximately 55% for high-income couples to over 85% for couples in the lowest income bracket, with middle-income workers needing to strive for a replacement rate of at least 65-70% of gross income (Rix, 1990).

The replacement rate formula results in a dollar amount which can be assessed according to each individual's financial situation. To begin, the woman's expenditures for her retirement years are estimated. These expenses include, but are not limited to, housing, utilities, food, clothing, transportation, travel, taxes, and insurance. For example, a 45 year-old woman with estimated annual expenses of about $25,000 per year will have to work another 21 years, or until age 66, to receive full Social Security benefits. For her to replace about two-thirds, or 65% of her income, the formula used is: $25,000 × .65 = $16,250. This formula works on the assumption that her income just covers her expenses [$25,000] (Rix, 1990). The uncertainties of inflation also need to be considered. For an inflation impact factor see Rix (1990).

Recommendations for Pre-Retirement/Life Planning

Employee assistance programs can be on the cutting edge of advocacy for older women not only by recognizing the need for retirement planning, but by providing the opportunity for women to take part in such planning. The time for planning is during midlife, between 35 to 55, regardless of social strata and regardless of whether a woman is single, married, divorced, widowed, working full-time, part-time or, unemployed (Hayes & Deren, 1990; Warshaw, 1988).

There must be accessible ways in which younger women can tap the information necessary for this "life-planning." Uncertainty about the future can be lessened when issues surrounding retirement are openly discussed and strategies for solving problems are presented (Atchley, 1982a, 1982b; Hayes & Deren, 1990; McKenna & Nickols, 1986). There are several avenues that exist for Employee Assistance programs to provide women with such training/ life-planning: (1) structured, formal educational workshop; (2) individual counseling sessions; (3) small group settings, classrooms, lunch rooms.

This author had the opportunity to do research with a group of people at the Long Island University, Southampton Campus, The National Center for Women and Retirement Research, who were instrumental in packaging a program, Pre-Retirement Education Planning for Women (PREP). The research led to the publication of four different life planning booklets for women: (1) Looking Ahead to Your Financial Future, (2) Social and Emotional Issues for Mid-life Women, (3) Employment and Retirement Issues for Women, and (4) Taking Control of Your Health and Fitness. PREP has also been responsible for sponsoring life-planning/pre-retirement education workshops throughout the country. Warshaw (1988, p. 28) summarizes the advice offered at the workshops:

1. Set up your own financial identity: your own checking and savings accounts and credit in your own name. Protect yourself with health insurance.
2. Make a list of all your assets and liabilities. Read all of your own and your family's financial and legal documents. Ask questions.
3. Evaluate your present job for its impact on your retirement. A cost benefit analysis will compare the expense of learning new skills to increase income against the amount of Social Security benefits you will receive if you stay in your present job. Find employment that provides a pension plan, even if the salary is less. Nontaxable and deferred tax benefits may be worth more to you in the long run than a few dollars in your paycheck.
4. Learn about Social Security benefits. Payments are tied to work credits. Dependent spouse benefits are 50% of the amount due to the working spouse. A widow can collect benefits at age 60 rather than waiting until she is 65, but her payments will be permanently reduced by almost 30% of the full benefit amount. A divorced woman may receive benefits based on her former spouse's work if the marriage lasted 10 years or more and both are 62 or older. However, if first claimed at age 62, the benefits would be reduced.
5. Go to the Social Security office and ask them for information about where you stand currently with your Social Security

benefits. Have them explain work credits and how many quarters of coverage you need for retirement.

6. If you have a pension plan, get a full explanation of the summary plan description, which includes who is covered and how benefits are disbursed.

7. Consider opening an IRA. Many women are eligible to take full tax deduction on IRA contributions. Income limits are $25,000 for an individual covered by a pension plan and $40,000 for a couple filing jointly. (There are no limits if you do not have a pension plan at work.) The money in an IRA earns compound interest. You may begin withdrawing from the account at age 59 1/2, but do not have to do so until you are 70 1/2. An annual IRA investment of $2,000 at 10% interest compounded quarterly will yield $229,957 after 25 years. Employee Assistant Professionals, or women desiring more information on pensions can contact the following:

1. American Association of Retired Persons (AARP). 1909 K Street, NW, Washington, DC 20049.
2. Displaced Homemakers Network. 1010 Vermont Avenue, NW, Suite 817, Washington, DC 20005.
3. Pension Rights Center, 1346 Connecticut Avenue, NW, Washington DC 20036.
4. Women's Equity Action League (WEAL). 1250 I Street, NW, Suite 305, Washington, DC 20002.
5. Older Women's League (OWL). 1325 G Street, NW, LLB, Washington, DC 20005.

Poverty in women's old age has become a fact of life in the 20th century. EAPs can work with younger women on long-term goals for retirement, providing retirement education in the context of immediate, wise financial management as part of their long-term goal.

REFERENCES

Atchley, R. (1982a). Retirement: Leaving the world of work. *The Annals of the American Academy of Policy and Social Science, 464*, 120-131.

Atchley, R. (1982b) The process of retirement: Comparing women and men. In M. Szinovacz (Ed.), *Women's retirement: Policy implications of recent research.* Beverly Hills: Sage.

Becker, G. (1975). *Human Capital*, (2nd ed.). New York: Columbia University.

Belgrave, L. (1988). The effects of race differences in work history, work attitudes, economic resources, and health on women's retirement. *Research on Aging, 10*,(3), 383-398.

Bergmann, B. (1971). The effect on white incomes of discrimination in employment. *Journal of Political Economy, 79*, 294-313.

Brown, R.D. (1988). *Employment and health among older black women: Implications for their economic status.* (Working Paper No. 77). Wellesley, MA: Wellesley College, Center for Research on Women.

Commonwealth Fund Commission on Elderly People Living Alone. (1987). *Old, alone, and poor: Technical analyses* (Report). Baltimore: Commonwealth Fund Commission on Elderly People Living Alone.

Cory, E. (1993, June 10). *National Public Radio–Morning Edition.* Report on women's salaries. Washington, DC.

Dowling, C. (1981). *The cinderella complex: Women's hidden fear of independence*, New York: Summit Books.

England, P., & Farkas, G. (1986). *Households, employment, and gender.* New York: Aldine Publishing Co.

Faludi, S. (1991). *Backlash: The undeclared war against American women.* New York: Crown Publishing, Inc.

Federal Register. "Notices," Vol. 56 (34) (Wednesday, February 20, 1991): 6860.

Gibson, R.C. (1983a). *Work and retirement [of] aging black women: A race and sex comparison.* Unpublished manuscript. Ann Arbor: The University of Michigan, The Institute of Gerontology.

Gibson, R.C. (1983b). Work patterns of older black female head of households. *Journal of Minority Aging, 8*, 1-16.

Gibson, R.C. (1986). Blacks in an aging society. *Daedalus, 115*(1), 349-371.

Gibson, R.C. (1987). Reconceptualizing retirement for Black Americans. *The Gerontologist, 27*(6), 691-698.

Gould, K.H. (1989). A minority-feminist perspective on women and aging. In J.D. Garner & S.O. Mercer (Ed.), *Women as they age: Challenge, opportunity, and triumph* (pp. 195-216). NY: The Haworth Press, Inc.

Hayes, C.L. & Deren, J.M. (1990). *Pre-retirement planning for women: Program design and research.* NY: Springer.

Jackson, J.L. (1985). Race, national origin, ethnicity, and aging. In R.H. Binstock & E. Shane (Eds.), *Handbook of aging and the social sciences* (2nd ed., pp. 264-303). NY: Van Nostrand Reinhold.

Jackson, J.L. & Gibson, R.C. (1985). Work and retirement among the black elderly. *Current Perspectives on Aging and the Life Cycle, 1*, 193-222.

Jacobson, S. (1975). The woman Alone. No Longer Young, *Occasional Papers in Gerontology* (Number 11). Ann Arbor: University of Michigan.

Kuhn, M.E. (1985). *Restructuring the workplace and non-retirement.* Philadelphia: Unpublished paper.

Levitan, S., Mangum, G., & Marshall, R. (1976). *Human resources and labor markets* (2nd ed.). NY: Harper and Row.

Livson, F. (1976). Patterns of personality, development in middle-aged women: A longitudinal study. *International Journal of Aging and Human Development, 7*, 107-116.

Madden, J.F. (1985). The persistence of pay differentials: The economics of sex discrimination. In L. Larwood, S. Stromberg, & B. Gutek (Eds.), *Women and work*. Beverly Hills: Sage Publications.

Malveaux, J. (1992). The economic predicament of low-income elderly women. (The Southport Institute's Series on Women and Population Aging, Monograph No. 6). Southport, CT: Southport Institute for Policy Analysis.

Martin, S.E. (1980). *Breaking and entering: Policewoman on patrol*. Berkeley: University of California Press.

McKenna, J. & Nickols, S.Y. (1986). Retirement planning strategies for mid-life women. *Journal of Home Economics*. Winter, 34-37.

Mor-Barak, & Tynan, M. (1993). Older workers and the workplace: A new challenge for occupational social work. *Social Work, 38*(1), 45-55.

National Commission on Working Women (1986). *Women at Work*. Spring/Summer, *3*, 2.

Older Women's League (1990). *Heading for hardship: Retirement income for American women in the next century*. Washington, DC: Older Women's League.

Perkins, K. (1991). Blue-collar women and retirement. *Social Work Research and Abstracts: Abstracts of Dissertations. 27*(3). (University Microfilms, University of Pennsylvania, No. 91-23424).

Perkins, K. (1992). Psychosocial implications of women and retirement. *Social Work, 37*(6) 526-532.

Perkins, K. (1993a). Working-class women and retirement. *Journal of Gerontological Social Work, 20*(1).

Perkins, K. (1993b). Recycling poverty: From the workplace to retirement. *Journal of Women and Aging, 5*(1) 5-23.

Polachek, S. (1980). Secular changes in female job aspirations. In C. Roberts (Ed.), *Retirement policy in an aging society*. Durham, NC: Duke University Press.

Puner, M. (1974). *To the good long life: What we know about growing old*. NY: Universe Books.

Report on the Status of Midlife and Older Women. (1986, May). Washington, DC: Older Women's League (OWL).

Rix, S. (1990). Who pays for what? Ensuring financial security in retirement. In C.L. Hayes & J.M. Deren (Eds.). *Pre-retirement planning for women: Program design and research*. NY: Springer.

Sontag, S. (1972). The double standard of aging. *Saturday Review of the Society*, September, 22-38.

Shaw, L. (1985). *Older women at work*. Washington, DC: Women's Research and Education Institute of the Congressional Caucus for Women's Issues.

Sheehan, J.W. (1986). Aging of tenants: Termination policy in public senior housing. *The Gerontologist, 26*, 505-509.

Silver, M. (1990, June). Hitting the unretirement circuit. *U.S. News & World Report*, p. 76.

Social Security Bulletin (1988). *51*(12), Washington, DC: Social Security Administration.

Stone, R. (1986). *The feminization of poverty and older women: An update.* Washington, DC: National Center for Health Services Research.

Stone, R., Cafferata, G.L., & Sangl, J. (1986). *Caregivers of the frail: National Profile.* Washington, DC: Older Women's League.

Snyder, E., Miller, J.E., Hollenshead, C., & Ketchin, J. (1984). *'Old' at 40: Women in the workplace.* Ann Arbor: University of Michigan, Institute on Gerontology.

U.S. Bureau of the Census. (1980). General population characteristics: United States summary. Washington, DC: U.S. Government Printing Office.

Walshok, M. (1981). *Blue-collar women: Pioneers on the male frontier.* Garden City NY: Anchor Books.

Warshaw, R. (1988, November 15). Women's retirement paradox. *Philadelphia Daily News.* pp. 25-28.

Watson, J. (1989). *Women and work.* National Commission on working women: Factsheet, Washington, DC.

Yalom, M. (1981). Introduction to Part IV. In E.O. Hellerstein, L.P. Hume & K.M. Offen (Eds.), *Victorian Women* (pp. 453-462). Stanford: Stanford University Press.

Family Relocation:
Family Systems, Gender
and the Role of EAP

Marta Lundy

SUMMARY. Family domestic relocations for the purpose of employment have increased and indications are that this will continue. Although there are various reasons for relocation which affect its influence, recent research on corporate moves suggests that there are unexplored discrepancies in the findings on how the two genders respond to the relocation. This paper will discuss these differences and will describe how professionals unwittingly can contribute to mother and/or wife blaming within the context of family relocation. The results are evident in the literature which produces: (1) a focus on women's responsibility and accountability for the family, to the exclusion of men, and (2) a lack of awareness of the societally prescribed contexts of work and family life that can be oppressive to both women and men. This paper also suggests practice principles that will guide work with family member's adjustment to relocation and that will direct future research.

Family relocation among corporate employees is an identified problem across the country. Changes within the corporate structure as well as personal upward mobility result in large numbers of

Marta Lundy, PhD, is a licensed Clinical Social Worker and faculty member at Loyola University of Chicago School of Social Work.
This paper is dedicated in loving memory to my sister.

[Haworth co-indexing entry note]: "Family Relocation: Family Systems, Gender and the Role of EAP." Lundy, Marta. Co-published simultaneously in *Employee Assistance Quarterly* (The Haworth Press, Inc.) Vol. 9, No. 3/4, 1994, pp. 99-112; and: *Empowering Women in the Workplace: Perspectives, Innovations, and Techniques for Helping Professionals* (ed: Marta Lundy, and Beverly Younger) Harrington Park Press an imprint of The Haworth Press, Inc., 1994, pp. 99-112. Multiple copies of this article/chapter may be purchased from The Haworth Document Delivery Center [1-800-3-HAWORTH; 9:00 a.m. - 5:00 p.m. (EST)].

employees and their families relocating. There are many reasons why families move. Some move for a better lifestyle, some for a greater personal challenge and some to continue in their chosen career. Others move to keep their jobs due to corporate mergers or layoffs. Families and family members may have different responses to moving. Relocation can be stimulating, bringing an awareness of regional and cultural diversity and a sense of capacity for change. For some families, the move brings a revitalized lifestyle, a fresh start after an unsuccessful period.

However, there are other families who have felt dissatisfied, uprooted and alone because of relocation. Social support systems are sacrificed, and the stress is manifested in individual behaviors. This paper will discuss these families and will describe how professionals can unwittingly contribute to mother and/or wife blaming within the context of family relocation. The results are evident in the literature which produces: (1) a focus on women's responsibility and accountability for the family, while excluding men, and (2) a lack of awareness of the societally prescribed contexts of work and family life that can be oppressive to both women and men. The focus of this paper is on domestic corporate transfers, but the problems and solutions cut across all family relocation.

THE ROLE OF EMPLOYEE ASSISTANCE PROGRAM PROFESSIONALS

Social workers are charged with facilitating social change. Employee Assistance Program (EAP) professionals are often social workers who have a strong professional ethic which alerts them to situations of oppression and inequity, however societally and individually manifested. EAP professionals play a significant role in managing the mental health care of employees. Their role is either advisory, as a consultant to the insurance carrier about employee services, or directly, with control over the contract and payment of services. They facilitate access to mental health services for a population that may not otherwise have access to or be aware of available help and support. In either capacity, they have the authority to focus and direct mental health services for employees. EAP professionals monitor the services and evaluate the outcome of treatment.

They are the pivotal point in identifying the problem and defining and ensuring equitable, effective services to employees and their family members.

This pivotal role is especially crucial when one considers the varied perspectives of mental health professionals. In the recent past, professionals often functioned as if mothers were accountable for all family matters, and were responsible for the amelioration of all family problems (Goldner, 1985). In a review of journal articles, 72 different psychological disorders have been attributed to mothers' failings (Caplan & Hall-McCorquodale, 1985). However, professionals have made strides in re-focusing family problems. The influence of feminist theory has resulted in the realization that there are alternative explanations and solutions for family problems. EAP professionals who use a feminist framework are better prepared to equitably assess more possibilities for the problems, and therefore have a larger set of interventions with which to accommodate families' situations.

FAMILY RELOCATION AND ITS EFFECTS

Americans are highly mobile and ambitious, moving up the corporate ladder with promotions that require relocation. In normal years, major corporations relocate an average of 100,000 employees and their families each year. High-tech employees and employees in managerial positions can expect a geographic transfer every two to three years (Anderson & Stark, 1988). It is acknowledged that geographic relocation is a major stress to families. Moving means loss and change in lifestyle for everyone in the family (Bloomfield & Holzman, 1988). There is a growing realization of the interdependence between families and work, resulting in work-family stress (Bowen, 1988; Raabe-Gessner, 1988). The combination of work-related and geographical stress can push some families' resourcefulness to a crisis stage.

Families are systems of interdependent people, each member influencing and being influenced by all other family members and by other systems. Family systems theory explains the impact of each family member's behavior on all other members and provides a rationale for exploring the family system as a resource for resolving

family and individual difficulties that arise due to relocation. Relocation stress includes normal feelings and tensions, which may be
exacerbated due to stress but are not necessarily indicative of psy-
chopathology (Gaylord, 1986). Problems arise when families move.

Certainly, there are families who highly prize goal achievement,
and for whom vocational rewards are a significant part of their value
system. For them, adjustment to relocation may come more easily.
However, there are other families for whom career achievement may
be a secondary priority. Unlike other social institutions which offer
rewards for goal achievement, these families offer rewards and place
greater emphasis on personal loyalty and mutually satisfying relationships (Boszormenyi-Nagy, 1981; Satir, 1967). This emphasis is
accomplished through reciprocity among family members. Family
cohesion and functioning depend upon a value system which rein-
forces the emotive and instrumental abilities of members to balance
individual growth and autonomy with family unity (Rankin, 1987).
More commonly, families are a blend of these two, with family
members continually adapting to accommodate the achievement as
well as personal needs of the family members. Corporate moves
create difficulties for some families when disparities in values among
family members are exacerbated, imbalancing the adaptation process, and often, requiring more from some members than others.
This greater responsibility usually falls to the mother. The systemic
nature of the family presupposes that the employee will be affected
by the experiences of the other family members, and that his/her
capacity and ability to work may be compromised. If the problems of
relocation are assessed with the idea that all members of the family
are equally effected, then the assessment has failed to acknowledge
the differences among family members.

Previous studies have suggested opposing explanations for the
consequences to individuals and families due to corporate relocation. Seidenberg (1974) concluded that there were deleterious effects to the mobile corporate life, specifically pointing out the com-
promises required of wives. Others have suggested that children
and wives are deprived of a fundamental human need for social
continuity and personal involvement. Boss, McCubbin and Lester
(1979), studied the coping patterns of sixty-six corporate executive
wives whose husbands were routinely absent from the home. The

wives reported three successful coping styles: (1) fitting into the corporate lifestyle; (2) developing self; and (3) establishing independence (Gullotta & Donohue, 1982). The explicit message of all three alternatives is that women must adapt. The first suggests that the woman identify with her husband's employment, with the implication that the vicarious experience will be sufficient. The other two suggest that the woman should be able to rely on herself for getting her needs met; there is no mention of her husband as a resource. It is her responsibility to either fit in or to take care of herself, through outside interests and activities. Thus, research reporting women's comments about their own coping efforts after relocation indicates that women also omit or minimize the role of the man not only in the family life, but also as a personal resource. Too often professionals do not help her or her family to conceptualize the problems differently. Rather, we continue to focus on the responsibility of women to organize, care for and shore up family problems–denying the man the opportunity to provide nurturing and support, and further imposing expectations on the woman.

These circumstances create a chasm between husband and wife, an invisible barrier that undermines the potential for mutual interdependence possible in the marriage unit. These alternatives also insidiously suggest that the woman may have serious personal problems if she is unable to accommodate to one of these three coping styles. It sounds chillingly familiar; women who have been raped have been re-victimized by being blamed for the rape. Mothers of schizophrenic children have been vilified as schizophrenogenic mothers, implying that they are the cause of the child's disorder. Once again, if women don't perform their societally prescribed roles, at best, they are categorized as irresponsible. At worst, they are ill. Perhaps most troubling is the realization that women accept these explanations as true. Weissman and Paykel (1972) noted a high correlation between mental depression in women and moving. They observed that the women had not noticed the association, having taken it for granted that moving and its associated discomforts was an accepted and integral part of American family life. According to the President's Commission on Mental Health:

Circumstances and conditions that American society has come to accept as normal or ordinary lead to profound unhappiness, anguish, and mental illness in women. Marriage, family relationships, pregnancy, childrearing, divorce, work and aging all have a powerful impact on the well-being of women . . . Compounding these ordinary events, women are also subject to some extraordinary experiences such as rape, marital violence, and incest, which leave them vulnerable to mental illness. (1978, p. 1038)

In contrast, a survey analysis of 500 employees from five companies concluded that the conceptualization of wives as victims was a poorly researched journalistic sensationalism that was not substantiated (Brett, 1982). The researcher suggests that there were very few differences between more and less stable people. In fact, mobile employees and their wives reported being more satisfied with their lives, families and marriages, but less satisfied with their social relationships than were stable employees.

More recent studies shed some light on the discrepancies between these findings. Husbands are exuberant whereas wives are lonely, bored and depressed, reactions attributed to career disruption and emotional uprooting (Bloomfield & Holzman, 1988).

A recent qualitative study focused on the personal experiences of relocation for forty-two women over two years (McCollum, 1990). The women reported experiencing loss of home and career, social network and a sense of self. The findings also suggest that recovery from the shock of the move is likely to take longer than the six months generally suggested as being necessary to adjust. One of the reasons that the shock of relocation is so profound is because of the roles the woman feels that she is expected to play in the family. Often, a contemporary woman must live up to the expectation that she care for the family and, at the same time, build a fascinating and financially rewarding career of her own. Regardless of her career responsibilities, she often also feels the responsibility for setting up the new household and responding to family needs for nurturance and support during this difficult time (Bloomfield & Holzman, 1988). She is expected to create the feeling of a secure home.

McCollum's study (1900) explored the interface between family and work and community systems, constructing the women's stories by examining the context of cultural, familial and societal expectations. It is from these perspectives that the study of women's experiences of relocation will be more fully understood. The implicit message of the study seemed to concur with others, suggesting that the women needed clinical intervention in order to understand and to overcome their reactions to the move. A woman's response to fulfill families' needs is not merely the result of her own sense of responsibility. She gets cues from her partner that "pressures are building on him at work," or that she must "understand" that he has less time for responsibilities at home (Bloomfield & Holzman, 1988). She is responding to either direct or indirect messages that she will have to pick up the pieces because there is no one else to do it. If she resents this additional responsibility or if she has trouble adapting to the role, she is perceived as inflexible and described as having difficulty adjusting to the relocation. The husband is not explicitly exonerated from responsibility, but the implicit message is that wives are in personal trouble when they don't conform to the needs of the primary breadwinner.

Studies suggest that "at some point in the marriage [it] has been renegotiated [that] the wife accept responsibility for family and the husband for income" (Gulotta & Donohue, 1982). In fact, 75% of American families are two income families (Collie, 1986), which means the wife works full time *and* assumes responsibility for the home and family, a fact which has been confirmed by recent sociological studies (Hochschild, 1989). Hochschild reported that mothers of three years olds who held full time jobs worked approximately 90 hours a week, in order to fulfill their household and job responsibilities. Finally, the conflict between her personal experiences and her family responsibilities has been identified. Women fulfill multiple roles. "There is now some general agreement that parenting contributes significantly to role overload, that women's participation in the labor force or lack thereof affects morbidity and mortality patterns, and that caring for [children and] elderly relatives costs the women bearing this burden dearly" (McBride, 1990, p. 382).

Furthermore, helping professionals often point out that the mother's personal adjustment to the move is the principal determinant of the functioning of the entire family (Stroh & Brett, 1988). Certainly, she is often the one responsible for the concrete needs of the family, e.g., finding a grocery store, locating the shoe repair shop, contacts with school districts, which of necessity places a large part of the responsibility for family resettlement on her shoulders. Recently, however, there has been acknowledgement that she, too, has many personal adjustments to make, e.g., loss of the extended family and social network, and the derailment of her career. One of the more progressive benefits of corporate relocation packages has been to include job relocation services to spouses, realizing that they often need help in locating adequate employment. Although this is an acknowledgement of the necessity and prevalence of two income households, it doesn't change the expectations for women about their family responsibilities. The concept of superwoman is alive and well in corporate America.

Our zealousness to offer a solution to the problems encountered by families when they move often results in our once again expecting the woman not only to facilitate the family's adjustment but also to accomplish the task quickly. This perspective is not the exclusive domain of helping professionals. Women derive great happiness and satisfaction from marriage and parenthood, but they also can be areas of extreme stress (Russo, 1990), especially if the woman is held primarily accountable for the success of family life. Not only does our thinking often lead us to focus blame on her, it helps us avoid involving the father in the process of family life. This societal structuring limits men's involvement with their families and is oppressive to women; each is restricted to a specific role. Both partners lose, the entire family suffers.

PRINCIPLES FOR EFFECTIVE PRACTICE

There are four predictable stages in the process of relocation: (1) the time before the move, preparing for the move; (2) the actual move and the early post-move stage; (3) the post-move crisis period, and (4) the post-move adjustment period. These are all critical periods during which different individuals will have different experiences. Each of the clearly defined stages and transition points of relocation needs to be understood within the context of a family member's individual, familial and societal experience. Each stage will have a different set of expectations for each person. Attention to unique concerns will affirm each person's experience of the move, and confirm the importance of the process, not just the result, of adjustment.

Although existing corporate priorities, societal influences, and family role expectations all play a part in sustaining the current limitations on family members, there are feminist principles which offer alternative perspectives for these problems. These principles are useful for both women and men, but they are especially relevant to the needs of women. They will guide EAP professionals in their work, connecting individual family members with useful internal and external resources.

However, EAPs are not always responsible for the needs of relocating families, especially just prior to and during the process of the move, and during the initial adjustment period. EAP professionals may not see the relocated family until they have completely re-settled and are in desperate need. The Human Resources department often has the most initial contact with families who are moving. In order to alleviate potential problems, EAPs and Human Resource personnel may want to consider developing an infrastructure that is designed to help relocating families. A coordinated relocation program, organized on feminist principles, could be available to families as they proceed through the process of a move, offering information, education and services all along the way.

The first principle involves an awareness of the socio-political constraints on women. Recent research on women's multiple roles and mental health suggests that a psychosocial approach is needed, one which assesses "both the advantages and disadvantages of [women's] multiple roles. . . ." (McBride, 1990). A psycho-social-cultural assessment of role expectations enables professionals to better understand the responsibilities that each woman has to juggle, as well as the particular circumstances. This orientation can alleviate the common pitfall of victim blame, which suggests that it is the woman alone who has the problem, that she must be referred to therapy, and that she must change in order to accommodate the situation. The most empowering message that we can give to her is that no one person can either cause or solve the family adjustment problems that may accompany a move.

Another principle on which to base a relocation program is the importance of the interface between the person, the family and the larger systems. The larger systems include the work place, neighborhood, community, city, church and other relevant organizations. Professionals must explicitly direct attention to the relevance of the environmental context in adjusting to relocation. Questions need to address the quality of the previous relationships and the anticipated level of satisfaction that she expects to derive from each, while also exploring the loss of significant interpersonal relationships. These expectations can be compared with previous experiences, providing a working foundation for the EAP practitioner and a point of reference, and of hope, for the client. The entire family must be included in this examination of anticipated relationships, giving the explicit message that each family member is responsible for developing and maintaining individual relationships within his/her own social support system. The mother is not the sole connection for the family with the community.

Another critical component is a sensitivity to the interlocking foci of concern for human dignity and the prevention of discrimination (NASW, 1980). This focus explicitly recognizes the importance of the individual within the social structure, questions authoritarian organizational concepts, including family patriarchy, and reconceptualizes power as a means to an end, not an end in itself. This is especially relevant to relocation as it gives an empowering message to all family members, but especially to women and children, that everyone is equally important. The conceptualization of the family as an environment that may be oppressive to women and burdensome to men is critical to the formation of a fair-minded approach. Although initially this may precipitate strife within the family, it will make explicit and perhaps understandable, interactions that have been covert, perhaps mysterious and unavailable for examination. Bringing problems into the daylight can be healing for the entire family.

The professional also must be able to reach into his/her own experience and share personal anecdotes about relocation, or other relevant events. The acknowledgement of commonalities helps normalize the experience for family members. Also, it introduces a different level of communication between the 'helper' and the 'helpee.' Once this level of personal involvement is established, the coordination of services and resources becomes a process of working together on a mutual project. This is a depathologizing and empowering process for the person who may be feeling especially inadequate during this time.

Using these feminist principles as the foundation, the relocation programs could include:

1. Seminars on how to prepare for a major relocation, including anticipated fears about making new contacts as well as how to achieve the kind of relationship each person wants from this new environment. Each family member will be given equal time and attention.

2. Practical arrangements about how to begin to settle in to a new neighborhood could be explained. For example, information could be available about local ordinances, and about the types, safety, and availability of public transportation. Information could be given about differences between the parts of the country, for example, the faster pace or the local customs. The relocation program professional may want to have available a list of various ethnic and/or culturally relevant markets and restaurants.

3. Information could be given about local child care facilities, including how often they are evaluated. Local agencies could make presentations.

4. Names of families who have recently relocated and have agreed to be available for questions could be distributed, indicating the same area from which they moved. Individual speakers could talk about their own adjustment experiences.

5. Discussion groups could be organized, providing family members with an opportunity to speak freely about their own experiences with relocation. Pivotal to the adjustment is a commitment to validate the woman's individual experience about the move and her feelings about her new home.

6. Telephone networking systems could be available to connect recently resettled family members with newly relocated family members within a particular company, or within a city.

7. For families who need therapy in order to work through the adjustment process, relocation programs could have a list of feminist family therapists who are knowledgeable in the area of family domestic relocation. Feminist family therapists dif-

fer from family systems therapists in that they focus on equitable relationships among all family members, and do not rely
on the traditional family structures of hierarchy and patriarchy. These family therapists, both men and women, will facilitate the work of the relocation programs, helping families to
adjust to their new environment as well as to one another.

By stating the facts and validating individual feelings about the
differences, as well as involving the whole family in the adjustment
process, professionals promote self-determination and empowerment for each person. It is imperative that societal expectations of
women, often shared by the women themselves as well as their
partners and families, must be considered. Too often professionals
give lip-service to the societal and familial expectations of caregiving that pervade women's experiences, but continue to refer to the
mother to resolve all the family problems. Meanwhile, the family
has firmly relocated, with the father working long hours and the
children all off to school, while professionals describe the isolated
woman as having "merged boundaries" with her partner and children, and suggest individual clinical treatment in order to understand 'what has happened to her.' Often there is no mention of
therapy for other family members, or of the insidious dictates of
society and family on the woman's choices. There is little substanti-
ation for the limited personal power that this arrangement affords
every woman. According to Fran Sussner Rodgers, founder and
president of Work/Family Directions, "The world has changed less
than we are led to believe by the anecdotes in the press on new roles
for men. In fact, gender roles are very slow to change and it is
useful to keep in mind the still-profound differences that separate
men and women. Women still bear the major share of the responsibilities for the care of children and the household . . . and family
responsibilities have an impact on the . . . lives . . . of women"
(Rodgers, 1992, p. 20).
   There is not enough acknowledgement that families need to find
solutions together. The ways in which family members adjust to the
needs of one another has to become a source of legitimate discussion, with a "focus on the transactions of individuals and their

environments . . . in a constant state of reciprocity, each shaping the other" (Compton & Galaway, 1989).

CONCLUSION

Research studies seem to have identified both ends of the continuum–women who do not indicate feeling victimized and oppressed, but rather quite fulfilled (Boss, McCubbin & Lester, 1979; Brett, 1982), and women who feel overwhelmed, unhappy and unable to make a satisfactory adjustment (Bloomfield & Holzman, 1988; McCollum, 1990; Seidenberg, 1974). The implications of these findings call for further research that explores women's experiences from a non-clinical as well as a clinical sample. Both need to focus on the systems in a woman's life: interpersonal, familial and societal gender role expectations. It is the interface between each woman and the systems that impinge upon her, including her family of origin, that is a missing and crucial perspective. Until we face our expectations and document our perceptions about women's roles, we will continue to expect women to accept personal responsibility for the amelioration of all family problems. This very different understanding about women and their lives will ultimately effect the personal and corporate adjustment of the relocated employee and family. It may be that the system, not the woman, has to understand and change.

REFERENCES

Anderson, C. and Stark, C. (1988) Psychosocial problems of job relocation: Preventive roles in industry. *Social Work*, 33(1), 38-41.

Bloomfield, K.M. & Holzman, R. (1988) Helping today's nomads: A collaborative program to assist mobile children and their families. *Social Work in Education*, 10(3), 183-197.

Boss, P.C., McCubbin, H.I., & Lester, G. (1979) The corporate executive wife's coping patterns in response to routine husband-father absence. *Family Process* (18), 79-86.

Boszormenyi-Nagy, I. & Spark, G.M (1984) *Invisible loyalties*. New York: Brunner/Mazel.

Bowen, G.L. (1988). Corporate supports for the family lives of employees: A conceptual model for program planning and evaluation. *Family Relations*, (37), 183-188.

Brett, J.M. (1982) Job transfer and well-being. *Journal of Applied Psychology*, 67(4) 450-463.

Caplan, P.J. & Hall-McCorquodale, I. (1985) Mother-blaming in major clinical journals. *American Journal of Orthopsychiatry*, 55, 345-353.

Collie, H.C. (1986) Corporate relocation: Changing with the times. *Personnel Administrator*, 101-103.

Compton, B. R. & Gallaway, B. (1989) *Social Work Processes*. Belmont, CA.: Wadsworth Publishing Company.

Gaylord, M. & Symons, E. (1986) "Relocation stress: a definition and a need for services," *Employee Assistance Quarterly*, Fall.

Goldner, V. (1985) Warning: Family therapy may be dangerous to your health. *Family Therapy Networker*, 9 (6), 19-23.

Gullotta, T.P. & Donohue, K.D. (1982). Preventing family distress during relocation: Initiatives for human resource managers. *Personnel Administrator*, 37-43.

Hochschild, A., with Anne Machung (1989) *The Second Shift*. New York: Viking Penguin, Inc.

McBride, A.B. (1990) Mental health effects of women's multiple roles. *American Psychologist*, 381-382.

McCollum, A. (1990) *The Trauma of Moving*. Newbury Park, CA: Sage Publications.

National Association of Social Workers. (1980) *Code of Ethics*. Silver Spring, MD: National Association of Social Workers.

President's Commission on Mental Health, Subpanel on the Mental Health of Women. (1978) *Report to the President* (Vol. 3, 1022-1116). Washington, DC: U.S. Government Printing Office.

Raabe, P.H. & Gessner, J.C. (1988) Employer family-supportive policies: Diverse variations on the theme. *Family Relations* (37), 196-202.

Rankin, E. (1984) The family life cycle, stress and caregiver burden in home-based care of the disabled elderly. Unpublished doctoral dissertation. University of Chicago, Chicago.

Rodgers, F.S. & Rodgers, C.S. (1993) The work and family agenda: Not for women only? *Family Resource Coalition*, 11 (2), 20.

Russo, N.F. (1990) Overview: Forging research priorities for women's mental health. *American Psychologist*, 368-373.

Satir, V. (1983) *Conjoint Family Therapy*. Third edition. Palo Alto, CA: Science & Behavior Books.

Seidenberg, R. (1973) *Corporate wives—corporate casualties?* Garden City, N.Y.: Anchor Press.

Stroh, L.K. & Brett, J.M. (1989) Corporate mobility: How do children fare in the shuffle? *Mobility*, February.

Weissman, M.M. & Paykel, E.S. (1972) Moving and depression in women. *Society*, 9, 24-28.

Violence Against Women
in the Workplace

Beverly Younger

SUMMARY. Although Employee Assistance Programs often incorporate workplace violence prevention and debriefings into their array of services, rarely has any attention been paid to the risks for workplace violence that female employees face. The prevalence in society of violence against women and the increase in violence at the work site could create a specific risk for women at work. An exploration of this risk was undertaken, using three apparent categories of workplace violence; random criminal (perpetrator unknown to victim), worker (perpetrator works at the same company as victim), and relationship or domestic (perpetrator is a family member or significant other of victim) violence. An analysis of the results of the 1991 Bureau of Labor Statistics Census of Fatal Occupational Injuries indicated that of all women who die on the job, 39% were the victims of assault, whereas only 18% of all male fatalities were murdered at work. Of the female homicides, over three-fourths were acts of random criminal violence. Worker violence and its potential for affecting female employees is discussed. Lastly, the effects of relationship violence entering the workplace are explored through the use of a case study. Information on assessment and prevention techniques useful to the EAP professional is included.

As Employee Assistance professionals, we are challenged not only by a number of familiar issues confronting employees but also

Address all correspondence to: Beverly Younger, Delphi Employee Services, P. O. Box 307, Riverside, IL 60546.

[Haworth co-indexing entry note]: "Violence Against Women in the Workplace." Younger, Beverly. Co-published simultaneously in *Employee Assistance Quarterly* (The Haworth Press, Inc.) Vol. 9, No. 3/4, 1994, pp. 113-133; and: *Empowering Women in the Workplace: Perspectives, Innovations, and Techniques for Helping Professionals* (ed: Marta Lundy, and Beverly Younger) Harrington Park Press an imprint of The Haworth Press, Inc., 1994, pp. 113-133. Multiple copies of this article/chapter may be purchased from The Haworth Document Delivery Center [1-800-3-HAWORTH; 9:00 a.m. - 5:00 p.m. (EST)].

by problems which go beyond the familiar, calling us to search for new information, resources, and interventions. As an EAP counselor, one day I was confronted by an employee's problem that I lacked an extensive resource file on–physical abuse in the workplace. The employee's problem was not merely an issue of relationship violence, sexual harassment or workplace violence, but rather an interplay of several concerns. After working with the woman who was physically and verbally abused *in the workplace*, I became aware that women have a particular vulnerability to abuse on the job. And, in spite of published evidence that "homicide is currently the leading manner of traumatic workplace death among women in the United States" (Bell, 1991, p. 729), little emphasis has been placed within the Employee Assistance field on the risks of workplace violence for women. The goal of this article is to call attention to the unique risks women face in the working world, with the hopes that other professionals will assist in the process of researching both occurrences and solutions.

VIOLENCE IN THE WORKPLACE

The increasing frequency of deadly outbursts in the workplace is evidenced by media reports of angry ex-employees who return to their former workplaces on killing sprees. Workplace murders occur twice as often now as they did 10 years ago (Stuart, 1992), with workplace homicides accounting for one third of all occupational deaths across the country (Richardson, 1993). Aggression at work is common as evidenced by a U.S. Postal survey which "found 300 cases of its employees attacking supervisors and about 100 cases of supervisors beating up employees in a three-year period" (Barnett-Queen & Bergmann, 1993).

Employee Assistance professionals are concerned about the influx of violence in the workplace, as confirmed by "workplace violence" being the most requested topic for the May, 1991 issue of *Employee Assistance* (Drotos, 1991). In response to increasing workplace trauma, Critical Incident Stress Debriefing techniques are now a standard function of many EAPs, especially when employees' lives are taken or threatened. Conflict assessment and resolution skills are becoming vital EAP tools. The more violent our world becomes, the more violent the workplace environment becomes and the harder we have to work to find solutions.

VIOLENCE AGAINST WOMEN

Girls do not usually learn to fight in the schoolyard the way boys do. Physical aggression has always been a stereotypical male response. Male on male violence is common, especially among gangs, where hand-to-hand combat is a form of competition for territory and status. Male on female violence implies, on the other hand, an unbalanced act of perpetrator on victim, in that females generally do not or can not fight back. It has been theorized that men, who commit 89% of all violent crimes in the U.S. (Levy, 1991), are socialized into believing that violence against women is an acceptable response, justified by a need to control women (Levy, 1991; Walker, 1989).

Although the total number of female victims of violence are less than the total number of male victims of violence, women are significantly less likely to be perpetrators, and appear to have a unique vulnerability to be attacked by men in specific ways (Koss, 1990). In the United States a women is raped every 6 minutes and every 18 seconds a women is beaten (Salholz, 1990). Males are "99% of persons charged with rape, and 86% of persons who committed offenses against family and children" (Koss, 1990, p. 374).

VIOLENCE AGAINST WOMEN AT WORK

The workplace is one area where women have confronted male dominance. Although in the recent past the workplace was populated primarily by men, by the year 2000 women are predicted to be the majority of all new workers entering the workplace (Clatterbaugh, 1991). The men's movement looks at the losses sustained by men stuck in the vanishing, traditional male role, that of "protector of family and the earth" (Kimbrell, 1991, p. 66). But few have asked about the anger that may accompany that loss. Susan Faludi's *Backlash* expounds on her perceptions of a forceful countermovement against the gains made by the women's movement, noting women's efforts to "improve their status, efforts that have been interpreted time and again by men`. . . as spelling their own masculine doom" (Faludi, 1991, p. 8). Whether men's frustration with the loss of control over the workplace is being translated into abusive behaviors towards women is an important, yet unanswered, question.

Reports on the incidence of sexual harassment, one form of abuse, are more common than reports of physical violence at work. A civil service study noted that during a two year period in a federal government setting, 42% of women employees said they were victims of sexual harassment (Spivack, 1988). Men and individuals in positions of authority are the most common perpetrators of female sexual harassment and young female workers are the most frequent victims (Ito, 1992). Verbal abuse is another form of workplace aggression which may be directed more easily at female employees, who are less likely than men to hold managerial or executive positions (U.S. Dept. of Labor, *Geographic Profile*, 1992) and, therefore, less likely to have the power to confront such abuse.

The occurrence of lethal violence against women in the workplace is just beginning to be documented. Data from the period of 1980 to 1985, from the National Traumatic Occupational Fatality (NTOF) survey conducted by The National Institute for Occupational Safety and Health (NIOSH), was used to compile statistics on the risks that women face from workplace homicide (Bell, 1991). This study indicated that 41% of all female fatalities were murder victims. A second review of the NTOF survey data from 1980 to 1988 stated the rate of female homicides within female occupational deaths to be 40% (Jenkins et al., 1992). Substantiating this figure, the 1991 Census of Fatal Occupational Injuries (CFOI) conducted by the Department of Labor Bureau of Labor Statistics (BLS) indicated that 39% of all female fatalities were the result of assault, whereas only 18% of all male fatalities were victims of assault (Dept. of Labor, 1992).

In order to better understand this trend, this article will summarize statistics on violent fatal acts against female employees as drawn from the 1991 Census of Fatal Occupational Injuries database, which the Bureau of Labor Statistics allowed the author to access directly. The findings of the 1991 CFOI are then compared to the previous 1991 study by Bell (1991) on data from the NIOSH survey. Initial exploration into workplace violence against women indicted that three categories of violence against women in the workplace exist: (1) random criminal violence (by a perpetrator unknown to the victim); (2) worker violence (by a perpetrator who works at the same company as the victim); and (3) relationship or domestic violence (by a perpetrator who is a family member or significant other of the victim). Each category of violence will be discussed and explored separately.

RANDOM CRIMINAL VIOLENCE IN THE WORKPLACE

For the purposes of this study, random criminal violence in the workplace is defined as an act of physical violence by an assailant unknown to the victim, such that the relationship between the perpetrator and victim is not a factor in the motive for violence. This type of violence could occur during a robbery or as the result of an explosive attack by a person in a psychotic or drug-induced state of rage. A review of the BLS study of the 1991 Census of Fatal Occupational Injuries revealed that over three-fourths of all female workplace homicides were perpetrated by an assailant unknown to the victim. The CFOI database was used to provide a clearer picture of this type of violence against women.

Method

A variety of variables from the CFOI database were examined. The CFOI database consists of fatality records for 32 participating states and New York City and does not represent the entire nation. The database was compiled from a variety of state and federal sources, including death certificates, state workers' compensation forms, State coroner reports, OSHA, and media and autopsy reports (the 1991 NIOSH survey included only death certificates). The database consists of 3,822 fatal occupational injuries. The injury was termed occupational if it occurred on the employer's premises, or off the employer's premises on a site where the person was there to work or was performing a work-related event. The CFOI data included reports of self-employed, government and small business workers.

This study looks specifically at one portion of the CFOI survey population—female employees killed by attack on the job. Frequencies of the coded CFOI variables were compiled to collect descriptive data on the reported fatalities. For the purpose of this study, only the variables of gender, age, race, industry, occupation, nature of injury, source and secondary source of injury, event, and a narrative description of the event were utilized. In addition to percentages compiled specifically for this study, percentages from unpublished tables prepared by the Bureau of Labor Statistics of the CFOI data were also utilized (herein noted as (BLS)).

Results

Gender

Of the 3,822 occupational fatalities reported, 3512 or 92% were male, and 310 or 8% were females. Seven hundred fifty or 19% of the 3,822 deaths were caused by some form of assault. Within the category of assault, 84 fatalities were self-inflicted assaults or suicides (five of these were women). By gender, 628 or 84% (BLS) of the assault fatalities were male, and 122 or 16% (BLS) were female. The percentage of male victims was disproportionately high, especially when compared with the national employment rates for 1991 which show 54% of the workforce being male and 45% female (U.S. Dept. Of Labor, *Geographic Profile*, 1992). Yet if results are considered within gender groups, 39% of all women who died of workplace injuries were the victim of assault, while only 18% of all men who died of workplace injuries were victims of assault (see Table I).

Industry and Gender

All Occupational Fatalities: Male occupational deaths were most likely to occur in the construction, transportation and manufacturing industries, with frequencies of 17%, 16% and 14% (BLS) of all

TABLE I
Comparison by Sex

Women	Percentages	Men
45%	Of employed nationally	54%
8%	Of all occupational fatalities	92%
16%	Of all assault fatalities	83%
39%	Of within gender assaults/ all gender fatalities	18%

male deaths. Female deaths were most likely to occur in the service (30%) and retail (26%) (BLS) industries.

Assault Fatalities Only: Of all male assault fatalities, 62% occurred within the retail or service industries, with retail accounting for 44%, and service for 18% of all male assault fatalities. In comparison, 81% of all female assaults occurred within the retail trade (52%) or service industry (29%). Using within gender percentages, women are shown more likely to be killed by assault than other forms of injury, within the retail and service industries.

Industry Employment Trends for Women: Based on demographic data for 1991 (Ibid.), it was found that 61% of all employed females work in technical, sales, and administrative support or service occupations, whereas only 32% of all employed men work in these occupations.

Race, Age, Occupation, Location,
Event, Source and Time

Looking specifically at the descriptive data on female assault victims supplied by the CFOI database, we can construct the following description of the typical female victim, with percentages based on all female assault victims:

A white female (79%), in her early 30s (mean age approx. 31), working as a sales person (31% worked in some category of sales occupations), in a convenient store (46% tending a retail establishment, 79% in a public building), was shot (59%) by an unknown assailant (88% unspecified person not known to victim), about 11 p.m. (12% from 10:00 to 11:00 p.m.).

As noted, the majority of women killed were white, but 16% were African American, and 8% were Asian American (Hispanic people were not recorded separately). The data for age was recorded in 10 year increments, and only a mean age was computed for this study. Occupation categories utilized 60 different occupational codes, but a couple of occupational clusters held the majority of cases. In addition to the large number of women killed in sales occupations, 16% of the victims were some type of manager or administrator, or 27% if sales supervisors are included.

The event of death included being "shot" (59%), "stabbed" (16%), "unspecified" (16%) and "hitting, kicked or beat" (4%), in addition to others. A large majority of assaults happened in a public building, with the next common setting, industrial settings, accounting for only 5%. Although the highest percentage of women killed during any hour was 12% from 10:00 to 11:00 p.m., overall the percentages for "hour of day" did not show any substantial differences. Listed as a secondary source, the type of assailant was most often unspecified. But 6%, or 7, of the female assault victims were killed by someone related to them, including husbands. Only 2%, or 3 women, were killed by co-workers. As an additional 4% were suicides, 88% were either acts of random criminal violence or lacked data on the perpetrator.

Comparison to the NIOSH NTOF Data

The National Traumatic Occupational Fatality survey results on female homicides from 1980-1985, as compiled by Bell (1991), was drawn from a broader base (all states and 5 years) than the CFOI data. Yet striking similarities exist between the two surveys. The CFOI data indicates that 39% of all female fatalities were victims of homicide, compared to the NTOF survey's 41%. Comparing industry of employment rates among the murdered women, the CFOI rate for the retail industry was 52% of all female fatalities, with the NTOF rate at 43%. The results on race in the NTOF survey indicted that "black women were 1.8 times more likely to be killed than Whites," with the rate derived by comparison with the larger employed population (Bell, 1991, p. 730). The CFOI results show only 16% of homicide victims were African American, whereas white murder victims accounted for 79%, but lacking survey population demographic information, a direct comparison between the studies is not possible. The most frequent age range for the NTOF homicide victims was 25-34 years of age (although proportionately women over 65 years of age had the highest homicide rate at 11.3 per million), while the CFOI mode was 31 years of age. Lastly the NTOF data supported that the cause of death is most likely "gunshot" (64%), as also was found in the CFOI results (59%).

Results Summary

The results of the findings from the CFOI database indicate that men are at a greater overall risk of death at work, mostly from non-violent injury. But, women, when considered separately from men, are more likely to die from assault than injury, especially when working in a job which serves the public, particularly in a store. The cause of assault is most likely to be an act of violence by an unknown perpetrator, using a gun or sometimes a knife. Unfortunately, the narrative descriptions of fatalities fail to detail motives or why females are targeted.

Although the CFOI data is only accumulated from 32 states plus New York City, the reliability and generalizability of the results are, for the most part, heightened by the NTOF data.

Discussion

Initially this author assumed that women attacked at work would be more at risk from estranged husbands or angry co-workers. But the evidence of this survey clearly indicates that women are more likely to be assaulted by a stranger, especially those women working in an position that involves serving the public, such as fast food server or store cashier. These jobs, which often are easily accessed, offer flexible hours and require minimal training, allow women to raise children, work their way through school, or break out of a cycle of poverty. So it is shocking to think that women carry the horrible risk of being murdered while working at the very job they need to survive.

Why is the risk of being murdered at work proportionally higher for women? Lacking data and therefore answers to these questions, we can only speculate. Perhaps just as women may be victimized by partners who are aware that many women do not or can not fight back, working women may be thought of by male criminals as easy victims.

It is the responsibility of the employer to protect people from assault at work. If male criminals consider female employees in retail and service positions easier targets than their male counterparts, then extra precautions may be necessary to protect women in these jobs. Although this is not an area of EAP expertise, we may be the only workplace professional listening to the fears that women have about working in unsafe settings or witnessing the pain suffered by family and co-workers following workplace murders. Employee Assistance professionals can advocate to increase their safety on the job, or implement women's groups which could challenge employers to increase security measures. Self-defense training for women may give them an edge on self-protection. EAPs who are aware of the risks for women of random criminal violence can be part of the solution.

WORKER VIOLENCE

One may easily assume that any violence occurring at work is related to something that happened at work (i.e., a conflict between a supervisor and a subordinate or an argument between two co-workers). Yet the CFOI 1991 data indicated that only 2% of the female assault fatalities were caused by a co-worker. With sparse data, it may be too soon to assume that it is not a significant workplace issue. As the Clinical Director of National Trauma Services, a company providing post-trauma workplace services, Dr. Thomas Harpley, Ph.D., is often called upon to respond to worker violence, (subordinate against supervisor, supervisor against subordinate, or co-worker against co-worker) and he believes that these type of incidents are increasing (Harpley, 1993). He also noted that women may increasingly be targets, primarily women in management positions. As women infiltrate the management strata, angry employees may vent their rage against them.

Out of the horror of the murders striking U.S. Postal Service work sites some good may arise if research funding and time are allocated to understand why employees resort to fatal violence to vent their work-related anger. Since 1985, 26 U.S. Postal employees have died as the result of revenge killings at work, most of the victims being supervisors (Stuart, 1992). To date, knowledge about the nature of worker violence at U.S. Postal Service locations has not been sufficiently gathered or analyzed. We do not know whether anger at work conditions or at supervisors is the cause or if certain workforces contain an abnormally large number of people with severe disorders triggering violent reactions. Further conclusions await research yet to be completed.

Some characteristics of the perpetrators of worker violence are known. Employees who may be at risk of attacking co-workers or supervisors are likely to threaten verbally or make reference to media reports of workplace violence, and are usually knowledgeable of weapons (Harpley, 1992). Differences between non-lethal and lethal violence indicators also exist. Lethal perpetrators are not likely to have a history of violent behaviors and are not likely to have a history of substance abuse, whereas non-lethal perpetrators have the opposite traits (ibid.).

Of the three types of violence discussed, worker violence may be the easiest to predict and prevent. The nature of random criminal violence clearly indicates that it is unpredictable. Although more is known about relationship violence, interventions are limited and the system may be resistant to change. In contrast, worker violence easily catches the attention of those employers who feel it is their responsibility to prevent supervisors or co-workers from being murdered by another employee.

Currently, no data exists to predict when workers may turn against female employees, in either lethal or non-lethal acts. Psychological issues regarding the unresolved anger of some men at women "taking over" their place of dominance and power at work must be explored. Workplace interventions to offset negative gender stereotyping and diffuse work-related anger at female employees may be necessary. Several workplace violence prevention services are cropping up across the country, focusing on prediction and prevention (one internal company model will be discussed later). The inclusion of a focus on the risks faced by female employees would strengthen such programs.

RELATIONSHIP VIOLENCE IN THE WORKPLACE

The results of the 1991 Census of Fatal Occupational Injuries show that only 6% of female assault deaths were caused by the violent act of a family member. However, this statistic describes *lethal* relationship violence in the workplace; EAPs must also be concerned about *non-lethal* relationship violence on the job. As indicated earlier, non-lethal workplace perpetrators tend to have a history of violent behaviors (Harpley, 1993). An abusive husband with a history of physical violence at home may attack his wife at home, on her way to work, or actually in the workplace.

When considering the frequency of relationship violence in the workplace, one must remember that the frequency of violence in the home is in dispute and under-reporting of domestic violence is a given, according to domestic violence researchers (Landes, Siegel & Foster, 1993). Nonetheless, one estimate of family violence states that "on average one wife or child in twenty-one has a chance of being physically abused from three to four times per year" (Gelles & Straus, 1988). Further, most researchers agree that females are the most frequent victims of family violence, with one study indicating wives were the victims in 75% of all family assaults (Pagelow, 1984). The most commonly stated percentage of married women who have been physically abused in a relationship is about 30% of all married women (Koss, 1990).

The frequency of domestic violence spilling out of the house and into the workplace is not well known and, like domestic violence itself, is probably greatly under-reported. Estimates of the costs of lost production time, absenteeism, turnover and medical benefits from employees victimized by domestic violence have been made and are fixed at $3-$5 billion annually (Amberson, 1991). Further, one can extrapolate from the existing data by assuming that violence is likely to occur between married or "involved" co-workers with the same frequency that it occurs between married couples in the broader population. Thus, if a company has 10,000 employees and 500 of the female employees are involved in significant relationships with a co-worker, then 30% or 150 of the females in those relationships may be subject to physical abuse. As employers become more aware of the frequency and costs of relationship violence, Employee Assistance professionals, many of whom may routinely screen clients for domestic violence risk, may be called upon to provide answers.

In order to introduce some of the characteristics of relationship violence at work, the following case study, a composite of three actual EAP cases, will be reviewed. The cases have been altered to preserve confidentiality but still retain the essence of relationship violence problems facing women at work.

Case Study

AB is a 38 yr old, divorced, African American female, mother of 2 children. She works in an industrial setting as a semi-skilled laborer. AB's ex-husband, was a cocaine addict and was both verbally and physically abusive to AB. AB's family of origin consisted of two very nurturing, highly religious parents, but her father died of diabetes when AB was 9. AB's mother is a strong-willed woman who has high expectations that AB be a good mother and wife. AB went through feelings of depression when her ex-husband left, feeling as if she had failed to create a good marriage and home life.

AB met CD, a 42 yr old, divorced African American male, who is a supervisor in another department. He also came from a religious family and was a father of three children. CD is known in his department for being "tough" with employees, but this is usually attributed to the difficulties a black supervisor faces in a largely white male management team. AB admired his leadership abilities and quickly fell in love with him. She became pregnant the first year of their relationship, and CD moved in to help support the parenting of the child.

Living together, AB became aware of CD's need to dominate the household, making all the decisions and criticizing AB's method of housekeeping and child-rearing. The criticism turned to physical violence during a time when CD was under a great deal of stress at work. AB attempted to control the violence at home by changing her behaviors, trying to placate CD. When this didn't work, and the violence increased, AB eventually asked CD to leave.

Due to the need to communicate with CD about parenting concerns (medical and child support issues), AB still had contact with CD, usually at work. CD was extremely angry at AB for ending the relationship and used these contacts to verbally and emotionally abuse AB at work. Usually CD was careful not to let others overhear their arguments, closing his office door. When she argued back or demanded her child support payments, CD also threatened to "make it difficult" for AB at work.

One day, in a fit of rage, CD struck AB. Having forgotten to close his office door, this was witnessed both by a fellow supervisor and a co-worker. CD spoke with the supervisor, telling him that AB was harassing him and that he had "just lost control." He also pulled the co-worker aside, who was someone that he supervised himself, and told him to keep to his own business, that AB had a "mental problem." AB later checked with these people to see if either would serve as a witness of the abuse, but both said that they didn't see anything. When AB confronted each about this, both related what CD had said. AB felt it was useless to try and convince either witness to come forward, or to confront CD's superiors.

When AB came to the Employee Assistance office, she was distraught, depressed, in financial difficulties, and experiencing a sense of helplessness to change her situation. She was also afraid of being physically attacked at home (CD had come to the home against her wishes in the past), of being verbally or physically attacked at work and of repercussions by CD at work.

Discussion

The case study presents a scenario in which such abuse actually entered the workplace. AB's treatment plan should include all the referrals given to any victim of domestic violence–a legal advocate, a support group for abused women, a therapist, a financial counselor, and government agencies assisting with child support and orders of protection. But these referrals would not be enough to help AB. A complicated workplace intervention should include documenting the incident and confronting, disciplining and referring CD to the EAP. Employee Assistance professionals sensitive to workplace relationship violence need to do the following: (1) assess and assist the woman to meet her goals to be free from abuse in or out of the workplace, (2) advocate for workplace interventions to stop the perpetrator, (3) advocate for changes in company policies and procedures to prevent such abuse.

This author has experienced a sense of frustration in trying to assist women in breaking the "cycle of violence" that entangles them. Although AB may have suffered from the loss of her father, the case study indicates that AB did not lack a strong family upbringing. Functioning well at work and at home, she was not a particularly damaged individual. Yet she entered and, for a period of time, stayed in an abusive relationship, continuing to be victimized at work in spite of ending the relationship.

Feminist psychological theory has helped us to reframe our understanding of the abused woman. The cycle of violence theory supported by Lenore Walker describes the phases of tension building, explosion and loving contrition that trap the victim into a psychological state of learned helplessness (Walker, 1989). Often the very strengths that women are encouraged by society to have—empathy, selflessness, nurturance—turn against them as they struggle to accept that the perpetrator victimizing them should no longer be taken care of and loved. Combining the instinct to be caretakers with a feeling of helplessness to stop or get away from the violence, women often can not see any way out. As clinicians assessing potential female domestic violence victims, we need to understand the nature of the trap that keeps them stuck before we can offer real and useful assistance.

Knowledge of the overt symptoms of domestic violence is required in order to screen potential victims. Koss (1990) describes the postvictimization distress response which may develop into symptoms of "fear/avoidance, affective constriction, disturbances of self-concept/self-efficacy, and sexual dysfunction" (p. 375). Further, Koss noted that victims of violence were significantly more likely to be diagnosed with "major depression, alcohol abuse/dependence, drug abuse/dependence, generalized anxiety, obsessive-compulsive disorder and posttraumatic stress disorder" as well as other chronic disorders (ibid., p. 376). The tendency to isolate is also a common denominator among abused women. Isolation may come in the form of physical isolation (e.g., avoiding other family and friends) or emotional isolation (e.g., feeling separate and different from the world) (Gary, 1991). Victims may also see themselves as "weak, needy, frightened and out of control" and may minimize or alter the meaning of the violent episodes (Koss, 1990). Effective screening should include asking all females who present any of the above symptoms or disorders about potential violence in the home or at work.

Assessing the risk for relationship violence in the workplace includes evaluating the risks inherent in the physical structure and the milieu of the work site. Asking the victim about the patterns of violence outside the job may help the EAP professional decide if the victim is also vulnerable at work. The EAP professional should ask the woman if she feels safe from the possibility of attack at work and, if not, how that attack may occur. If the perpetrator is a co-worker, assess how the couple's work interactions may trigger abuse at work. Does the environment allow for such incidents? Are secluded places available in which abuse could occur or does the victim work in isolation? Is the parking lot or driveway to the workplace open to stalkers? Does a power differential exist between the victim and perpetrator such that the perpetrator can threaten the victim's job security if she talks about the abuse? Does the workplace culture embody negative gender stereotypes about women or place a value on male dominance? As shown in the case study, CD had the privacy of his own office, the control over other co-workers necessary to deny the incident, and the support of a fellow male supervisor.

Screenings of potential workplace perpetrators should utilize the current knowledge base on domestic violence. Common character traits of perpetrators include "a history of family violence, abuse or neglect; chronic family chaos or disorganization; lack of acceptance of, or interest in, family members; (and) poor intra-family communication skills" (Miller & Veltkamp, 1991, p. 36).

A history of substance abuse may also be an indicator of family violence, although it is not a known cause. In a study by Maiden and Tolman (Edleson & Tolman, 1992), 80% of the EAP cases in which substance abuse was diagnosed were likely to have some incidence of family violence. Maiden (1993) found in a study of the interaction between alcoholism and domestic violence that 47% of the men with alcoholism who were interviewed "reported moderate to severe physical violence before alcoholism treatment" (p. 95-96). Maiden also found that moderate physical violence continued in 20% of recovering alcoholics' relationships, with verbal aggression continuing in 75% of those surveyed (p. 97).

In addition to assessing the potential victim and/or perpetrator, workplace interventions are the second concern that EAPs have when confronted with the risk of relationship violence at work. However, workplace violence prevention programs may not be sufficient to assist women victims of relationship violence at work. Policies and procedures may need to be changed to enable the company to act on relationship violence issues. Just as the police officer leaves the "domestic squabblers" to fend for themselves, company management may consider relationship workplace violence the private concern of the employees involved and not the concern of the employer. The employer needs to accept, as does the criminal justice system, that women are at risk from men when the system allows for violence motivated by male needs for dominance.

In summation, relationship violence in the workplace may cause women to become entrenched in cycles of physical abuse and the workplace itself may protect the perpetrator from consequences. Employee Assistance professionals who have special knowledge of the symptoms of abused women or male perpetrators will increase their ability to identify such risks. Lastly, efforts to advocate for system changes which protect female employees from physical abuse by male partners are sorely needed.

WORKPLACE SOLUTIONS: VIOLENCE PREVENTION PROGRAMS

Employee Assistance professionals alone cannot solve the problems of workplace violence or secure safe job sites for female employees. To work effectively, we need the cooperation of the many arms of the employer.

In response to the potential for violence in the workplace, Abbott Laboratories, a large health care company in the Chicago area, recently instituted a comprehensive violence prevention program (Dainas, 1993). The first step was the implementation of a Taskforce on Workplace Violence, the goal of which was to devise the policies and procedures needed to predict and act upon workplace violence risks. With the involvement of progressive Human Resource and Employee Assistance departments, a unique team-based model was designed. A team consisting of representatives from the EAP, Security, Legal, Public Affairs, Human Resources and Employee Health departments was assembled at the corporate facility. Risk assessments of potentially explosive employees are performed by the Workplace Violence Prevention team. Supervisors, trained in identifying which employees may be violent, report any volatile behaviors that could lead to workplace violence. Upon receiving notice of a risk situation, the team assembles immediately, having designated back-up members in the event of absences. The team's task is to assess the potential risk and, if a risk is present, to formulate a plan of action to prevent violence from occurring.

The role of Abbott's EAP in the team is vital. An employee identified by the Workplace Violence Prevention team as a real risk may be referred to Employee Assistance for a thorough assessment, including a screening for homicidal or suicidal tendencies. If necessary, hospitalization of the employee may be facilitated. With the use of a four page risk assessment/management form, the EAP is able to document potential risk in concrete terms. The presence of Employee Assistance staff members on the team ensures that their professional skills are utilized to the fullest extent in the development of appropriate responses to troubled employees. On occasion, the employee presenting the risk may already be an EAP client. Having learned of the situation during team meetings, the EAP may act quickly and confidentially to intervene with the employee.

An important element in the success of Abbott's Workplace Violence Prevention program is the training of supervisors and other relevant employees in the identification of potentially risky situations. The information presented at the trainings includes a profile of the symptoms of violence perpetrators and a checklist to help effectively identify risk. Once trained, supervisors can serve as part of a prevention network, funneling referrals to the Workplace Violence Prevention team for further action. Experience shows that the concept works well. The goal of the EAP is to participate in expanding the Workplace Violence Prevention program throughout various company sites, setting up prevention teams at all locations.

Workplace Violence Prevention programs, like the one at Abbott Laboratories, can help protect female and male employees from workplace violence. But if these programs do not highlight the unique risks faced by women and include special policies and procedures which specifically assist female employees, then women will still be vulnerable. Thus, companies should build on Abbott's Workplace Violence Prevention model by including safety and security measures for females who work in public or isolated settings, who are at risk of any kind of relationship violence, or who are the target of the anger of male employees. Offering special support groups or self-protection trainings for females at risk is an option for expanding workplace violence prevention efforts. Further, training programs need to include consciousness-raising educational efforts, the identification of risks to women, special safety measures, and methods for assessing different types of risk. When prevention programs are able to focus on dangers to female employees, women may be safer from assault at work.

CONCLUSION

Studying the topic of violence against women in the workplace has been both enlightening and frustrating. Pursuing this inquiry has seemed like taking a walk on a moonless night; little data exists to clearly describe or understand the issues. Undoubtedly women are sexually harassed, discriminated against, verbally abused, physically assaulted and murdered in the workplace. However, we still lack an adequate description of the scope or frequencies of workplace abuse.

The role of the Employee Assistance professional in preventing workplace violence against women is, as are all EAP roles, an extremely demanding one. In addition to motivating the company to utilize preventative measures to ensure the safety of women, the EAP also needs to actively identify risks of all types of violence and intervene accordingly. The company may be resistant to change, choose to ignore the risks, or be effectively involved. Employee Assistance Programs often have their hands tied until a tragedy does hit, at which time the employer may be more receptive to change. Efforts to educate the employer is one way that an Employee Assistance professional can help reduce the risks for women of being victimized on the job.

Should a private employer be more concerned than society at large about the risks for violence against women or about brutality in general? Society continues to struggle to even acknowledge the victimization of women by domestic violence, rape, or murder. As society becomes more hostile and more accustomed to violence, will we still be able to know that physical aggression is wrong? Will males, socialized to use violence, be able to see that dominating women with physical abuse is horrendously wrong? Or will women have to embrace violence as a means of protection? Employers, or even society itself, may not yet be motivated to address such questions. But as violence escalates, the costs to human beings, especially women, escalate. Employee Assistance professionals exist in order to help maintain the value of the employee for the employer. What could be more important to this duty than the maintenance of life itself?

REFERENCES

Amberson, J. (1991). Family violence and the workplace. *EAPA Exchange, 21(6)*, 28-29.

Barnett-Queen, T., & Bergmann, L. (1993). Coping after crisis. *Employee Assistance, 5(8)*, 6-11, 34.

Bell, C. (1991). Female Homicides in United States Workplace, 1908-1985. *American Journal of Public Health, 81(6)*, 729-732.

Clatterbaugh, K. (1991). Changing men, as reprinted in *Utne Reader (May)*, 82-83.

Dainas, C. (1993). Personal communication, Abbott Laboratories Employee Assistance Program, August 4.

Drotos, C. (1991). Violence in the workplace. *Employee Assistance, 3(10)*, 6.

Edelson, J., & Tolman, R. (1992). *Intervention for men who batter: An ecological approach.* Newbury Park, CA: Sage Publications.

Engel, F. (1991). Assault and violence in the workplace. *Employee Assistance, 3(10)*, 34-37.

Engelken, C. (1987). Employee assistance: Fighting the costs of spouse abuse. *Personnel Journal, 66(3)*, 31-34.

Faludi, S. (1991, September). Blame it on feminism. *Mother Jones*, 24-29.

Gary, L. (1991). Feminist practice and family violence. In Bricker-Jenkins, M. Hooyman, N. & Gottlieb, N. (1991). *Feminist social work practice in clinical settings.* Newbuy Park CA: Sage.

Gelles, R. & Straus, M. (1988). *Intimate violence.* New York: Simon & Schuster.

Harpley, T. (1993). Personal correspondence, National Trauma Services, July 5.

Ito, R. (1992). Beyond hostility. *Employee Assistance, 5(5),* 12-16.

Jenkins, E., Layne, L. & Kisner, S. (1992). Homicide in the workplace: the U.S. experience, 1980-1988. *AAOHN Journal, 40 (5),* 215-216.

Kimbrell, A. (1981, May). The new politics of masculinity. *Utne Reader,* 66-783.

Koss, M. (1990). The women's mental health research agenda: Violence against women. *American Psychologist, 45(3),* 374-380.

Landes, A., Siegel, M. & Foster, C. (Eds.) (1993). *Domestic Violence: No longer behind the curtain.* Wiley, Texas: Information Plus.

Levy, D. (1991). Why Johnny might grow up to be sexist. *Time,* September 16, 16-19.

Maiden, P. (1993). The relationship of alcoholism recovery and the reduction of domestic violence among employee assistance program clients. Ph.D. Dissertation, University of Maryland.

Miller, T. & Veltkamp, L. (1991). Recognizing spouse abuse. *Employee Assistance, 12(1),* 36-39.

Oloroso, A. (1993, June 21-28). Explosive issue: Guns in the workplace. *Crains Chicago Business,* pp. 1, 44-45.

Pagelow, M. (1984). *Family Violence.* New York: Praeger.

Richardson, S. (1993). Workplace homicides in Texas, 1990-1991. In U.S. Depart. of Labor, Bureau of Labor Statistics, (1993) *Fatal workplace injuries in 1991: A collection of data and analyses, Report 845,* Washington, DC: U.S. Government Printing Office, 39-44.

Salholz, E. (1990). Women under assault. *Newsweek,* July 16, 23-24.

Spivack, M. (1988). Uncle Sam's cabin. *Ms.,* November, 83.

Stuart, P. (1982). Murder at work. *Personnel Journal, 71(2),* 27.

Toscano, G. & Windau, J. (1993). Fatal work injuries: Census for thirty-one states. In U.S. Dept. of Labor, Bureau of Labor Statistics, (1993). *Fatal workplace injuries in 1991: A collection of data and analysis, Report 845.* Washington, D.C.: U.S. Government Printing Office, 1-6.

U.S. Department of Labor, Bureau of Labor Statistics, (1991). Census of fatal occupational injuries, 32 participating states and New York City, 1991.

U.S. Department of Labor, Bureau of Labor Statistics, (1991). 1991 CFOI Database User Reference, Version 2 and unpublished tables.

U.S. Department of Labor, Bureau of Labor Statistics, (1992). *Geographic profile of employment and Unemployment, 1991, Bulletin 2410.* Washington, D.C.: U.S. Government Printing Office.

Walker, L. (1989). Psychology and violence against women. *American Psychologist, 44(4),* 695-702.

Women and HIV:
An EAP Professional's Concerns
with Prevention,
Identification and Assistance

Sally Mason

SUMMARY. Women constitute one of the fastest growing groups of people infected with HIV. Women have always been *affected* by HIV as informal or formal caregivers. Despite this, HIV services and education have been directed almost exclusively towards men. Given that women comprise half of the workforce, the change in the face of the epidemic requires a reexamination of the EAP professional's approach to AIDS education and services. This article delineates HIV-related issues specific to women and their impact on the functions of the EAP. Suggestions are made for targeting AIDS workplace education and prevention to women. The implications of women's issues on early identification, counseling, and referral by EAP professionals are also explored. Consideration is given to the cultural and socioeconomic diversity of women affected by HIV.

Since the beginning of the epidemic, women have been affected by HIV. Though not infected in large numbers, women felt the impact of AIDS through their relationships with men, having cared

---

Sally Mason is affiliated with Jane Addams College of Social Work, University of Illinois at Chicago.

[Haworth co-indexing entry note]: "Women and HIV: An EAP Professional's Concerns with Prevention, Identification and Assistance." Mason, Sally. Co-published simultaneously in *Employee Assistance Quarterly* (The Haworth Press, Inc.) Vol. 9, No. 3/4, 1994, pp. 135-147; and: *Empowering Women in the Workplace: Perspectives, Innovations, and Techniques for Helping Professionals* (ed: Marta Lundy, and Beverly Younger) Harrington Park Press an imprint of The Haworth Press, Inc., 1994, pp. 135-147. Multiple copies of this article/chapter may be purchased from The Haworth Document Delivery Center [1-800-3-HAWORTH; 9:00 a.m. - 5:00 p.m. (EST)].

135

for ailing sons, brothers, friends and partners. As nurses and social workers, women have served people with HIV in hospitals, nursing homes, hospices, and social service agencies. Some women have done double duty–employed as professional caregivers of people with HIV and then coming home to support an ill family member or friend (Kaspar, 1989).

In the last few years, feminists and AIDS activists have drawn the public's attention to the more direct impact of the epidemic on women. The number of women with AIDS in the U.S. is still relatively small, representing a little more than 11% of the diagnosed cases, but women have been identified as one of the fastest growing categories of people with AIDS (Ellerbrock et al., 1991). With the revision of the Centers for Disease Control definition of AIDS in January 1993, public health officials anticipate that the numbers of women diagnosed with AIDS will double in 1993 (G. Mueller, personal communication, March, 1993).

In a phenomenon that started during World War II, women have also entered the workforce in ever increasing numbers. The "revolution" in women's employment patterns in the U.S. has most notably involved married women and women with children (Brewer, 1991, p. 394; Chafe, 1991). For example, since 1960, the percentage of married women with children under 6 years old employed outside the home has increased 40% (U.S. Bureau of Census, 1992). The coincident rise in the numbers of employed women and the numbers of women affected by HIV challenges EAP professionals to plan HIV services relevant to women and families.

ISSUES SPECIFIC TO WOMEN

Slightly over half of women with AIDS have been infected through injected drug use; heterosexual transmission accounts for about a third of the cases in women. However, transmission from injected drug use has been steadily decreasing over the years while heterosexual transmission increased dramatically (11% to 34%) from 1984 to 1990 (Smeltzer & Whipple, 1991). The majority of diagnosed women (85%) are of reproductive age, African-American or Hispanic (72%) and residents of large metropolitan areas

(Ellerbrock et al., 1991). Indeed, the overrepresentation of African-Americans and Hispanics among AIDS cases is even more pronounced for women than it is for men.

People affected by HIV, male or female, face common difficulties. However, women as a group have specific concerns based on the history of the epidemic and women's roles and status in our society.

Lack of Identification as Infected or at Risk for HIV Infection

The first woman was diagnosed with AIDS in 1981, the same year that marks the beginning of the epidemic in the U.S. Yet, public perception only recently has adjusted to include women as people at risk for HIV. The early emphasis on risk groups, rather than risk behaviors, affirmed what many wanted to believe: women and even heterosexual men could not get HIV unless sharing unclean needles. Statistically, this became a self-fulfilling prophecy as the Centers for Disease Control definition of AIDS, based on men's anatomy, did not include gynecologic infections common to women with AIDS. When women were diagnosed, it was much later in the illness when treatment was less effective. Even when women revealed their risk for HIV, physicians repeatedly discounted the possibility of infection as the cause of their symptoms. Women were statistically invisible, therefore doctors did not suspect and, subsequently, test for HIV infection (Anastos & Marte, 1989).

Where HIV-infected women have been visible is in research on transmission of HIV to children and to men through prostitution (Anastos & Marte, 1989; Smeltzer & Whipple, 1991). Women have been viewed as a public health threat to men and children rather than people having their own needs and as "victims of transmission from the men in their lives" (Anastos & Marte, 1989, p. 10). As a result of their invisibility in the epidemic, women have been excluded from clinical trials for experimental medication and neglected in prevention or early intervention efforts. Only recently have researchers focused on the psychosocial needs of women affected by HIV.

Prevention and Education

Statistically, women are at greater risk than men of encountering an HIV-infected heterosexual partner (Shayne & Kaplan, 1991). Plus, the relative efficiency of male to female transmission may be greater than from female to male (Shayne & Kaplan, 1991; Smeltzer & Whipple, 1991). However, for reasons mentioned above, education has not been geared to women. When education is available, it represents only the first step in preventing HIV infection.

Several studies indicate that women know about safe sex and condoms but this knowledge is not directly associated with use (Smeltzer & Whipple, 1991). Women have to feel empowered within their personal relationships to request that a partner use condoms (Anastos & Marte, 1991). The reality is that many women are not equal partners in relationships and few experience equality with men in society at large. Suggesting use of a condom to a male partner implies a lack of trust in him or that the woman has been "promiscuous." Women fear that asking a man to use a condom will precipitate violence or drive him away (Anastos & Marte, 1989; Smeltzer & Whipple, 1991; Springer, 1992). Without a man, many women feel inadequate and unprotected. For low-income women, the financial support of a man may be crucial to maintaining her family.

HIV prevention goes beyond teaching women how to use a condom. Women need skills development and peer support to negotiate safe sex with their partners (Shayne & Kaplan, 1989, p. 16). Men must be included in the responsibility of safe sex. More research needs to be done on attitudes and practices towards condom use, especially with different cultural groups. Another option is to make methods available that women can use and do not require the cooperation of a male partner (Stein, 1990).

Lack of Support

Women with HIV are just as likely as men to be abandoned by family and friends. In a 1990 needs assessment of HIV-infected women in Chicago, more than half of the women had little or no support from family or friends: 32% of the total had only one friend or relative to help them cope with their illness or that of their children; 22% had no one available to help them cope (Carr, 1990). Asking someone for help means also disclosing infection with HIV and, perhaps, even that a child is infected. The potential target of fear, anger, and blame, a mother may keep her HIV status a secret from family and friends in order to protect her family thus depriving herself of support from other infected women and from family and friends (Smeltzer & Whipple, 1991).

Women with HIV are less likely than men to have peers to turn to for advice or information (Weitz, 1989). Still a relatively small group and without the forms of community available to gay men, women with HIV have no reason to know one another. Access to groups of other women with HIV infection or AIDS may be difficult because women are not tested early or diagnosed properly. Without diagnosis, women are prevented from receiving benefits and services associated with a diagnosis of AIDS (Anastos & Marte, 1989; Pfeiffer, 1991; Shayne & Kaplan, 1991). When diagnosed, services geared to gay men do not fit women's needs or women are reluctant to accept help from them. As women appear to be unaffected by the epidemic, relevant services have been slow to develop.

Decisions About Childbearing

Estimates of rates of transmission of HIV from mother to fetus range from 25-50% (ACT UP/NY Women, 1990). A study in New York examined the factors that influence the decisions of pregnant HIV positive women to continue or terminate a pregnancy (Selwyn et al., 1989). Although risk of perinatal transmission was a reason to terminate pregnancy in some instances, transmission was not the best predictor of termination. Rather, women decided to terminate the pregnancy because they had a previous abortion, had not planned the pregnancy, or were unhappy about the pregnancy. Women who chose to continue their pregnancies did so because of family influence, religious beliefs or because they wanted a child.

The importance of childbearing to women cannot be ignored (Stuntzner-Gibson, 1991; Smeltzer & Whipple, 1991). The loss of child-bearing potential sparks profound grief and the desire to have a child is a powerful influence in decision-making. The common recommendation of deferring childbearing until more is known about perinatal transmission probably seems absurd to a woman who anticipates a significantly shortened life span.

Multiple Roles

Women are universally the informal caregivers in this country, especially for children. In addition, women take care of sick partners and elderly parents. Increasingly women are also bread-winners for their families employed outside the home in addition to doing a second shift of cooking, cleaning, and child-rearing (McBride, 1990).

In one study of caregivers of HIV-infected children, women represented 83% of the sample (Reidy et al., 1991). These women were natural mothers, friends, relatives, and foster parents; many of the women were HIV infected themselves. With estimates ranging from over 50% to 99%, the majority of women with HIV have children (Walker, 1990). A Chicago needs assessment indicates that, in addition, most HIV-infected mothers are single parents (Carr, 1990). About half had infrequent or no help ever with child care. Because of failing health or fatigue, one third needed frequent help with tasks such as meal preparation, cleaning, laundry, and shopping (Carr, 1990). Women with HIV, alone and ill, are increasingly unable to care for their families.

Services, especially AIDS programs, are usually not designed to serve families; a family-centered or systems approach is especially critical when women are involved. Women are connected to a network of people for whom they provide support and whose needs they put before their own, sometimes to the detriment of their own health (Pfeiffer, 1991). Women's responsibilities within the family create special needs for outreach, support, and concrete services such as transportation and child care.

Permanency Planning

Recent estimates of the number of children who will lose their mother to AIDS by 1995 in the U.S. are 45,600 (Michaels & Levine, 1992). The vast majority of these children will be healthy, either born before the mother was infected or not infected perinatally. The stigmatization that isolates HIV-infected women from friends and family can also leave a mother with few options for placement of her children at her death. Even if extended family are willing, a mother may consider them inappropriate caregivers, lacking the stability or nurturance that she wants for her children.

When a mother finds someone to care for her children, the legal system is not well suited to the circumstances of HIV-infected women. Neither of the traditional mechanisms, guardianship or adoption, meets the needs of a parent who wants to make arrangements for her children but retain custody until she is incapacitated or dies. Appointing a guardian in a will, although not ideal, is still the best option in most cases allowing the mother to retain her rights until death. Unfortunately, there is no guarantee that the mother's choice for guardian will be upheld by the court (Cooper, 1992).

Women with HIV disease understand that their death and the subsequent changes for the children, such as new caregivers, a different home and school, will be painful. Anything that the mother can do to reduce that distress and ensure some stability for her children contributes to her sense of well-being. One woman wrote:

> Since the birth of my children, they have been my only concern. And now it is them I worry about when I think of having AIDS. They really have no one else but me. So when I lie in bed at night, it is for them that I cry. I have no say in what is going to happen to me. I have no idea when this will kill me. I only know that it will. And it would be much easier for me to die with this if I could know that they will be all right, have a family, stay together, be taken care of afterwards. (Confidential, personal communication, May, 1992)

Women in the Labor Force

Women are more likely than men to be low income, lacking health benefits or disability, and susceptible to a job loss. In the workplace, women are segregated into low-paying jobs–clerical, service, and sales–with little potential for promotion or on-the-job training where a woman may increase her marketability (Fox & Hesse-Biber, 1984). In order to reduce health and life insurance costs, lower level jobs are increasingly being filled with "part-time employees, temporary employees, leased employees and contractual service agreements" (Klingner, 1991, p. 132). The top tier of employees (managers, executives, and union employees) not only receive higher levels of pay but, even more importantly, health and disability benefits. The bottom tier, hired on an as-needed basis, do not receive benefits. Female employees are overrepresented in the bottom tier.

An employee in the bottom tier is also more easily let go without cause. She may be discharged because she has AIDS or a family member has AIDS but as long as the company claims that the temporary worker's services were no longer needed, the employee has little recourse (Klingner, 1991). Women who are infected or caring for an ill person are likely to take more sick days or need more time off which makes them especially vulnerable to firing.

If health benefits are tied to the job, a job loss may mean a permanent loss of health coverage for the employee and her family. If her employer has over 20 employees then, according to federal law (COBRA), she must be offered an extension of health coverage for 18 months beyond termination of employment. However, the ex-employee must pay the entire premium plus 2%, often a prohibitive cost. Even with future employment and related health benefits, at the end of the COBRA extension the woman may be without coverage for HIV disease under her new policy because of its exclusion as a pre-existing condition (Hermann & Schurgin, 1992).

THE ROLE OF THE EAP PROFESSIONAL

Employee Assistance programs were developed to handle employee problems that affect work performance (Klingner, 1991; Masi, 1990). In 1991, women represented 45% of the civilian labor force in the United States (U.S. Bureau of Census, 1992). As the numbers of women affected by HIV increase, the impact on the workplace is inevitable. The areas in which EAP professionals can apply their knowledge of women and HIV are: education for women at risk; early identification of infected women; case management of affected women; and organizational policies. The following suggestions are based on the issues delineated above.

Education

1. Target behaviors, not groups. Let employees know that risk behaviors are the concern, not risk groups. Anyone participating in those behaviors, no matter what their gender, color, or sexual orientation, may be at risk.
2. Raise employees' awareness of women at risk while letting them know that you are concerned. Make sure your educational materials include women in pictures, language, and content. When possible, provide in-house forums to discuss sensitive information. Saying "practice safe sex" is not enough; talk about how a person negotiates safe sex with a partner.
3. Include heterosexual men in your education; make everybody part of the responsibility to prevent HIV infection.
4. Recognize that employees are mothers (and fathers); include education on how to talk to children about HIV.
5. As African-American and Hispanic women appear to be most at risk, check your material and presentation content for cultural sensitivity.

Identification

1. Be "suspicious" of HIV in women as well as men; incorporate HIV into all of your psychosocial assessments.
2. Educate yourself on the symptoms of HIV in women. Gynecological exams may reveal the earliest symptoms of HIV disease. Vaginal candidiasis or vaginal yeast infections, pelvic inflammatory disease, abnormal pap smears, and genital warts are common early indications of HIV. These conditions are, of course, also seen in the general population of women. However, if the infections are recurrent or severe, the physician should suspect HIV and recommend testing (NIAID, 1993; Pfeiffer, 1991; Smeltzer & Whipple, 1991).

Case Management/Counseling

1. Add resources for women and families to your list; advocate for services when not available.

2. Utilize a family-centered approach defining "family" broadly to cover non-traditional households and/or informal support systems. Recognize that women are the hub of a network of children, parents, friends, and partners. Offer family education and counseling when appropriate. Remember that a female employee may not herself be infected but be deeply impacted by the illness of a child, partner, or friend.

3. Prepare for counseling around issues of childbearing: grief for loss of the potential or decision-making about pregnancy. The best approach to pregnancy counseling is non-directive and non-judgmental (Hauer, 1989). ". . . learn from the woman why she favors one or the other option and combine that knowledge with the relevant factual information in order to reach a decision" (Kass, 1991, p. 324). Examine your own attitudes about reproductive choice, especially in light of the potential infection of a child.

4. Consider future planning for children. Emphasize that planning for her children does not mean that her death is imminent or that she has to "give up" her children before she is ready. Offer to provide education and counseling with a family member or friend who might be a potential caregiver. Help parents understand the legal options such as adoption or guardianship and how to make arrangements for them. Screen your legal referrals for sensitivity to HIV-related issues.

Policy

1. Review policies for gender-inclusive language. Don't inadvertently contribute to the perception that women need not be concerned.

2. Promote flexibility in work schedules. Assist affected women in making arrangements for work around doctor appointments or another caregiver's schedule.

3. Review the benefits available to employees. Determine what can be done in your company to blunt the impact of the two-tiered labor market on women of color, a group disproportionately affected by HIV. Advocate for change.

The above guidelines presuppose that the EAP professional has existing AIDS programs on which to build; the employer and the EAP have already recognized AIDS as a problem and now must adjust their services, education, and policies to be gender-, race-, and class-appropriate. However, despite the potential impact of HIV on the workplace, it appears that "only 10% of employers formally address AIDS in the workplace" (Klingner, 1991, p. 101).

If the company that you work with has not implemented AIDS programs, use the excellent resources available, such as books and journal articles, to establish a program of education and support for employees and managers. Contact a local or national AIDS organization and ask if they have a workplace curriculum that meets your needs. Again, be sure that the curriculum is inclusive of women as people who are infected and as caretakers. The epidemic is clearly changing to encompass more women and children and, since the beginning, women have been deeply involved in the care and support of people with HIV.

Most importantly, do not wait for your 'first case,' male or female, before implementing relevant services and education. An employee may already have been affected but did not come forward for fear of discrimination. Being proactive can avert a crisis and reassure employees that you are willing and able to handle HIV-related problems. The Employee Assistance Program can play an important leadership role in developing AIDS workplace programs.

REFERENCES

Anastos, K., & Marte, C. (1989). Women–the missing persons in the AIDS epidemic. *Health/PAC Bulletin, 19*, 6-18.

Brewer, R.M. (1991). Working women. In H. Tierney (Ed.), *Women's studies encyclopedia: Views from the sciences*, (pp. 392-395). New York: Peter Bedrick.

Carr, A. (1990). *Summary of research report: The health care and social service needs of HIV-positive women and children in metropolitan Chicago*. Visiting Nurse Association of Chicago.

Ellerbrock, T.V., Bush, T.J., Chamberland, M.E., & Oxtoby, M.J. (1991). Epidemiology of women with AIDS in the United States, 1981 through 1990. *Journal of the American Medical Association, 265*, 2971-2975.

Fox, M.F., & Hesse-Biber, S. (1984). *Women at work*. Mayfield Publishing Co.

Hauer, L.B. (1989). Pregnancy and HIV infection. *Focus: A guide to AIDS research and counseling, 4*, 1-2.

Hermann, D.H.J. & Schurgin, W.P. *Legal aspects of AIDS: 1992 cumulative supplement.* Deerfield, IL: Clark, Boardman, Callaghan.

Cooper, E.B. (1992). HIV-infected parents and the law: issues of custody, visitation and guardianship. In N.D. Hunter & W.B. Rubenstein (Eds.), *AIDS agenda: emerging issues in civil rights,* (pp. 69-117). New York: New Press.

Kaspar, B. (1989). Women and AIDS: A psycho-social perspective. *Affilia, 4* (4), 7-22.

Kass, N.E. (1991). Reproductive decision making in the context of HIV: The case for nondirective counseling. In R. Faden, G. Geller, & M. Powers (Eds.), *Women, AIDS and the next generation,* (pp. 308-327). Oxford: University Press.

Klingner, D.E. (1991). *Workplace drug abuse and AIDS: a guide to human resource management policy and practice.* Westport, CT: Quorum.

Masi, D. (1990). *AIDS issues in the workplace: A response model for human resource management.* Westport, CT: Quorum.

McBride, A. B. (1990). Mental health effects of women's multiple roles. *American Psychologist, 45,* 381-384.

Michaels, D., & Levine, C. (1992). Estimates of the number of motherless youth orphaned by AIDS in the United States. *Journal of the American Medical Association, 268,* 3456-3461.

National Institute of Allergy and Infectious Diseases (NIAID). (1993). *Backgrounder.* Bethesda, MD: National Institutes of Health.

Pfeiffer, N. (1991). Highlights from the National Conference on Women and HIV infection. *AIDS Patient Care,* April, 67-69.

Reidy, M., Taggart, M.-E., & Asselin, L. (1991). Psychosocial needs expressed by the natural caregivers of HIV infected children. *AIDS Care, 3,* 331-343.

Selwyn, P.A., Carter, R.J., Schoenbaum, E.E., Robertson, V.J., Klein, R.S., & Rogers, M.F. (1989). Knowledge of HIV antibody status and decisions to continue or terminate pregnancy among intravenous drug users. *Journal of the American Medical Association, 261,* 3567-3571.

Shayne, V.T. & Kaplan, B.J. (1991). Double victims: Poor women and AIDS. *Women and Health, 17(1),* 21-37.

Smeltzer, S.C. & Whipple, B. (1991). Women and HIV infection. *Image: Journal of Nursing Scholarship, 23,* 249-256.

Springer, E. (1992). Reflections on women and HIV/AIDS in New York City and the United States. In J. Bury, V. Morrison, & S. McLachlan (Eds.), *Working with women and AIDS: Medical, social and counseling issues* (pp. 32-40). London: Routledge.

Stein, Z.A. (1990). HIV prevention: The need for methods women can use. *American Journal of Public Health,* April, 460-462.

Stuntzner-Gibson, D. (1991). Women and HIV disease: An emerging social crisis. *Social Work, 36,* 22-28.

U.S. Bureau of the Census (112th ed.). (1992). *Statistical abstract of the United States, 1992.* Washington, D.C.

Walker, J. (1990). Mothers and children. In ACT UP/NY Women & AIDS Book Group (Eds.), *Women, AIDS & activism* (pp. 165-171). Boston: South End Press.

Weitz, R. (1989). Uncertainty and the lives of persons with AIDS. *Journal of Health & Social Behavior, 30,* 270-81.

Women Survivors of Sexual Abuse: EAP Providers Play a Pivotal Role

Mary Jo Barrett
Wayne Scott
Joanna Gillespie
Becky Palmer

SUMMARY. This article discusses issues that employees bring to the workplace and to the EAP counselor when childhood incest is the referring problem. It examines three broadly related areas of potential difficulty that EAP counselors, employers and coworkers can anticipate from a coworker who is an incest survivor: power, control and connection. The impact of these dynamics on the workplace and the EAP counselor is explored. Treatment goals and interventions emphasize five key areas of intervention: (1) therapeutic relationship; (2) rituals; (3) flexible boundaries; (4) recognizing family and workplace patterns; and (5) creating workable realities for the survivor.

Current research suggests that nearly seventy percent of women seeking services from mental health clinicians are survivors of childhood sexual abuse (Briere and Zaidi, 1989). Sexually abused clients are more likely than non-abused people to experience emotional problems in adulthood (Rew, 1989). Among women hospitalized on a psychiatric unit, sexually abused women were more likely

---

Address all correspondence to the authors at: The Center for Contextual Change, Ltd., 9239 Gross Point Road, Skokie, IL 60077.

[Haworth co-indexing entry note]: "Women Survivors of Sexual Abuse: EAP Providers Play a Pivotal Role." Barrett, Mary Jo et al. Co-published simultaneously in *Employee Assistance Quarterly* (The Haworth Press, Inc.) Vol. 9, No. 3/4, 1994, pp. 149-159; and: *Empowering Women in the Workplace: Perspectives, Innovations, and Techniques for Helping Professionals* (ed: Marta Lundy, and Beverly Younger) Harrington Park Press an imprint of The Haworth Press, Inc., 1994, pp. 149-159. Multiple copies of this article/chapter may be purchased from The Haworth Document Delivery Center [1-800-3-HAWORTH; 9:00 a.m. - 5:00 p.m. (EST)].

149

to experience symptomatic and maladaptive behaviors, including: suicidal ideation, self-mutilation, serious sexual problems, severe marital conflicts, low self-esteem, distorted body images, and impaired social relationships (Briere and Zaidi, 1989; Finkelhor, Hotaling, Lewis and Smith, 1989; Jackson et al., 1990; Shearer, Peters, Quaytman, and Ogden, 1990). Given this complex and diverse array of symptomatology, women referred to an EAP provider for therapeutic intervention with any of the difficulties listed may be expressing symptoms associated with early sexual victimization.

The EAP provider has a pivotal role in facilitating the recovery of the survivor of childhood sexual abuse. The goal of this article is to help the EAP provider make an appropriate assessment and referral for the adult survivor of childhood sexual abuse. The article includes a theoretical framework for understanding intrafamilial and extrafamilial (where the offender is known to the victim) sexual abuse and its repercussions in the adult lives of women survivors. It also briefly describes some aspects of what a referring party should observe in a successful treatment program. Lastly, the article outlines where the EAP provider fits into the treatment process and ways the EAP provider can facilitate recovery.

CONCEPTUALIZING THE PROBLEM: THE VULNERABILITY FRAMEWORK

The Multiple Systems model for treating childhood sexual abuse, developed by Trepper and Barrett (1986), has been successful in treating adult survivors of sexual abuse. The model consists of three stages of treatment with each including: (family of origin, childhood issues, and current life situation) (1) family; (2) work; and (3) social contexts where the repercussions of the abuse are manifested. The Multiple Systems model combines individual, family, group and couple modalities, depending on the particular needs of the client. The success of this model rests on the clear understanding of how sexual abuse impacts one's life. Using the client's "survival" strengths, the clinician helps the client to focus on the particular areas that she wants to change. A particular treatment model is not necessary in the treatment of adult survivors of abuse, but rather, there are certain qualities of treatment programs that provide the most respectful, efficient, and safe therapy possible.

THREE STAGES OF TREATMENT

The following description of the stages of treatment are not meant to be a description of specific therapeutic techniques. The purpose is to provide the reader with a map to follow while looking for appropriate resources for the adult survivor. The EAP provider may keep these stages in mind in order to understand the process the client is going through, and to remain clear about their role, whether as direct service provider or as facilitator to a provider.

The first stage of treatment is: *Creating a Context for Change.* The following major goals need to be accomplished during stage one: (1) Most significantly, establish a safe environment *with* the client; (2) Create a therapeutic context where change is possible and expected; (3) Define the problem in a way that makes sense to everyone involved, including significant others; and (4) Acknowledge that change is difficult and anticipate inevitable intrapsychic and interpersonal setbacks and difficulties. This assessment revolves around understanding the early abuses as well as how the problems are currently maintained.

Stage two, *Challenging Patterns and Expanding Realities*, focuses on reducing the vulnerabilities identified in stage one. As a facilitator, the EAP professional may encourage the client to remain in therapy, acknowledging the difficulty and the duration of the work, while monitoring the work for the relevant processes. As the direct service clinician, the EAP professional identifies dysfunctional behavioral and emotional patterns, belief systems and interactional sequences by suggesting alternative ways of behaving and feeling. During stage two the client identifies and prioritizes the context (familial, work, and social) on which she will concentrate in treatment. Even though she may focus on one area, she will work on broadening these changes to all areas of her life.

The final stage of treatment, *Consolidation*, involves an integration of the previous changes in therapy and a discussion of future solution-focused plans for maintaining the changes (Trepper & Barrett, 1989).

For the purpose of the following discussion, it is important to focus on Stage One, the phase of treatment where the EAP provider plays the most crucial role. In order to do that, however, it is important to explore some of the essential theoretical underpinnings of the Multiple Systems perspective on childhood sexual abuse.

The Vulnerability Framework. The vulnerability framework has one basic assumption: there is no one cause for sexual abuse and no one cause for the subsequent symptoms of a particular person. Rather, individuals are endowed with a degree of vulnerability based on environmental factors, (social, political, gender, racial, cultural, economic and religious); family factors (family of origin, current family, current partner); and individual factors (biological, intrapsychic, spiritual, coping skills), that as adults may be expressed in different behaviors and feelings. Thus, treatment is based on the client's unique vulnerabilities and areas of resilience.

While survivors of childhood sexual abuse suffer the effects of specific events of sexual molestation (e.g., threats, manipulation, fondling, intercourse), they may also suffer from the larger systemic vulnerabilities that enabled the sexual abuse to occur, and from continuing victimization and exploitation in their adult lives. Within the family of origin and the current marriage and family situation, these vulnerabilities are manifested in: (1) enmeshed or disengaged interpersonal boundaries (Larson & Maddock, 1986); (2) communication problems (Trepper & Barrett, 1986); (3) oppressive family hierarchies (Minuchin, 1974, 1981); and particularly, (4) denial about the sexual abuse and its impact; and (5) family members' experiences regarding responsibility for the abuse (Barrett, Sykes & Byrnes, 1986; Barrett & Trepper, 1991, 1992). In addition, these families are influenced by larger sociocultural belief systems that accept the idea that one should use any means to gain power and control over those of less power, and that accept and believe in male supremacy and female submission, which encourages the abuse of women and children (Herman & Hirschman, 1977). The survivor has learned from the world and her family that she is not in control of her life or her body. She has learned that other people are concerned about their own needs first and that she will be abused if it will help satisfy their needs for power or connection (emotional or sexual).

These vulnerabilities, characteristic of the early family and social/political environment that enabled the sexual abuse to occur, continue to haunt the adult survivor in other aspects of her life. Her primary relationships, her work relationships, and her capacity to seek help from others are all hampered by this early experience of betrayal. Most significantly, her attempt to reach out for help from her Employee Assistance Program may be characterized by mistrust, a pervasive sense of revictimization (powerlessness) and a loss of control. Understanding the background experience of the adult survivor can sensitize the EAP professional to these complicated dynamics and lead to more supportive intervention. It is crucial that the EAP clinician does not become another powerful other, who attempts to control the employee's life to meet their own needs or is controlling even in the service of the client and thus represents another abusive experience. This is the challenge for all professionals working in the area of childhood trauma.

STAGE ONE: CREATING A CONTEXT FOR CHANGE

Three major themes–power, control and connection–are interwoven throughout assessment and referral, treatment and other aspects of the survivor's life. Simply, someone sexually abuses a child because they themselves are vulnerable: they experience themselves as *powerless* in their environmental and intrapsychic contexts, *out of control* of their world, their impulses and their belief systems, with an overwhelming desire to *regain control* at any cost. The abusers are *disconnected* from their own feelings and experiences, and the feelings and experiences of those more vulnerable than they. Subsequently, the abused child experiences a similar *powerlessness*: helpless in her environment and in her internal world, often feeling *out of control* in her life. Depressed, she may develop almost a panic to find some way to *regain control* and *disconnect* from those around her. Her efforts to regain control may be manifested in various problems, for example, eating disorders, substance abuse, anxiety attacks, and other forms of self abuse. She also may disconnect from her own feelings and experiences as a way of protecting herself and regaining control (dissociation).

These therapeutic themes provide the clinician with a conceptual framework to understand the presenting problems of the employee.

For the survivor of sexual abuse who struggles with issues of power, control and connection, the initial contact with the EAP provider has as much potential for healing as for confusion and destructiveness. In order to make an appropriate assessment and referral, the EAP provider needs to understand that the sexual abuse happened within the context of a relationship where the offender, often while professing care and concern for his victim, had more power and control than she did, displayed outward caring for her even while planning to exploit her, and was disconnected from the ultimate impact of his actions on her emotional well-being. The EAP provider, by virtue of his or her professional relationship to the survivor, can potentially replicate the frightening dynamics of the original abuse: he or she is in a more powerful position than the survivor, outwardly displays benevolence, and may appear disconnected to the intensity of pain that the survivor experiences.

THE ASSESSMENT PERIOD

The assessment period provides an excellent opportunity to begin to create a context for change. The EAP clinician can set the stage for the course of treatment and provide a safe, supportive place for the survivor to identify areas that need work, whether or not the client identifies the problem as childhood sexual abuse. It is crucial to accept the client's definition of the problem, even if the EAP provider strongly suspects she may be a survivor of sexual abuse. For example, labeling the client with a premature diagnosis or trying to determine the direction of the treatment can be the replication of the abusive dynamics that were mentioned earlier. The client needs to feel in control of her treatment by not fighting assumptions or interpretations made by the provider.

In our experience, many survivors present with concerns that fall in one or more of the following three areas: (1) current intimate relationships with friends, lovers, spouses, and/or children; (2) work difficulties with peers, supervisors, and/or effectiveness; and (3) family of origin relationships. Discussion and prioritization of these areas during assessment will enable the client and future therapist to organize the treatment. Traditionally, treatment of sexual abuse survivors has been assumed to be a long process, encompassing many areas of the client's past and present experiences. In order to follow a time-sensitive approach, help the survivor to focus on one broad area that encompasses the specific concerns she describes. For example, if a suspected survivor presents with problems with her partner/spouse, focus on the broad issue of relationships. The EAP and treatment provider can weave in the themes of *power, control and connection* discussed earlier without ever knowing if the client has been abused. If the client identifies herself as an abuse victim, a clinician can help the client to further prioritize the areas she would choose to focus on in treatment. As the client becomes more clear about her priorities, it will enable the provider to do the most effective job in matching the client with the most appropriate treatment program/provider.

In our experience, the treatment process for people who have been abused as children is often serial. The client may need to pursue certain problem areas in her life at different times and with different treatment modalities. A survivor may first want to address her marital problems and after establishing a safe relationship decide to stop therapy. A year later she may choose to join a group to focus more directly on past abuse issues. Perhaps after some individual treatment she may want to focus on work with her family of origin, choosing a therapist who is experienced in this area. Flexibility in designing individual treatment goals is crucial.

FORMULATING GOALS: THE CONCEPT OF RESILIENCE

To provide respectful, thorough and efficient treatment to the survivor of childhood sexual abuse we developed guidelines that are based on the work of Wolin and Wolin (1992). Briere has warned the profession repeatedly of the danger of pathologizing adult survivors of childhood sexual abuse who might present with extreme symptoms with traditional labels such as Borderline Personality Disorder. Concentrate on people's strengths, rather than their deficits. The Wolins studied survivors of trauma who were functioning well in their adult lives with minimal disruptions.

These five guidelines will help survivors identify their individual resilience–socially, professionally and personally.

1. Establish healing, "therapeutic relationships." The client must feel valued and acknowledged for her life experience in order for her to continue the process of healing.
2. Recognize interaction patterns that are hurtful, abusive or oppressive. Survivors often believe that all relationships are abusive, which makes them normal. However brief the contact, every clinician can help the survivor recognize destructive patterns and must not be abusive or oppressive toward the client.
3. Recognize personal strengths. Identify when the problems are not intruding painfully into her life. Point out functional behavior, and positive life experiences. The therapist can help the client recognize when she is functioning well.
4. Formulate appropriate and adaptable boundaries regarding: how much information to share with others; how emotionally, physically close to become with others; how rigid or flexible to be in interactions.
5. Create workable realities. Maintain hope and create solutions that feel attainable and important in the client's life and in her work in therapy.

THE REFERRAL TO AN OUTSIDE PROVIDER

Matching a client and her needs to the appropriate therapist can be a frustrating task. In fact, it is like shopping for an important item. Sometimes the treasured object is found on sale with relatively minimal effort, but more often finding exactly what is needed takes time and lots of shopping. For the survivor of sexual abuse, finding a therapist who is a good match often can shorten the length of treatment.

It is important to work with the client, focusing on her needs during the selection of the therapist. Many clients have ideas about what they want to do in therapy and what kind of therapist they would feel safest with in order to do their work. The following points may be taken into consideration when helping a client choose a potential therapist:

1. What is the therapist's experience and conceptual model about sexual abuse? In our experience a good clinician has experience with sexual abuse but also has a generalized practice. They integrate the abuse experience into the therapy, but it is not the total focus. If there are no experienced therapists in the area, suggest to your referring therapist some of these readings:

   Therapy for Adults Molested as Children, John Briere, 1989;
   Trauma and Recovery, Judith Herman, 1992;
   The Systemic Treatment of Incest: A Therapeutic Handbook, Terry Trepper and Mary Jo Barrett, 1989;
   Working with Adult Incest Survivors, Sam Kirschner, Diane Kirschner, and Richard Rappaport, 1993;
   Healing the Incest Wound, Christine Courtois, 1989

2. Many clients feel very strongly about the gender of their therapist. It is important to listen to these feelings and not try to convince the client that "gender does not matter." During different stages of treatment the client might choose to work with different genders depending on the treatment issues; this is very common and many times a good idea.
3. Therapists should be willing to work as a team, not just with the EAP provider, but with group or family therapists.
4. It is helpful if the treatment provider is willing to work with significant partners or spouses. One of the goals of treatment is to help the client identify her role in problematic relationships, either as a victim or as an abuser, consequently working with partners often is included in the treatment.
5. If the client wants to work on her family of origin relationships, particularly if she is deciding to communicate about the abuse with the family for the first time, it is extremely important that the therapist have experience with these types of sessions. This work takes much preparation and tolerance for high emotional intensity.

6. Ascertain how this therapist is supervised and by whom. How often do they use consultation and under what conditions?
7. Discuss the therapist's views about boundaries and safety in the therapeutic environment. If they do not understand the relevance of the question, this is cause for concern.

It might be necessary to help facilitate a transition meeting between the therapist and the client. After a few sessions talking with you it might feel overwhelming to begin talking with another person. The EAP involvement in the transition can be pivotal to its success. Experienced therapists will understand this need and will cooperate with the request of working together. One cautionary point: the suggestion for the EAP provider to be involved in the transition is not meant to have the provider take control or become overly involved in the process, rather to respect *mutual* work and *boundaries* with the client.

The efficiency of such a conceptual framework cannot be underestimated. EAP professionals are often confronted by clients whose life situations appear extremely complicated, if not overwhelming, and appear to defy a short-term, time-sensitive model of treatment. The conceptual framework presented in this paper enables the EAP professional, the survivor and the therapist to work together to establish a mutually respectful relationship.

REFERENCES

Barrett, M.J., & Trepper, T. (1992). Unmasking the incestuous family. *Family Therapy Networker, 16,* 39-46.

Barrett, M.J., & Trepper, T. (1992). Treatment of denial in families where there is child sex abuse, In LeCroy, C.W., *Case Studies in Social Work Practice,* 57-68, Belmont, California: Wadsworth Publishing Company.

Barrett, M.J., & Trepper, T. (1991) Treating women drug abusers who were victims of childhood sexual abuse. *Journal of Feminist Family Therapy, 3,* (4) 127-145.

Barrett, M.J., Sykes, C., & Byrnes, W. (1986). A systemic model for the treatment of intrafamily child sexual abuse. In Trepper, T. and Barrett, M.J. (Eds) *Treating Incest: A Multiple Systems Perspective.* New York: The Haworth Press, Inc.

Briere, J. & Zaidi, L.Y. (1989). Sexual abuse histories and sequelae in female psychiatric emergency room patients. *American Journal of Psychiatry, 146,* 1602-1606.

Briere, J. (1989). *Therapy for Adults Molested as Children*, New York: Springer Publishing.

Finkelhor, D., Hotaling, G.T., Lewis, I.A., & Smith, C. (1989). Sexual abuse and its relationship to later sexual satisfaction, marital status, religion and attitudes. *Journal of Interpersonal Violence, 4*, 379-399.

Herman, J.L. (1992). *Trauma and Recovery.* Basic Books: New York.

Herman, J.L., & Hirschman, L. (1977). Father-daughter incest. *Signs, 4*, 735-756.

Hunter, J.A. (1991). A comparison of the psychosocial maladjustment of adult males and females sexually molested as children. *Journal of Interpersonal Violence, 6* (2),205-217.

Hillenberg, J.B. & Wolf, K.L. (1988). Psychological impact of traumatic events: Implications for employee assistance programs. *Employee Assistance Quarterly, 4*, (2), 1-13.

Jackson, J.L., Calhoun, K.S., Amick, A.E., Maddever, H.M., & Havif, V.L. (1990). Young adult women who report childhood intrafamilial sexual abuse: Subsequent adjustment. *Archives of Sexual Behavior, 19*, 211-221.

Kirschner, S., Kirschner, D., & Rappaport, R. (1993). *Working with Adult Incest Survivors.* Brunner Mazel: New York.

Larson, N.R. & Maddock, J.W. (1986). Structural and functional variables in incest family systems: Implications for assessment and treatment. In Trepper, T. & Barrett, M.J. *Treating Incest: A Multiple Systems Perspective.* New York: The Haworth Press, Inc.

Minuchin, S. (1974) *Families and Family Therapy.* Cambridge, MA: Harvard University Press.

Minuchin, S. & Fishman, H.C. (1981). *Family Therapy Techniques.* Cambridge, MA: Harvard University Press.

Schwartz, R. & Barrett, M.J. (1988). Women and eating disorders. In Braverman, L., *Women, Feminism, and Family Therapy.* New York: The Haworth Press, Inc.

Shearer, L., Peters, C.P., Quaytman, S. and Ogden, R. (1990). Frequency and correlates of childhood sexual and physical abuse histories in adult female borderline patients. *American Journal of Psychiatry, 147*, 214-216.

Trepper, T. & Barrett, M.J. (1989) *Systemic treatment of incest: A therapeutic handbook.* New York: Brunner Mazel.

Trepper, T. & Barrett, M.J. (1986) Vulnerability to incest: A framework for assessment. In Trepper, T. & Barrett, M.J., *Treating incest: A multiple systems perspective.* New York: The Haworth Press, Inc.

Wolin, S.J., & Wolin, S. (1993). *The Resilient Self.* New York: Villard Press.

Van Den Bergh, N. (1991). Workplace Mutual Aid and Self-Help: Invaluable Resources for EAPs. *Employee Assistance Quarterly, 6* (3), 1-20.

From Invisibility to Voice:
Providing EAP Assistance to Lesbians
at the Workplace

Nan Van Den Bergh

SUMMARY. The purpose of this article is to articulate the salient issues of gay and lesbian employees, both in the workplace and in general. Hence, it also serves to sensitize Employee Assistance professionals and their interventions to the problems and needs of gays and lesbians. As less research and fewer publications have been focused on lesbian issues, this article offers a specific focus on the problems and needs lesbians experience in the workplace. Within the last year, there has been more visibility focused on lesbians and gays due to both state referenda seeking to curtail their civil rights protections and Federal initiatives to lift the military ban on homosexuals. Therefore, it is pertinent and timely for EAP professionals to become familiar with the issues that confront this group of employees, to ensure that Employee Assistance interventions can be developed which will be both appropriate and effective.

The year of 1993 could be considered the "Year of Pride," as increased attention has been placed on lesbian and gay issues and concerns. Although there are varying opinions concerning the percent of the U.S. population assumed to be lesbian or gay, with estimates ranging from 3% to 10% (Rogers, 1993), there is consen-

Nan Van Den Bergh, PhD, is affiliated with the School of Social Work, Tulane University, New Orleans, LA.

[Haworth co-indexing entry note]: "From Invisibility to Voice: Providing EAP Assistance to Lesbians at the Workplace." Van Den Bergh, Nan. Co-published simultaneously in *Employee Assistance Quarterly* (The Haworth Press, Inc.) Vol. 9, No. 3/4, 1994, pp. 161-177; and: *Empowering Women in the Workplace: Perspectives, Innovations, and Techniques for Helping Professionals* (ed: Marta Lundy, and Beverly Younger) Harrington Park Press an imprint of The Haworth Press, Inc., 1994, pp. 161-177. Multiple copies of this article/chapter may be purchased from The Haworth Document Delivery Center [1-800-3-HAWORTH; 9:00 a.m. - 5:00 p.m. (EST)].

sus that lesbians tend to be more "invisible" than gay men. Consequently, estimates on the lesbian presence within the U.S. range from two to thirteen million–the lack of certainty in quantification being based on the assumption that most lesbians are not "out" or self-disclosing about their sexual preference. The April, 1993 March on Washington for gay/lesbian rights, coupled with increased media attention to "gayness," (Salholz et al., 1993; Shapiro et al., 1993) suggests, however, that lesbians and gay men are becoming more willing to be visible and to organize for rights, opportunities and equal protection under the law.

The purpose of this article is to address the needs of lesbian women in the workplace and to suggest appropriate interventions for EAP professionals to undertake with lesbian clients. Prior to an explication of those specific issues, information will be shared on the needs of lesbians and gay men in general and at the workplace.

GAY AND LESBIAN ISSUES: AN OVERVIEW

"Coming Out"

The above colloquial term concerns the process that lesbians and gay men go through in acknowledging their sexual preference. It is crucial to realize that there is not one normative course an individual follows in acquiring a lesbian/gay identity. Some persons may be clear from the time they are youth that they have an "affectational/sexual preference" for their same gender; others may not acquire a lesbian/gay identity until they have experienced heterosexual realities, including marriage and raising children. Although attention has been given in the recent past to suggesting that homosexuality may have a genetic predisposition (Shapiro et al., 1993), other causative propositions have posited a "cultural" etiology (Ettore, 1980). The latter explanatory argument has been applied particularly to lesbians, stating that women become lesbian-identified through their awareness of the oppressive conditions for women which exist within patriarchal and capitalist societies. Regardless of etiology, "coming out" for lesbians and gay men is a critical psychological and developmental process which includes stages varying from quandary to identity synthesis to acceptance (Cass, 1979; Lewis, 1984).

The ease with which one navigates the coming out process depends upon the social support one receives, as well as the access to information and opportunities one has to develop camaraderie with other lesbians and gays. A failure to receive positive feedback or support can cause an individual to experience depression, anxiety or the self-destructive abuse of alcohol or drugs. It is important to emphasize that "unconditional positive regard" and nonjudgemental attitudes are extremely helpful in deterring any negative aspects of the "coming out" process. The experience of derogatory treatment can lead lesbians and gay men to develop "internalized homophobia," or a self-hatred based on one's sexual preference. Such a phenomenon invariably leads to mental health problems and accompanying behavioral impairments.

"We Are Family"

Frequently overlooked, but highly salient for lesbians and gay men, is the need to feel that their committed domestic partnerships and parenting status are accepted by others. It is estimated that there may be as many as five million lesbian mothers (Steinhorn, 1983). Although the majority of lesbian and gay parents become so by virtue of prior heterosexual unions (Tully, 1989), there has been a growth in lesbian/gay adoptions, as well as lesbian birthing through the use of artificial insemination (Gibbs, 1989; Levy, 1992). Family policy issues can have import for lesbians/gays, particularly for lesbians who may be subject to litigation surrounding the retention of child custody. Setting a positive example, the Massachusetts Supreme Court ruled in 1993 that a lesbian couple could legally adopt a child conceived by one of the women through the use of artificial insemination *(Times Picayune, 1993)*. Joint adoption was pursued in order for both women to share parental rights. Unfortunately, there have also been lesbians (more so than gay men) who have lost custody of their children because they were "out" about their sexual preference (Shapiro et al., 1993). Fears of losing one's children, concerns that the children will be rejected by others or worries that the children will reject the parents are driven by homophobia, prejudicial attitudes and discriminatory behavior. There is no research that indicates children raised by lesbian parents are in any way different from youth raised by heterosexuals (Gibbs, 1989; Levy, 1992; Lott-Whitehead, 1993).

The recognition of lesbian and gay domestic partnerships as viable legal entities is an extremely prominent issue. Although lesbians have traditionally been more likely to form monogamous conjugal units, gay men have increasingly done so, particularly since the outbreak of HIV infection. A trend which has gained increasing acceptance since the 1980's has been the actual formalization of lesbian and gay partnerships by a ceremony (Butler, 1990; Cherry & Mitulski, 1990). Increasingly, municipalities are allowing lesbians and gays to register as "domestic partners." For example, in May of 1993 the Hawaii Supreme Court ruled that gay marriage can be legal. New York City, San Francisco, Los Angeles, New Orleans, Seattle and twenty-five other cities now allow lesbians/gays to register as domestic partners (Shapiro et al., 1993). The opportunity to codify relationships in this manner can help to secure lesbian/gay couples' economic and legal rights.

There are workplace-related implications associated with recognizing gay and lesbian domestic partnerships. Members of such unions might then be considered eligible for receipt of employee benefits coverage as the official "partner" of a covered employee. A few organizations currently offer such coverage to partners of gay/lesbian employees, including Ben and Jerry's Ice Cream and the American Psychological Association. In a related vein, there are a few universities–notably Stanford, Columbia, Harvard and the University of Oregon–which extend housing and other benefits to same-sex couples (Achtenberg and Newcombe, 1991).

Civil Rights

Organized advocacy to secure equal protection under the law for lesbians and gays most notably dates from the "Stonewall Uprising" in June, 1969, precipitated by police harassment of individuals at a gay bar in Greenwich Village, New York. A riot was triggered which mobilized the gay community. Every June, throughout major U.S. cities, gay rights celebrations are held to commemorate Stonewall. Exemplifying earlier attempts to network and affiliate with lesbian/gay kindred spirits are the founding of both the Mattachine

Society (primarily male) and the Daughters of Bilitis in the 1950's. However, greater willingness to take an ardent stand for gay rights emanated from the general civil rights tenor of the sixties and feminist organizing efforts in the 1970's.

The hallmark anti-discriminatory law, Title VII of the 1964 Civil Rights Act, does not preclude sexual orientation discrimination. To date, the Supreme Court has refused to hear any cases applicable to sexual orientation discrimination. Additionally, the U.S. Equal Employment Opportunity Commission has refused to accept claims of sexual orientation discrimination and most state anti-discrimination laws do not protect lesbians and gay men (Poverny & Finch, 1985). This is because the courts have not as yet placed lesbians and gays in a "suspect class" category, meaning a group with an immutable trait (such as skin color) which has subjected them to a history of discrimination and political disadvantage (Shapiro et al., 1993). Research attempting to discern a biological precursor to lesbian or gay existence may pose an interesting legal challenge regarding the possibility of an "immutable" homosexual reality.

The reality is that lesbians and gays do face discrimination, as can be witnessed by the fact that there were 1,898 hate crimes against such persons in 1992, within only five major U.S. cities (ibid.). In November, 1992, Oregon voters defeated a ballot initiative declaring homosexuality as "abnormal, wrong, unnatural and perverse"; however, a more subtly phrased measure passed in Colorado (ibid., p. 46). Similar antigay measures are being promoted in seventeen states and numerous cities.

Despite a societal milieu which tends towards homophobia, by 1993 twenty-four states had decriminalized homosexuality and eight states and more than 100 municipalities had passed gay-rights laws. There are currently approximately 120 openly gay officials in public office, more than double the number in 1991 (ibid.). Roberta Achtenberg, the Assistant Secretary of Housing and Urban Development, a Clinton appointee, is the first openly lesbian or gay person to be confirmed by the United States Senate for political office.

The most prominent current issue with public policy import pertains to lifting the military ban on homosexuality. In reality, this is a lesbian issue, bespeaking the tendency towards the "invisibility" of lesbian needs and concerns. It is assumed a higher percentage of lesbians than gay men are in the military. However, women have been left out of the debate over lifting the ban on homosexuals, despite the fact that across all services women are three times more likely to be investigated and discharged for homosexuality. Within the Marine Corps, they are six times more likely to be scrutinized (Salholz et al., 1993). Although there has been fervent activity to "rout out" lesbians in the military, a less than assiduous stance has been demonstrated regarding the sexual harassment complaints of female military personnel. Often women reporting sexual harassment have found their own sexual practices investigated; both gay and straight women have acknowledged having sex with men to deter accusations of lesbianism (Salholz et al., 1993).

Subsequent to whatever outcome resolves the current debate over lifting the ban on homosexuality within the military, the next major civil rights battle will ensue over a Federal Gay Civil Rights bill. Senator Edward Kennedy and Representative Henry Waxman plan to introduce a bill that would protect gays from discrimination by employers, landlords, hotels, restaurants and other public places. This bill will be modeled after the Americans with Disabilities Act. Moving towards actualization of such a goal, the Leadership Conference on Civil Rights, the main Washington civil rights coalition, voted in November of 1992 to make gay rights a legislative priority. Supporters included the National Association for the Advancement of Colored People and the AFL-CIO (Shapiro et al., 1993).

The HIV/AIDS Epidemic

No discussion of contemporary lesbian/gay issues, in general or at the workplace, would be complete without mention of the HIV/AIDS epidemic. Since the early 1980's when the disease began to manifest itself, it is estimated that there have been approximately 230,000 AIDS cases reported in the United States, with approximately 40% of those being in six metropolitan areas: New York City, Los Angeles, San Francisco, Miami, Washington DC and Newark, New Jersey. The World Health Organization estimates that, worldwide, about nine million persons may be infected with HIV, with one million of those living in North America (Lynch, Lloyd & Fimbres, 1993). AIDS can manifest itself in any of several "opportunistic" diseases up to ten years subsequent to the exposure of the HIV infection; hence, to be HIV positive is not necessarily to manifest AIDS symptomology at the time of infection.

Women are not immune to AIDS; in fact, they are the fastest growing group with the disease, especially women of color who are significantly at risk (Lynch, Lloyd & Fimbres, 1993). The primary ways in which females acquire HIV infection are either by unprotected sex with an infected partner or by intravenous drug use (51% of all female AIDS cases are due to the latter) (ibid.). Although the majority of HIV infected women have been either heterosexual or bisexual, lesbians are not immune; such cases have been reported. A common HIV/AIDS phenomenon impacting lesbians is the more virulent homophobic response generated by the people who believe that HIV is prevalent amongst all persons who are homosexual and that HIV can be spread by casual contact. Prejudicial attitudes of this sort can create a hostile work environment, one which manifests itself in either overt or latent discrimination against lesbians (i.e., avoiding contact with them, social ostracizing, etc.).

WORKPLACE-BASED ISSUES FOR LESBIANS AND GAYS

Although the advocacy of lesbian and gay issues has received national attention in recent years, concern about sexual preference discrimination at the workplace has a longer history. Dating to the McCarthy years of the 1950's when surveillance activities took place against Americans considered "security risks," security clearances have frequently been denied to gays on the basis that they could be susceptible to blackmail. During the 1950's, police raids on gay clubs often resulted in the employers of arrested gays being contacted to inform them that one of their employees had been engaging in homosexual activity.

One difficulty in documenting gay and lesbian employment discrimination is that employees are forced to "come out" in order to seek redress for their grievances. Needless to say, neither the workplace nor society has been supportive of such forthright action. Research data suggest that lesbians and gays believe that disclosure of their sexual preference will have an adverse outcome on their employment. In two studies on this subject, 20 to 25% of respondents did report actual experiences with workplace-based sexual preference discrimination (Stoddard, 1986; Homosexual women . . . 1986). In another study, the Oregon Task Force on Sexual Preference found that many lesbians and gay men were denied employment or terminated when their sexual orientation was made known (Povemy & Finch, 1985).

Although the New York City Commission on Human Rights has indicated that the majority of lesbian/gay employment discrimination cases have probably *not* been reported, such complaints rose from 139 to 339 in just one year, 1986. It is assumed that the increase was directly associated with an ordinance issued in that same year, prohibiting discrimination based on sexual orientation (Povemy & Finch, 1988). In the 1960's, the Gay Activist Alliance in New York City identified job discrimination as the most likely issue around which gays could organize.

Despite a social policy environment which has not unilaterally protected lesbians and gay men from myriad forms of discrimination, employment suits have still been undertaken. The most successful legal actions have been those concerning public sector workers in which the Fifth Amendment due process caveat was employed. In such cases a judicial recognition was made that discrimination based on sexual orientation deprives one of due process; a discharging agency must demonstrate some rational basis for its job termination decision (Norton vs. Macy, 1969). In employment discrimination cases undertaken thus far, there has been an inverse relationship between job rank and likeliness to file a suit, such that professional, managerial and administrative lesbians/gays have *not* been predominant among those filing sexual orientation discrimination charges (ibid.).

The question needs to be raised as to how gay/lesbian employment discrimination is manifested. As recently as 1991, the Cracker Barrel restaurant chain fired several openly gay employees (Shapiro et al., 1993). In the recent past, there have been lesbian military personnel who have fought dishonorable discharges when their sexual preference was made known (Salholz et al., 1993). Historically, job discrimination has been manifested in the acts of: (a) being fired; (b) not being promoted or experiencing demotion; (c) being denied raises; or, (d) being restricted in job responsibilities (Povemy &

Finch, 1988). More recently, acts of job discrimination have centered around AIDS-related issues; that is, being associated with persons who have AIDS or being presumed to be HIV+. The Americans with Disabilities Act precludes any adverse employment action towards individuals who have AIDS, as the disease is considered a disability. Several enlightened companies have passed anti-discrimination policies based on sexual orientation, notably, American Express, Bank of America, General Electric, ABC, CBS, American Motors and Anheuser Busch. The reason for undertaking such action is to protect the "bottom line"–it precludes costly litigation.

In addition to the kind of overt discrimination mentioned above, certain aspects of organizational culture can generate discriminatory workplace behaviors. For example, workplace social activities which consider only employees and their *spouses* discriminate against not only lesbian and gays but also heterosexual couples who are not married. In a related vein, office banter about out-of-work activities that assumes all "coupling" is heterosexual causes lesbian and gay men to feel the need to be "closeted." Organizational culture is important because it sets up the context for what is valued and rewarded within an organization and clarifies behavioral norms and expectations. Hence, when a climate is *heterosexist,* it sends the message that to be lesbian/gay is aberrant–that reality needs to be covert.

An area directly related to the workplace, which is receiving increasing attention as a focal point for lesbian/gay activities, pertains to employee benefits plans and receipt eligibility for same-sex partners. This issue deserves attention, as it has implications for the way "family" is defined and, in a more general sense, who is eligible to be covered as a dependant. Even twenty years ago, households were not constituted as they are now. For example, the U.S. Census defines family as two or more persons related by birth, marriage or adoption who live together. Yet, 1980 census data indicated a 538% increase, since 1940, in households not meeting that definition. The percent of American households made up of unrelated adults increased from 21% in 1968 to 34% in 1984 (Poverny & Finch, 1988). Hence, employee benefit receipt strategies based upon the census formulation of a traditional family are clearly anachronistic and deserve revision.

Lesbians and gay men living in domestic partnerships have been denied coverage on their partner's health insurance and retirement plans, and eligibility for family leave to care for an ill partner. Lesbians and gay men involved in coparenting or adoption have also been unable to utilize family leave options. Although not specifically related to the workplace, federal and state preclusions have existed in filing joint income tax, qualifying as a head of household or serving as beneficiaries for Individual Retirement Account (IRA) disbursements. However, there is a precedent for allowing same-sex partners the kind of financial and legal protections noted above. In Denmark, lesbians and gays have protection with inheritance benefits; in the Netherlands there are income tax advantages which can be accrued.

Finally, although the Americans with Disabilities Act precludes discrimination against individuals who have AIDS, there is some concern that fears related to contagion have caused antigay discrimination to be more overt. As noted earlier, lesbians are not excluded from receiving this type of homophobic response. The following are examples of AIDS-hysteria discriminatory behaviors:

- an employee of the New Orleans Hilton lost his job after revealing to fellow workers that a friend had AIDS;
- a Houston public school teacher was removed from classroom teaching after posing for a photograph to be used in an article about AIDS;
- in Los Angeles, a gay chef was fired because of his employer's fear of contracting the virus, even though the employee did not have AIDS (Poverny & Finch, 1988, p. 22).

The above has served as an overview of lesbian and gay workplace issues. It is now appropriate to address those concerns which are more specific to lesbians.

LESBIAN-SPECIFIC WORKPLACE CONCERNS

The areas of discrimination most specific to lesbians relate primarily to their status as women. That is to say, the problems which lesbians face in the workplace are based on the confluence of sexism and homophobia.

For example, lesbians can be subject to sexual harassment centered on the theme of "not having found the right man." This kind of taunting suggests that the lesbian's willingness to engage in heterosexual activity would be the "cure" for her homosexuality. Male vociferousness around "lesbian-baiting" is, in itself, an interesting commentary on female sexuality and how it is normatively viewed. Lesbians clearly represent women who believe in the positive expression of female sexuality and who have not subscribed to parochial beliefs that sex is for procreative purposes, or to please men.

Similarly, lesbians represent women who are autonomous and not dependent upon men for their economic survival. Such a behavioral statement can raise the ire of males who have a need to be dominant over women, in order to indicate their strength and value. Hence, women who are openly lesbian can be extremely threatening to individuals who are traditionally patriarchal in their view of male and female relationships. Violence by men against known lesbians is often predicated upon the male desire to re-establish control over a female who has ostensibly not subscribed to traditional gender relations.

The statements of lesbian military personnel substantiate that women have experienced sexual harassment by male colleagues who presume their lesbianism and feel threatened by their break from traditional roles. One noncommissioned army officer stated, "If I act like a female they think I'm weak and can't do my job; if I'm aggressive they think I'm manly and must be queer" (Salholz et al., 1993, p. 60). Another example was given by a lesbian air force officer who rebuked a male colleague's sexual advances toward her. An investigation was then initiated into her intimate relationship with another woman, who "confessed" to being in a lesbian involvement in order to receive an honorable discharge (Beck et al., 1993, p. 60).

The point is that discrimination against lesbians is highly associated with discrimination against women who are not behaving according to traditional gender role precepts. Historically, lesbians have played a dominant role in most social movements from

19th century abolition and temperance activism to 20th century civil rights movements. Lesbians are better educated than the overall population (Salholz et al., 1993) and tend to be concentrated in nontraditional roles (for women), including management, professional, supervisorial or skilled craft capacities (Ettorre, 1980). Consequently, lesbianism minimizes women's traditional role to reproduce, in favor of a more productive role, one which is usually reserved for men. Thus, lesbianism suggests the abrogation of beliefs that women are inferior, weak, subservient, dependent and without power. The harassment of lesbians in the workplace may be based upon the need to re-establish traditional gender dynamics on the part of individuals who are more patriarchal in their view of male/female relationships. Interestingly, to be lesbian becomes a kind of political statement, as well as an indicator of personal empowerment. In summation, derisive statements toward lesbians are potentially motivated by a need to re-establish male power and control.

In addition to experiencing overt sexual harassment, lesbian-specific discrimination can be manifested by a failure to allow lesbian coparents to utilize any extant family leave opportunities for parenting responsibilities. Given that the passage of family leave actions is very recent (1993 federal and state initiatives), there appear to be no cases which have challenged the use of that option for lesbians/gays. Federal family leave guidelines do not extend to same sex partnerships; states have the option of being more inclusive in defining who is covered. This issue underscores the need to have broader interpretations of what constitutes "dependents" within dependent care policies, to include same sex partners and any children they are jointly raising.

EAP INTERVENTIONS WITH LESBIAN CLIENTS

Direct Services

When providing direct services, the EAP practitioner must ensure that s/he is able to assess a lesbian client's problem in a gay-sensitive fashion. Primarily, this means viewing the client's sexual preference as a descriptive reality, rather than a diagnostic category. For lesbians who may present with the duress associated with "coming out," either at the workplace or in general, an empathic, supportive response is necessary, as well as a willingness to provide community resources for lesbians. Unconditional positive regard is requisite for work with lesbians and gays who are coming out; the establishment of an accepting "holding environment" will do much to quell the client's anxiety and angst. Also, sharing reading materials with clients on lesbian and gay realities is recommended; there are many volumes with "coming out" stories that can be found in bookstores.

If alcohol or drug dependence appears to be part of the problem, the EAP practitioner is well advised to refer the client to lesbian/gay recovery resources. Although addiction is an equal opportunity disease, the ability to honestly self-scrutinize and to share with others is facilitated by being with "like kind." Most major metropolitan areas have lesbian/gay-specific 12 Step meetings as well as recovery programs. Investigation of those resources is crucial in order to offer optimal recovery resources. Bookstores which have gay/lesbian titles will carry national and international directories of gay/ lesbian community social and cultural resources; virtually all of those volumes will note telephone numbers for lesbian/gay AA meetings. Additionally, there is a group known as the National Association of Gay and Lesbian Alcoholism Professionals which can be contacted. PRIDE Institute, located outside of Minneapolis, Minnesota, is a nationally recognized lesbian/gay addictions treatment resource which can also be contacted for both inpatient and outpatient treatment, as well as to provide training on gay/lesbian issues (800-547-7433).

If lesbian clients present with either relationship or parenting issues, it is crucial to understand the specific stresses lesbian couples/families experience due to homophobia. In addition to the normal vicissitudes inherent in coupling or raising children, lesbian units have to endure shaming, pejorative, judgmental and sometimes physically threatening abuses. A sensitive practitioner may look for signs of internalized homophobia or other self-deprecating beliefs which may impact the ability of a couple or family to resolve problems. Again, it can be extremely helpful for lesbian couples and parents to be referred to community resources focused on lesbian issues, as one can often acquire solutions through mutual aid and peer support. If information is needed on legal matters, such as child custody, there are several options. First, metropolitan areas with a lawyer's bar association will be able to provide referrals to attorneys having specialization on gay/lesbian topics. Secondly, the National Gay and Lesbian Task Force could be contacted for referrals and information (202-332-6483).

Dealing with grief and loss associated with HIV/AIDS is a phenomenon which many lesbians have been confronted with over the last decade. Clients experiencing symptoms associated with protracted grief often need assistance in re-establishing a sense of meaning and purpose to life (spiritual concerns), as well as setting new boundaries and priorities. Sustained involvement with loss and bereavement can engender trauma symptomology, such as a sense of emptiness, exhaustion, futility and anger. Most metropolitan areas have support groups for friends and family of persons with HIV/AIDS; encouraging a client to avail herself of such resources would be an appropriate intervention.

Clients who have experienced discriminatory behavior, such as sexual harassment or other actions associated with their sexual preference, require several types of intervention. First, a supportive, listening stance needs to be provided that is initially not outcome-oriented. Typically women experiencing gender-related discrimination have trepidation in reporting the issue and taking action, as they may fear being held responsible for the discrimination. "Blaming the victim" is prevalent, unfortunately, and women often fear rebuke or retaliation by others in the workplace. It is imperative for the EAP professional to provide an empathic stance, "starting where the client is at," while also providing information on options which could be undertaken, pursuant to filing harassment or discrimination claims.

It would behoove the EAP professional to serve in the broker or mediator role while clarifying the steps a client can take, should that be her desire. Such actions might include acquiring information through an organization's labor relations and affirmative action departments on the processes involved in filing a grievance. It is crucial that an EAP practitioner encourage the client to contact him or her for support or clarification on an ongoing basis. Legal actions of any sort are protracted processes, which can be frustrating and discouraging for clients.

Indirect Services

Employee Assistance professionals are encouraged to advocate within their organizations for the development of policies which preclude de facto discrimination against lesbians/gays in hiring, retention or promotion. As was noted previously, not only is there "bottom line" prudence to such actions as they deter potential litigation, but such actions also help establish an organizational culture which supports its human resources. In times affected by recessionary budgets, where downsizing and reorganization are prevalent, such practice policies engender employee loyalty and can positively impact productivity.

Additionally, the creation of policies and procedures regarding HIV/AIDS also assists all lesbian/gay employees, as the impact of such actions can be to mitigate homophobia. Employee education on HIV/AIDS also can reduce their fear and anxiety which, if ignored, may lead to ostracizing or maligning lesbian/gay employees.

When planning supervisory or employee training, assume that 10% of participants are lesbian or gay and, accordingly, honor their reality. It is important to use nomenclature inclusive of gay/lesbian lifestyles. For instance, relationship, family or couple problems should not be addressed with a sole focus on heterosexual, nuclear family units. Diversity training should also include information on lesbians and gays, both in terms of their prevalence and some of the special needs related to that population, as addressed previously.

Efforts to preclude dejure discrimination, such as the inclusion of lesbian/gay domestic partners within benefits plans, are very important. The concept of "dependent," and the guidelines of eligibility for that status, could be redefined as a co-resident of a household which has existed over time. This broadened definition of family and dependent will be particularly valuable for lesbian employees who, historically, have experienced more of a need for policy and social supports of their domestic partnerships and coparenting families.

A highly significant way to preclude discriminatory behavior towards lesbians and gay men is to ensure that the organization acknowledges the existence of lesbians and gays as a part of its culture. Encouragement to include employees' *partners,* as opposed to invitations addressed exclusively to spouses, sends the message that it is O.K. to be "out." It might also be possible to encourage lesbian/gay employees to share about their experiences, either as part of "learn-at-lunch" convenings, or within organizational newsletters. In companies which have diversity committees or task forces, it would be crucial to ensure lesbian/gay employees are represented. Yearly, October 12th is commemorated as National Coming Out Day; it would be highly appropriate to encourage workplace recognition of that event.

CONCLUSION

A momentum has been engendered in recent years, considered as the "gay nineties," which encourages lesbians and gays to have pride, to be visible, to organize and to advocate for equal protection, opportunities, and rights. Employee Assistance professionals can serve as facilitators of lesbian and gay pride by becoming educated about lesbian/gay realities, developing community and treatment resources which are lesbian-gay sensitive and by serving as advocates and facilitators for the articulation of a lesbian and gay pride voice, at the workplace.

REFERENCES

Achtenberg, R. & Newcombe, M. (Eds.) (1991). *Sexual orientation and the law* (Release 4). New York: Clark, Boardman, Callaghan.

Associated Press. (1993, September 11). Lesbian couple can adopt girl. *Times-Picayune,* D-9.

Beck, M., Glick, D., Annin, P. (1993, June 21). A quiet uprising in the ranks. *Newsweek,* 60.

Butler, B. (1990). *Ceremonies of the heart.* Seattle: WA Seal Press.

Cass, V. (1979). Homosexual identity information: A theoretical model. *Journal of Homosexuality,* 4(3), 219-235.

Cherry, K. & Mitulsik, J. (1990). Committed couples in the community. *Christian Century,* 107(7), 218-220.

Ettorre, E. (1980). *Lesbians, Women and Society.* London: Routledge & Kegan Paul.

Gibbs, E. (1989). Psychosocial development of children raised by lesbian mothers: A review of research. *Women & Therapy,* 8 (1/2), 65-75.

Homosexual women said to face job discrimination. (1986, October 24). *The Chronicle of Higher Education.*

Levy, E. (1992, January). Strengthening the coping resources of lesbian families. *Journal of Contemporary Human Services,* 23-31.

Lewis, L. (1984). The coming-out process for lesbians: Integrating a stable identity. *Social Work,* 29 (5), 464-469.

Lynch, V., Lloyd, G., Fimbres, M. (1993). *The Changing Face of AIDS: Implications for Social Work Practice.* Westport, Conn.: Auburn House.

Norton. V. Macy, 417 F. 2d 1161, 1964 (D.C. Cir. 1969).

Poverny, L. & Finch, W. (1985). Job discrimination against gay and lesbian workers. *Social Work Papers,* 19, 35-45.

Poverny, L. & Finch, W. (1988). Integrating work-related issues on gay and lesbian employees into occupational social work practice. *Employee Assistance Quarterly,* 4, (2), 15-30.

Rogers, P. (1993, February 15). How many gays are there? *Newsweek,* 46.

Salholz, E. Glick, D. Beachy, L., Monserrate, C., King, P., Gordon, J. Barrett, T. (1993, June 21). The power and the pride. *Newsweek,* 54-60.

Shapiro, J., Cook, G. Krackov, A. (1993, July 5). Straight talk about gays. *Newsweek,* 42-48.

Steinhorn, A. (1983). Lesbian mothers. In H. Hildalgo, T. Peterson, N. Woodman (Eds.), *Lesbian and Gay Issues: A Resource Manual for Social Workers,* 33-37. Silver Spring, MD: NASW.

Stoddard, T. (1986, February 14). It isn't a 'Gay Rights' bill, *The New York Times,* National Edition: 15.

Tully, C. (1989). Caregiving: What do mid-life lesbians view as important? *Journal of Gay & Lesbian Psychotherapy,* 1 (1), 87-103.

Women and Alcohol, Tobacco, and Other Drugs: The Need to Broaden the Base Within EAPs

Beth Glover Reed

SUMMARY. Increased numbers of women in the work force provide opportunities for services for problems with alcohol, tobacco and other drugs (ATOD) that are long overdue. Drawing from the contributions of wellness programs, and the research and literature on women, this paper describes how to more effectively reach and assist women at risk of alcohol, tobacco and other drugs by broadening Employee Assistance Programs.

The increase of women in the work force provides an opportunity to assist women who have problems with alcohol, tobacco, or other drugs (ATOD). Jobs are still quite gender-segregated, and the major techniques and programs for intervening with alcohol problems are "largely man-made for male employees and based on data and experience with male alcoholics and problem drinkers" (Trice & Beyer, 1980, p.74). The goal of this paper is to describe how to more effectively reach and assist women at risk of alcohol, tobacco, and other drug problems by broadening the base of Employee Assistance Programs (EAPs). To be optimally useful for women, services must be created

---

Beth Glover Reed is affiliated with the University of Michigan.

[Haworth co-indexing entry note]: "Women and Alcohol, Tobacco, and Other Drugs: The Need to Broaden the Base Within EAPs." Reed, Beth Glover. Co-published simultaneously in *Employee Assistance Quarterly* (The Haworth Press, Inc.) Vol. 9, No. 3/4, 1994, pp. 179-201; and: *Empowering Women in the Workplace: Perspectives, Innovations, and Techniques for Helping Professionals* (ed: Marta Lundy, and Beverly Younger) Harrington Park Press an imprint of The Haworth Press, Inc., 1994, pp. 179-201. Multiple copies of this article/chapter may be purchased from The Haworth Document Delivery Center [1-800-3-HAWORTH; 9:00 a.m. - 5:00 p.m. (EST)].

for women, based on an understanding of gender. Simply adding components for women is not sufficient. The critique and expansion should also attend to other dimensions important for many women, for example, ethnicity and sexual orientation, although few examples of these differences among women can be given in this article.

ATOD USE AND PROBLEMS IN WOMEN

The patterns of gender differences related to ATOD parallel those described in most scholarship on women and gender; they derive from the condition of being female in this society, and not from ATOD use. Different standards of acceptable behavior stigmatize women who develop problems with drugs. The stigma appears in every culture, is often internalized as low self-esteem and shame, helps to prevent many from acknowledging ATOD problems in women, and inhibits direct help-seeking for ATOD problems (Fillmore, 1984; Gomberg, 1982).

Many studies suggest that differences in ATOD use between women and men have been declining since World War II, especially among younger groups (Blume, 1990; National Institute on Drug Abuse (NIDA), 1991; Wilsnack & Wilsnack, 1991; Windle, 1991). For instance, one third to half of new tobacco smokers are young women (NIDA, 1991). However, in general, women use lower levels of alcohol and illicit drugs than men, but are twice as likely to use prescribed drugs, alone and in combination with alcohol or illicit drugs (Fillmore, 1987; Roth, 1991; Worth, 1991). Seventy per cent of the prescriptions for tranquilizers, sedatives, and stimulants are still being written for women (Galbraith, 1991; Roth, 1991). The effects of drugs used in combination are multiplied, often in unpredictable, life-threatening ways.

Some estimate that women's problems with psychoactive substances equals men's, especially if all psychoactive drugs are included (e.g., Sandmeier, 1980), although most studies of alcohol problems find that fewer women than men develop ATOD-related problems (e.g., Ferrance, 1980). At least one in 25 women employed full time have psychoactive drug disorders (Anthony, Eaton, Mandell, & Garrison, 1992), and rates among women who work part time or who experience conflict about working are higher

(Wilsnack & Wilsnack, 1991; Wilsnack, 1993). Many types of problematic use patterns in women go undetected since the criteria were developed for men and the focus is on the types of problems and settings that are more likely for men.

In addition to problems arising from their own use, many women in the work place are affected by the ATOD problems of partners and family members. Many also experience emotional or behavioral interactions from medications being taken for physical conditions (prescribed or self-administered) and those they may take for recreation that often go unrecognized or are interpreted as psychological problems.

The few outcome studies that differentiate by gender suggest that women who reach treatment do as well as comparable men once they are engaged in treatment (Chatham, 1989; Institute of Medicine, 1990). The major challenge within services for women is the systematic barrier to women's access to treatment. Proportionally, many fewer women than men currently reach traditional ATOD treatment programs (NASADAD, 1990). The best estimates suggest that at least one of three persons with alcohol-related problems is a woman, and only one in twenty of these women is in treatment in a given year. For other drugs, two of 5 persons experiencing problems are likely to be women; only one in fifty is in treatment (Chatham, 1989; Wilsnack, 1989). Women comprise only 22.3 percent of patients in federally funded alcohol treatment programs and 33 percent in federally funded drug treatment programs (NASADAD, 1990). When women seek treatment, they often encounter programs that are not suited to women, and that may actually increase self-blame and depression.

A number of studies document that different types of outreach activities and other programming relevant to women's styles and needs are able to engage more and different women, although these programs are scarce (Copeland & Hall, 1992; Dahlgren & Willender, 1989). These studies are the best evidence that many women in need of services are not being reached through current referral mechanisms. In fact, available data suggest that currently women with ATOD-related problems in the work place are less likely than men to be detected and referred for services (Brodsincki & Goyer,

1987; Coudriet, Hall, Vacc, & Kissling, 1991; Young, Reichman, & Levy, 1987).

THE NEED TO BROADEN EAPs

To be more successful in reaching women, work place programs must address the incompatibilities between women's patterns of seeking and achieving help with ATOD problems, and available treatment methods and models. Broadened EAPs that incorporate knowledge about women and gender are likely to lessen the severity of problems that develop by intervening earlier. Techniques from the new scholarship on women will alert EAPs to gender-related assumptions that misdirect traditional services. EAPs must strengthen outreach by adding wellness programs, and increasing attention to health, mental health, family, social and economic consequences, which are co-occurring conditions that are inevitably linked to compulsive substance use. The common presence of these co-occurring conditions which require a variety of services, leads to a more holistic approach toward women's problems. Few programs acknowledge, and fewer still coordinate this array of services for women. In the next sections are more specific examples of women's patterns that suggest that work place programs must be broadened.

I. Referral

EAPs have used consultation and training of supervisors, union representatives and co-workers to identify work performance problems, recognize ATOD problems, and promote referrals. At least one study found that increasing knowledge about ATOD and the EAP's policies and procedures through training increased referrals for men, but not for women, suggesting that current training lacks ingredients important to initiate referrals of women (Young et al. 1987).

Training designed to detect developing problems and to promote referrals must incorporate information about women's patterns without using male standards of health, or implying pathology. In order for the referral process to be effective for women, training programs need to address several important gender-based issues: (1) the prevalent stigmatizing attitudes about women and ATOD use; (2) the various ways that ATOD use affects women; (3) the common co-occuring conditions with ATOD use, i.e., health, mental health, family, social and economic consequences; (4) women's different ways of knowing, help-seeking, and expressing difficulties; (5) the presence of violence and the implications for intervening with battered women; and (6) the ways to provide support for women (Cahill, 1983; Reichman, 1983).

Attitudes about women also must be addressed. Supervisor referrals are low because supervisors do not perceive individual strengths and needs, and often they believe that women are interchangeable and easily replaced within the work force (Aaron, 1991). Knowledgeable supervisors with the skills to provide support and feedback also need positive incentives related to referral success. An evaluation procedure that rewards positive referrals will have more impact on attitudes and behavior than educational strategies alone.

Special outreach programs designed to reach women, co-workers, and family members are especially likely to increase referrals for women since many cite mothers, children, and women friends as primary sources of referral. Within EAPs, several studies have found that women are more likely than men to self refer if accurate and non-blaming information about problems and options is available, although the studies differ in whether this is more likely with ATOD problems or for less stigmatized conditions (Brodzinski & Goyer, 1987; Coudriet et al., 1987; Hall et al., 1991). Studies in emergency rooms (Andersen, 1986), crisis centers (Soler & Dammann, 1980), and women's centers (Roth, 1991), demonstrate that women will accurately describe their ATOD use and problems if asked in a straightforward, non-accusatory manner. Women will refer themselves to services if given information that helps them correctly identify key elements of their problems, and locate and access available and appropriate services. Since women's problems are not correctly labeled, written materials must be specific about substances, amounts and behaviors. Messages to women must support the worth of every employee as well as every person's right to assistance.

Easily administered detection and screening tools can help to identify common ATOD problems. Unfortunately, most ATOD screening instruments were developed from samples of men or without attention to gender. In studies of effectiveness with women (Blume, 1991; New York State Division of Alcohol and Drugs, 1991), of the standardized instruments available, the AUDIT (Babor, Krenzler, & Lauerman, 1989; Saunders & Aasland, 1987) and the TWEAK (Russell et al., 1991) have performed best thus far at detecting alcohol problems in women. It is important to remember that such instruments focus primarily on identifying well entrenched and serious problems. They will miss many developing problems, those which do not fit criteria for traditional forms of treatment, or problems that involve prescription drugs, or low levels of several drugs taken in combination.

II. Identification and Assessment

Additional services pose basic questions about how ATOD problems are understood and identified, and the structure and organization of treatment. ATOD problems must be broadened to include prescribed and over the counter drugs, and the concurrent use of multiple drugs, even if each is used in relatively small amounts. Women are more likely than men to seek help for problems, but perceive their ATOD problems as intertwined with mental health, health, and social problems, and seek help for these other co-factors (Beckman & Amaro, 1984; Smith, 1992). Co-factors must be expanded from work performance issues to a wider range of psychological, health and family issues, and more subtle signs in the workplace.

For example, psychologically, women with ATOD problems in most studies report higher levels of depression, anxiety and shame than comparable men, and lower levels of self-esteem or self-efficacy. Multiple studies report that symptoms of post-traumatic stress disorder (PTSD) and other signs of trauma are common among women with ATOD problems. Women with ATOD problems share others' negative assessments about women who develop problems with ATOD, are more likely than men to blame themselves for difficulties in their lives, and less likely to perceive or acknowledge their strengths (Boyd, 1992; Gomberg, 1988). Referral for mental health problems without an ATOD assessment can lead to polydrug problems if the ATOD issues continue to be missed and additional psychoactive medications are prescribed.

Interpersonally, women's sense of self is more interconnected, with more awareness and responsiveness to others (Brown & Gilligan, 1992; Jordan, Kaplan, Miller, Stive & Surrey, 1991). This self-in-connection orientation and societal role expectations create more feelings of guilt about families and children than men report. Women are more likely to be and feel responsible for the care of their children, to be blamed if children have problems, and to have no safe, acceptable source of child care that allows them to seek many forms of treatment. They also report more significant losses and life changes than men, and perceive their use of ATOD as a way of coping with stress and life problems (Gabe & Thorogood, 1986). Services for children and family members provide opportunities to assist women to assess whether ATOD problems are an issue in their lives.

Social support is very low for women with ATOD problems, much smaller than men's. Indeed, their significant others often oppose their efforts to seek help (Boyd & Mieczkowski, 1990; Schilit & Gomberg, 1987). Their mother is often described as their major supporter even if the relationship is stressful. Male partners often also have ATOD problems which contributes to their lack of support for treatment. Most studies report that ninety per cent of men leave a relationship with a woman as the woman develops problems, while 90 percent of men with such problems have women partners who can be enlisted to provide support for treatment. The low levels of social support are especially important, given the pervasive evidence that support is a major factor in depression, maintaining health, working on mental health problems, and recovering from trauma (Hall, Vacc, & Kissling, 1991; Huselid, Self & Gutierres, 1991; Lutz, 1991).

Violence is a major factor for high percentages of women who develop ATOD problems–including child sexual abuse, rape, and battering (Amaro, Fried, & Cabral, 1990; Hurley, 1991; Miller, Downs, & Gondoli, 1989; Paone, Chavkin, Willets, Friedman & Des Jarlais, 1992; Reed, 1991; Root, 1989; Young, 1990). The trauma symptoms described earlier are linked to experiences with violence, and they also contribute to low self-esteem and depression. For example, women in violent relationships accurately fear reprisal of physical and emotional battering if they follow through with getting help. Programs must be sensitive to this problem, with specific guidelines for supervisors to follow.

Physically, consequences develop earlier for women and are more severe at lower levels of use for alcohol and other drugs (Piazza, Vrbka, & Yeager, 1989). More physical problems are also found during and after detoxification (Andersen, 1980).

Important differences among women require attention, for example, ethnicity, race, age, regional location, sexual orientation, social class and other important contributors must be identified and their social circumstances explored (Gabe & Thoroughgood, 1983; Saulnier, 1991). Some women's patterns look more like men's and may be missed if stereotypes about women persist. Subsets of women experience other problems, for instance, eating disorders endogenous depression, PTSD, gynecological problems, pain, and sexual dysfunctions. In different women, these appear to begin concurrently with the ATOD problems, may precede the development of ATOD problems, or occur after ATOD. In most cases, these problems also need attention.

III. Conceptual Issues Around Services

Once a woman connects with an EAP, the task is to screen for the presence of problems that require treatment and ascertain her willingness for treatment. An assessment determines (1) the barriers to treatment that require attention, and (2) the information relevant for identifying an appropriate program for her. A major recurring issue within the EAP and ATOD literature is the difficulty of getting someone to recognize the presence of an ATOD problem and the need for treatment.

However, providing support and reducing barriers to treatment may be all that is required for many women to seek treatment. An EAP may need to worry more about a partner's opposition, even violence, if a woman wishes to seek treatment. Evidence is also accumulating that once engaged in recovery, the longer term challenge is to prevent relapse and increase the quality of life for women who are survivors of violence (Paone et al., 1992; Root,

1989; Young, 1990). Ruling out the presence of violence in key relationships will be VERY important before any interventions involving a partner are undertaken, since such interventions can trigger episodes of violence. Without such care, a woman may have to choose between honesty within a family session and risking her safety. Further, an EAP may need to assist her in locating child care, transportation and other relevant services while also identifying an appropriate program. Women also will likely need assistance in constructing alternative support networks (work place groups, community networks and resources), if existing support systems are too small, stressed, conflicted, or destructive.

Constructive Confrontation

Constructive confrontation is a common activity within EAPs to motivate treatment for men. Key people in the workplace and sometimes family members and friends are helped to present evidence about the negative consequences accruing from the use of alcohol or other drugs. The context is one of concern about the person, hope about the possibility of recovery, and support for treatment (Erfurt, Heirick, & Foote, 1992; Trice and Beyer, 1979). These techniques were developed as a way to pool information and to coordinate and change the social system dynamics in order to present a consistent message to the affected person about the severity of the problems. It was also intended to offer support, and sometimes demand, that the person seek treatment or risk losing their support, the job, and various other valued assets. Individuals who care about the person often hide evidence of the problem from others, either because they are trying to help the person or fear consequences to themselves. Confrontation is often described as a tactic for breaking through a person's denial, and escalating an already impending crisis in order to motivate the person to seek treatment before the person loses everything.

When conducted, constructive confrontations with women are more likely to be effective if they include much more support, education about the connections between ATOD use and other problems, identification of strengths, bolstering of self-esteem, and much less strong confrontation (Trice & Beyer, 1979). This does not imply softening the message that serious problems are present, but does take into account a woman's greater awareness of and responsiveness to those around her, a woman's tendency to feel shame, to take responsibility for others' pain, and to misperceive or not recognize the considerable strengths she often demonstrates.

ATOD Assumptions

Assumptions about ATOD problems and theories derived from experience with men limit treatment for women. For example, the "disease" framework is certainly a great improvement over earlier definitions as problems of will-power or morality. Certainly there are health and medical aspects that must be addressed, and for many people, problems with ATOD do develop progressively. The evidence about genetic risk factors is stronger for men. Most importantly, the disease label has helped many women to accept that they have problems and has challenged the stigma and blame, with the result of improved health care and insurance coverage.

However, if defined primarily in biological, psychological and health care contexts, its use can medicalize what also has complex sociocultural dimensions, can lead to misinterpretations of women's behaviors, and to serious gaps in understanding factors important for treatment, especially for women, people of color, and others who experience discrimination, or who do not fit well with dominant models for prevention and treatment (Kurz, 1987; Schur, 1984). Factors often obscured for women in the popular understanding of disease are (1) major societal dynamics that perpetuate difficulties for women for example, stigma, violence, child responsibilities; (2) ways in which women's behaviors and thinking have been in the service of their survival in difficult circumstances, and (3) gaps and barriers in referral systems, treatment models, and programs (Reed, 1987). Broadening the definition to a family disease begins to incorporate key relationships, but with little understanding of how families are gendered in ways that need attention, for example, violence and childcare, or with how the family is influenced by the larger environment.

Denial, commonly used in the ATOD fields, is actually a combination of defense mechanisms: denial, projection, and rationalization (Bean, 1981). These defenses block uncomfortable feelings and unacceptable problems from consciousness. They also protect self-esteem by attributing the unacceptable behaviors and feelings to others, or by developing face-saving explanations for unacceptable acts. These mechanisms interfere with an individual's ability to perceive and accept the need to change, the willingness to seek treatment, and do the work required to change behaviors. Typical early intervention and treatment focus on ways to break through or reduce this barrier in order to motivate recovery. Interpreting everything that impedes seeking treatment as denial has delayed attention to the factors that block women's access to treatment. As a result, the development of referral systems and treatment models better tailored to women's styles and needs is only beginning.

The levels of depression and self-blame common for many women (and some men) with ATOD problems suggest that denial is not the dominant defense mechanism. Women may not understand that ATOD use is a primary problem, but most acknowledge that problems exist, and a large proportion report multiple attempts to seek help. For example, women have reached out to many different services, health care; mental health; family; child-related professionals; clergy; neighborhood and community gate-keepers; employers; police. Most did not assess ATOD problems, and many ignored obvious signs; when a woman asked about them directly, they were punitive and rejecting (Reed, 1991b; Smith, 1992).

People with low self-esteem and depression don't believe they are worth being helped, and often behave in ways that confirm their deep self-loathing and lack of hope that anything can make a difference. This pattern is certainly a barrier to help-seeking and investing in treatment, but will not be reduced and may be worsened by the typical techniques used to address denial, e.g., summary and recitation of consequences; stressing the need to accept being powerless to control the problem and accept help; sometimes confrontation. The most effective strategies for women appear to be those that build self-esteem, create empowering conditions, and build a sense of worth, regularly and repeatedly reaching out, providing support and conveying respect and confidence.

Enabling and co-dependency are especially popular in the literature on alcohol problems. Enabling refers to often well-meaning efforts that family members and friends make to cover for the person, but which also protects the person from experiencing the full negative consequences of their substance use. Co-dependency describes the under-responsibility/over-responsibility dynamics that develop in many relationships marked by ATOD problems.

These concepts arose from experiences with men with ATOD problems and their women partners and family members. Thus, behaviors described as enabling and co-dependent include major role expectations for women, including great unrecognized sacrifice. Neither term acknowledges that female socialization prepares women to be caretakers, tuned into others' needs, and to minimize their own needs. The recognition of gender-related behaviors in co-dependent relationships is absent (Haaken, 1993). As a result, many women, especially survivors of violence, are not able to recognize their own needs or expect them to be met, even without ATOD problems. Learning to identify one's own needs and to express them openly and directly, without guilt, is a major challenge for many women.

Further, neither concept acknowledges the absence of social support in the lives of women with ATOD problems, or the often violent opposition to treatment and recovery that many women experience from the men in their lives. They incorporate no understanding of battered women's syndrome and the dynamics of battering relationships. In fact, being labeled as codependent can be dangerous for battered women, if the battering is minimized, unacknowledged, and prolonged.

IV. Linkages with Community Services

Even when problematic use is identified and the need for treatment accepted, ATOD services equipped to respond to women's needs, and able to accommodate children, are very difficult to locate. Despite evidence that some program characteristics and specialized services for women attract more and different women to treatment, very few programs have incorporated these elements. Only 28 percent of treatment programs surveyed in a 1987 national study of 7,000 treatment programs reported providing any specialized services for women (Wilsnack, 1989) [alcohol only units, 30 percent; drug abuse only units, 23 percent; combined units, 28 percent]. Most ATOD programs have difficulty working effectively with women, partly because they lack the resources, knowledge, skills, and program models to provide women-sensitive services

(Reed, 1987). The current influx of programs concerned about pregnancy and early parenting is improving this situation somewhat, but women must be pregnant or have very young children to qualify for many of these programs.

V. Alternatives to Community-Based Treatment Programs

Providing brief treatment options is an additional focus within EAPs that is likely to improve outreach and effectiveness with women. Consistent with IOM recommendations, several brief treatment options are available, which can be conducted right in the workplace by the EAP or contractually, although these are not common within EAPs currently. These educational and self-help approaches enable a person to (a) identify problematic patterns and co-conditions related to those patterns; (b) practice activities to strengthen healthier patterns; and (c) develop ways to monitor progress. Evaluations suggest substantial effectiveness with some types of ATOD problems, and that long term effectiveness is greater for women than for men (Sanchez-Craig et al. 1989; 1991). If the problematic patterns continue, a referral can still be made to a treatment program, and research suggests that people are more willing to consider more intensive treatment after a brief treatment trial has failed.

Developing alternatives to ATOD programs by strengthening attention to them in other types of agencies will be useful for many women. Too often, women seeking help encounter a fragmented and bureaucratic helping network that does not respond to their level of need in effective and timely ways. Depending on her responsibilities and the co-conditions that she experiences, a woman may have to go to multiple settings to acquire the range of services she needs, each of which has different requirements, waiting lists and timetables (Beckman & Amaro, 1984). As an alternative to women-sensitive ATOD treatment programs, EAPs might want to assist women's centers and other programs that follow a holistic approach, to develop their capacity to provide brief ATOD interventions.

EAP staff need to be knowledgeable about available services that are sensitive to women's needs. A number of studies have now identified key components of treatment for women and produced remarkably similar lists (Kumpfner, 1991; Paone & Chavkin, 1991; Reed, 1987; Toneatti, Sobell, & Sobell, 1992). EAPs may be able to provide some elements of these directly if ATOD programs cannot, or help to coordinate the efforts of several service providers. Key elements include women-focused outreach activities, an intensive engagement process, and ways to reduce the multiple barriers women encounter. A rapid intake process can make a difference between connecting with her or losing her. Continuity and multiple types of services are preferred through all phases—outreach, engagement, planning/setting priorities, with the ability to work on multiple issues. Programs at different levels of intensity and location are also useful, e.g., residential, short and longer term; brief models; half-way houses, and so on.

Within a program, MINIMUM requirements are a safe, non-exploitative environment that takes into account women's roles, status, and socialization. Role models of strong women staff and some women-only services are also important. Different types of counseling are useful, including journals, art/poetry therapy, drama, dance, sports and body work. Women's groups are especially important as is a focus on increasing self-esteem. Counseling for non-drug issues and co-factors is likely to be important, especially those related to trauma and violence.

In addition, many women will need comprehensive health care, respite care, support for parenting, services for children, and assistance with any survival needs. Housing, food, transportation, and clothing may be issues even for women who are fully employed, especially if they are trying to leave a battering relationship. Continuing education, attention to job performance factors, and advocacy with child protection and legal systems may be useful for some women. Culturally sensitive, skilled staff with training in mental health, family issues and violence are important. A focus on empowerment runs through many of the descriptions of treatment, strengthening a woman's skills and confidence. Self-help groups can provide important support and learning systems for women, through meetings and sponsors. Especially if all-women 12 step groups or alternatives like Women for Sobriety are not available, an EAP staff member needs to be aware that women can be sexually propositioned and harassed within self-help meetings, a situation common enough that some ironically refer to this as "the thirteenth step." A vigilant sponsor, plus some preparation and on-going support by a counselor can minimize this probability and the resulting negative consequences. If women-only groups are not available, an EAP concerned about women might approach other service providers and the local self-help councils to see if such a group can be started. Ideally, a program should provide continuing support and intervention, with assistance for multiple transitions over time.

VI. Reconceptualize Treatment

After successfully ceasing destructive ATOD use in a treatment program, a woman often faces a hostile, less compassionate society with less social support than does a man. Aftercare needs to be redefined as a continuing and important phase in recovery, not just post-treatment support. The scope and duration of changes necessary for recovery suggest a need to reconceptualize treatment. Insurance programs and funders commonly define treatment as the initial transition from destructive use to abstinence, followed by aftercare. For most women, different and longer engagement periods are necessary, primarily to reduce barriers and to build self-esteem, trust and hope. The term aftercare implies primarily post-treatment support. Given the complex changes that most women must negotiate, this term is a misnomer and needs to be redefined into additional phases of change. Many workplace activities can be useful to help promote empowerment, support recovery and prevent relapse. For women, assertiveness and communications skills training as well as the development of interpersonal skills and ways of thinking and problem-solving would help them to identify and intervene at the source of problems, rather than return to self-blame and helplessness. For instance, women can learn to provide support for each other by conducting educational and support groups. Supervisors can be helped to understand what it is like to live without ATOD use, and to assist them in useful and empowering ways.

EAPs may want to help women access specific services, such as voluntary sober social clubs or non-alcoholic group activities. Work place programs could support these activities for workers and encourage their development in the community. At least some of these activities would ideally involve children, since many women who are recovering may not have much experience just having fun with their children. A parent's changes during recovery can be very unsettling for children who at least knew what to expect before. Services for the mother must be coordinated with health check-ups and mental health and support services for the children.

WELLNESS PROGRAMS AND IMPLICATIONS FOR WOMEN

Historically, EAPs have mirrored the larger society by focusing primarily on disruptive use of alcohol or any use of illicit drugs, impaired work performance and other costs to the employer. Although little data from worksite programs are as yet available to support this contention, the evidence about women's co-factors, help-seeking patterns, and perceptions of their ATOD use suggest that well-linked EAP and wellness programs will identify more women and intervene more effectively with them than traditional EAPs, *IF* programming incorporates knowledge about women and gender patterns. Erfurt, Foote, and Heirich (1992) describe important commonalities in the tasks of EAPs and wellness programs. For example, both focus on behavior change, attend to health, work to reduce health/behavior problems, and use organizational knowledge and skill. EAPs deal mostly with people with immediate problems, that are usually detected by impaired workplace functioning. Wellness programs target and screen everyone to identify physical or behavioral health risks in those apparently functioning well. Both kinds of programs attend to risk-factors and workplace stressors related to their broader foci. Both settings also train and work with supervisors to reduce workplace risk-factors and increase participation in the programming. EAPs may increase their effectiveness by incorporating some ideas from wellness programs.

Erfurt et al. (1992), define six current dimensions that pertain primarily to wellness programs in the workplace, but that may be extremely useful when adapted to EAPs: (1) establish constructive policies about wellness, screening all employees for health risks; (2) provide a menu for health improvement; (3) conduct personalized outreach and regular follow-up counseling; (4) conduct organization-wide wellness events; and (5) conduct on-going evaluation of how the program is working and (6) evaluate the program's success in reducing health risks. Two future trends are turning fitness centers into wellness centers and expanding programming to include family members. These dimensions are likely to improve detection and interventions with women for the following reasons.

1. Barriers to help, especially stigma, will be eliminated if EAPs (a) embed ATOD assessment questions within a larger health context; (b) assess everyone; and (c) train staff about women's ATOD patterns, co-factors, and consequences. Scrutinize activities and advertisements to ensure that they are affirming and do not inadvertently reinforce the stigma that women with ATOD problems often experience.

2. A holistic health/mental health framework is compatible with women's perceptions of themselves and ATOD use. Health should be defined to build on the strengths of women as well as men, and to *not* reflect limiting stereotypes about appropriate feminine behaviors. Educational sessions can focus on over-the-counter and prescribed medications, drug and drug-food interactions, and typical family health problems.

3. Promote positive development and maintenance of health which bolsters self-esteem and increases coping skills.

4. Expand to include family health, and thus draw in many women who will seek assistance first for family problems, but they will be inside the health organization.

5. Include personalized components such as outreach and follow-up counseling which are compatible with women's interpersonal orientations. Monitor work-place stressors, and define interventions that support wellness or recovery. Develop outreach, support, and educational materials that target common co-factors, e.g., domestic violence, depression, stress and coping, effective parenting.

6. Acknowledge the life issues that remain for women after treatment for ATOD problems, and strengthen recovery and relapse by helping women to learn coping and resilience skills, and developing and strengthening support systems.

Messages that are supportive and appeal to women's contextual, self-in-connection and holistic orientations are likely to be more

effective for women, than those that stress the negative consequences likely if use continues (Jordan et al., 1991). Attention to
policies and programs that assist women with multiple roles, provide assessment and referrals for family members, and support
families in parenting and childcare, e.g., flextime, childcare options,
will create more options to identify women with ATOD problems
and support their recovery.

Finally, to be optimally effective for women at risk of problems
with alcohol or other drugs (and many other types of problems as
well), both wellness and EAP programs should find ways to generate or influence health protection strategies that address environmental risk factors for women, both in and outside the worksite.
These include past and current climate for and patterns of sexual
and racial harassment, salary structures that pay women less than
men for the same work, devalued monotonous jobs, and the organizational and interpersonal processes that contribute to the glass
ceilings that truncate women's opportunity structures.

Directly relevant for preventing ATOD problems are practices
that overprescribe psychoactive medications to women, and health
care systems that attend less to the particular health problems of
women. Worksites could be influential in reducing the stigma
against women with ATOD problems, in the workplace and the
community, through training and advocacy activities. Protesting
highly publicized court cases against women with ATOD problems
who are pregnant, for instance, can educate the public, make a
statement to women employees about the worksite's health rather
than punitive orientation and prevent the stigma from increasing.
Without at least some of these activities, worksite programs may
actually perpetuate ATOD problems in women.

Subtle or more blatant patterns of harassment, limiting gender
expectations, and the general culture of fear for women are all
important factors. Clearly, chronic post-traumatic stress issues will
undermine efforts to get and remain abstinent, and will often take
years of hard work to achieve, with alternating periods of crisis,
progress, and stabilization. Our current funding policies and treatment systems are not structured to undertake the intermittently intensive work with intervening plateau periods that are required if
both ATOD and the effects of chronic trauma are involved. EAPs

could also advocate strongly with insurance companies to provide coverage for those women who must deal with the consequences of early and severe violence in their lives in addition to or concurrently with their work to recover from problems with ATOD. Broader funding patterns for increased duration and variety of services might be more expensive initially, but are likely to increase the effectiveness of current services over time.

FURTHER IMPLICATIONS / CONCLUSION

This paper has identified existing problems and barriers in services for women and has made suggestions for needed change. It identifies elements of the wellness model that when integrated with expanded EAPs and brief intervention strategies suggests a potentially more effective program for women. Many of the issues noted in this paper have policy implications that suggest a needed and long overdue transformation in programs for women, including strong evaluation and outcome studies on programs for women. Programs must be held accountable for the quality and effectiveness of their services. There is a paucity of research about what works for women, and especially for women of color and other women. EAPs should be involved in identifying workplace factors that (1) contribute to problem development and to low rates of detection and referral; (2) promote resilience among women; (3) identify, recognize, and intervene with important co-conditions; (4) evaluate outreach and prevention.

REFERENCES

Aaron, M. (1991). Issues for women in the workplace. In P. Roth (Ed.). *Alcohol and drugs are women's issues*. Metuchen, NJ: Scarecrow Press, 120-124.

Amaro, H., Fried, L. E., & Cabral, H. (1990). Violence during pregnancy and substance abuse. *American Journal of Public Health, 80(5)*, 575-9.

Andersen, M. D. (1980a). Medical needs of addicted women and men and the implications for treatment. In A. Schecter (Ed.). *Drug dependence and alcoholism* (pp. 23-33). New York: Plenum Press.

Andersen, M. D. (1986). Personalized nursing: An effective intervention model for use with drug-dependent women in an emergency room. *International Journal of the Addictions, 21*, 105-122.

Anthony, J. C., Eaton, W. W., Mandell, W., & Garrison, R. (1992). Psychoactive drug dependence and abuse: More common in some occupations than others? *Journal of Employee Assistance Research, 1(1)*, 148-186.

Babor, T. F., Kranzler, H. R., & Lauerman, R. J. (1989). Early detection of harmful alcohol consumption: Comparison of clinical, laboratory, and self-report screening procedures. *Addictive Behaviors, 14*, 139-157.

Bean, M. H. (1981). Denial of the psychological complications of alcoholism. In M. H. Bean & N. E. Zinberg (Eds.). *Dynamic approaches to the understanding and treatment of alcoholism.* New York: Free Press, 55-96.

Beckman, L. J., & Amaro, H. (1984). Patterns of women's use of alcohol treatment agencies. In S. C. Wilsnack & L. J. Beckman, *Alcohol problems in women: Antecedent, consequence, and intervention* (pp. 319-348). New York: Guilford Press.

Blume, S. B. (1991). Women, alcohol and drugs. In N. B. Miller (Ed.). *Comprehensive handbook of drug and alcohol addiction* (pp. 147-177). New York: Marcel Dekker.

Boyd, C., & Mieczkowski, T. (1990). Drug use, health, family and social support in "crack" cocaine users. *Addictive Behaviors, 15*, 481-485.

Brodzinski, J. D., & Goyer, K. A. (1987). Employee Assistance Program utilization and client gender, *Employee Assistance Quarterly, 3*(10), 1-13.

Brown, L. M., & Gilligan, C. (1992). *Meeting at the crossroads.* Cambridge, MA: Harvard University Press.

Cahill, M. H. (1983). Training employees and supervisors to increase use of EAPs by women. *Alcohol Health Research World, 7*(3), 18-22.

Chatham, L. R. (1989). Understanding the issues: An overview. In R. C. Engs (Ed.). *Women: Alcohol and Other Drugs* (pp. 3-14). Dubuque, IO: Kendall/Hunt Publishing Company.

Copeland, J., & Hall, W. (1992). Comparison of women seeking drug and alcohol treatment in a specialist women's program and two traditional mixed-sex treatment services. *British Journal of Addiction, 87*(9), 1293-1302.

Coudriet, T. W., Swisher, J. D., & Grisson, G. (1987). The role of gender in requests for help in Employee Assistance Programs. *Employee Assistance Quarterly, 2*(4), 1-12.

Dahlgren, L., & Willander, A. (1989). Are special facilities for women alcoholics needed? A controlled two year follow-up study from a specialized female unit (EWA) versus a mixed male/female treatment facility. *Alcoholism: Clinical and Experimental Research, 13*(4), 499-504.

Erfurt, J. C., Foote, A., & Heirich, M. A. (1992). Integrating employee assistance and wellness: Current and future core technologies of a megabrush program. *Journal of Employee Assistance Research, 1*(1), 1-31.

Fillmore, K. M. (1984). When angels fall: Women's drinking as cultural preoccupation and as reality. In S. C. Wilsnack & L. J. Beckman (Eds.). *Alcohol Problems in Women* (pp. 7-36). New York: Guilford Press.

Fillmore, K. M. (1987). Women's drinking across the adult life course as compared to men's. *British Journal of Addiction, 82*, 801-811.

Gabe, J., & Thorogood, N. (1986). Prescribed drug use and the management of everyday life: The experiences of black and white working class women. *The Sociological Review, 34*, 737-772.

Galbraith, S. (1991). Women and legal drugs. In P. Roth (Ed.). *Alcohol and Drugs are Women's Issues: Vol. 1. A review of the issues* (pp. 150-155). Metuchin, NJ: Women's Action Alliance and Scarecrow Press.

Gomberg, E. S. L. (1982). Historical and political perspective: Women and drug use. *Journal of Social Issues, 38*(2), 9-24.

Gordon, M. T., & Riger, S. (1989). *The female fear: The social cost of rape.* New York: Free Press.

Haaken, J. (1993). From Al-Anon to ACOA: Codependence and the reconstruction of caregiving. *Signs, 18*(2), 321-345.

Hall, L., Vacc, N., & Kissling, G. (1991). Likelihood to use employee assistance programs: The effects of sociodemographic, social-psychological, sociocultural, organizational, and community factors. *Journal of Employment Counseling, 28*(2), 63-73.

Hurley, D. L. (1991). Women, alcohol and incest: An analytical review. *Journal of Studies on Alcohol, 52*(3), 253-268.

Huselid, R. F., Self, E. A., & Gutierres, S. E. (1991). Predictors of successful completion of a halfway-house program for chemically dependent women. *American Journal of Drug and Alcohol Abuse, 17*(1), 89-103.

Institute of Medicine. (1990). *Broadening the Base of Treatment for Alcohol Problems.* Washington, DC: National Academy Press.

Jordan, J. V., Kaplan, A. G., Miller, J. B., Stive, I. P., & Surrey, J. L. (1991). *Women's Growth in Connection.* New York: Guilford Press.

Kumpfner, K. L. (1991). Treatment programs for drug-abusing women. *The Future of Children, 1*(1), 50-60.

Kurz, D. (1987). Emergency department responses to battered women: Resistance to medicalization. *Social Problems. 34*(1), 69-81.

Lutz, M. E. (1991). Sobering decisions: Are there gender differences? *Alcoholism Treatment Quarterly, 8*(2), 51-65.

Miller, B. A., Downs, W. R., & Gondoli, D. M. (1989). Spousal violence among alcoholic women as compared to a random houschold sample of women. *Journal of Studies on Alcohol, 50*(6), 533-540.

National Association of State Alcohol and Drug Abuse Directors (NASADAD). (1990). *State resources and services related to alcohol and other drug abuse problems: An analysis of state alcohol and drug abuse profile data, fiscal year 1990.* Washington, DC: Author.

National Institute of Drug Abuse. (1989). *National household survey on drug abuse: Population estimates 1988-1989.* Washington, DC: Department of Health and Human Services.

New York State Division of Alcoholism and Alcohol Abuse. (1991). *Alcohol abuse and alcoholism among women: A three-tiered approach to screening* (pp. 2-11). New York: Author.

Paone, D., & Chavkin, W. (1991). *Treatment for crack-using mothers: A study and guidelines for program design.* New York: Beth Israel Medical Center.

Paone, D., Chavkin, W., Willets, I., Friedman, P., & Des Jarlais, D. (1992). The impact of sexual abuse: Implications for drug treatment. *Journal of Women's Health, 1*(2), 149-153.

Piazza, N. J., Vrbka, J. L., & Yeager, R. D. (1989). Telescoping of alcoholism in women alcoholics. *The International Journal of the Addictions, 24*(1), 19-28.

Reed, B. G. (1991). Linkages: Battering, sexual assault, incest, child sexual abuse, teen pregnancy, dropping out of school and the alcohol and drug connection. In Roth, P. (Ed.). *Alcohol and Drugs Are Women's Issues: Vol. 1. A review of the issues.* Metuchen, N.J.: Scarecrow Press.

Reed, B. G. (1987). Developing women-sensitive drug-dependence treatment services: Why so difficult? *Journal of Psychoactive Drugs, 19*(2), 151-164.

Reed, B. G., & Leibson, E. (1981). Women clients in special women's demonstration drug abuse treatment programs compared with women entering selected co-sex programs. *International Journal of the Addictions, 16,* 1425-1466.

Reichman, W. (1983). Affecting attitudes and assumptions about women and alcohol problems. *Alcohol and Health Research World, 7*(3), 6-10.

Root, M. P. P. (1989). Treatment failures: The role of victimization in women's addictive behavior. *American Journal of Orthopsychiatry, 59*(4), 542-549.

Roth, P. (Ed.). (1991). *Alcohol and drugs are women's issues: Vol. 1. A review of the issues & Vol. 2. The model program guide.* Metuchen, NJ: Scarecrow Press.

Russell, M., & Bigler, L. (1979). Screening for alcohol-related problems in an out-patient gynecological clinic. *American Journal of Obstetrics and Gynecology, 134,* 4-12.

Russell, M., Martier, S. S., Sokol, R. J., Jacobson, J., & Bottoms, S. (1991). Screening for pregnancy risk-drinking: TWEAKING the tests. *Alcoholism: Clinical and Experimental Research, 15*(2), 368.

Sanchez-Craig, M., Leigh, G., Spivak, K., & Lei, H. (1989). Superior outcome of females over males after brief treatment for the reduction of heavy drinking. *British Journal of Addiction, 84*(4), 395-404.

Sanchez-Craig, M., Spivak, K., & Davila, R. (1991). Superior outcome of females over males after brief treatment for the reduction of heavy drinking: Replication and report of therapist effects. *British Journal of Addiction, 86*(7), 867-876.

Saulnier, C. L. (1991). Lesbian alcoholism: Development of a construct. *Affilia, 6*(3), 66-84.

Saunders, J. B., & Aasland, O. G. (1987). WHO collaborative project on the identification and treatment of persons with harmful alcohol consumption: Report on Phase I. Development of a screening instrument. Geneva: World Health Organization.

Schilit, R., & Gomberg, E. S. (1987). Social support structures for women in treatment for alcoholism. *Health and Social Work, 12*(3), 187-195.

Schur, E. M. (1984). *Labeling Women Deviant: Gender, Stigma, and Social Control.* Philadelphia: Temple University Press.

Smith, L. (1992). Help seeking in alcohol-dependent females. *Alcohol and Alcoholism, 27*(1), 3-9.

Soler, E. G., & Dammann, G. (1980). Women in crisis: Drug use and abuse. *Focus on Women, 4*(1), 227-241.

Toneatti, A., Sobell, L. C., & Sobell, M. B. (1992). Gender issues in the treatment of abusers of alcohol, nicotine, and other drugs. *Journal of Substance Abuse, 4*(2), 209-278.

Trice, H. M., & Beyer, J. M. (1979). Women employees and job-based alcoholism programs. *Journal of Drug Issues, 9,* 371-385.

Wilsnack, S. C. (1989). Alcohol abuse and alcoholism: Extent of the problem (pp. 17-30). In R. Engs (Ed.). *Women, Alcohol, and Other Drugs.* Dubuque, IO: Kendall/Hunt Publishing Company.

Wilsnack, S. C., & Wilsnack, R. W. (1991). Epidemiology of women's drinking. *Journal of Substance Abuse, 3,* 133-157.

Wilsnack, R.W. (1993). Unwanted statuses and women's drinking. *Journal of Employee Assistance Research, 1,* 239-270.

Worth, D. (1991). American women and polydrug abuse. In P. Roth (Ed.). Alcohol and Drugs are Women's Issues: Vol. 1. A review of the issues (pp. 1-9). Metuchin, NJ: Women's Action Alliance and Scarecrow Press.

Young, E. B. (1990). The role of incest issues in relapse. *Journal of Psychoactive Drugs, 22*(2), 249-258.

Young, D. Reichman, W. R., & Levy, M. F. (1987). Differential referral of women and men to employee assistance programs: The role of supervisory attitudes. *Journal of Studies on Alcohol, 48*(1), 22-28.

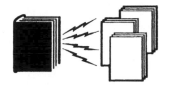

Haworth
DOCUMENT DELIVERY
SERVICE

This new service provides a single-article order form for any article from a Haworth Journal.

- *Time Saving:* No running around from library to library to find a specific article.
- *Cost Effective:* All costs are kept down to a minimum.
- *Fast Delivery:* Choose from several options, including same-day FAX.
- *No Copyright Hassles:* You will be supplied by the original publisher.
- *Easy Payment:* Choose from several easy payment methods.

Open Accounts Welcome for ...
- Library Interlibrary Loan Departments
- Library Network/Consortia Wishing to Provide Single-Article Services
- Indexing/Abstracting Services with Single Article Provision Services
- Document Provision Brokers and Freelance Information Service Providers

MAIL or *FAX* THIS ENTIRE ORDER FORM TO:

Attn: **Marianne Arnold**
Haworth Document Delivery Service
The Haworth Press, Inc.
10 Alice Street
Binghamton, NY 13904-1580

or FAX: (607) 722-1424
or CALL: 1-800-3-HAWORTH
(1-800-342-9678; 9am-5pm EST)

PLEASE SEND ME PHOTOCOPIES OF THE FOLLOWING SINGLE ARTICLES:
1) Journal Title: _____
   Vol/Issue/Year:_____Starting & Ending Pages:_____
Article Title:_____

2) Journal Title: _____
   Vol/Issue/Year:_____Starting & Ending Pages:_____
Article Title:_____

3) Journal Title: _____
   Vol/Issue/Year:_____Starting & Ending Pages:_____
Article Title:_____

4) Journal Title: _____
   Vol/Issue/Year:_____Starting & Ending Pages:_____
Article Title:_____

(See other side for Costs and Payment Information)

COSTS: Please figure your cost to order quality copies of an article.

1. Set-up charge per article: $8.00
   ($8.00 × number of separate articles) _____

2. Photocopying charge for each article:

   1-10 pages: $1.00 _____

   11-19 pages: $3.00 _____

   20-29 pages: $5.00 _____

   30+ pages: $2.00/10 pages _____

3. Flexicover (optional): $2.00/article _____

4. Postage & Handling: US: $1.00 for the first article/
   $.50 each additional article _____

   Federal Express: $25.00 _____

   Outside US: $2.00 for first article/
   $.50 each additional article _____

5. Same-day FAX service: $.35 per page _____

GRAND TOTAL: _____

METHOD OF PAYMENT: (please check one)

❑ Check enclosed   ❑ Please ship and bill. PO # _____
(sorry we can ship and bill to bookstores only! All others must pre-pay)

❑ Charge to my credit card: ❑ Visa;   ❑ MasterCard; ❑ American Express;

Account Number:_____ Expiration date:_____

Signature: ✗_____ Name: _____

Institution: _____ Address: _____

City: _____ State:_____ Zip:_____

Phone Number: _____ FAX Number: _____

MAIL or *FAX* THIS ENTIRE ORDER FORM TO:

Attn: **Marianne Arnold**
Haworth Document Delivery Service
The Haworth Press, Inc.
10 Alice Street
Binghamton, NY 13904-1580

or **FAX:** (607) 722-1424
or **CALL:** 1-800-3-HAWORTH
(1-800-342-9678; 9am-5pm EST)